THE EC AND THE UNITED STATES

Other books by Peter Coffey

European Monetary Integration (with John R. Presley). Macmillan, London, and St. Martin's Press, New York, 1971.

The Social Economy of France. Macmillan, London, and St. Martin's Press, New York, 1973.

The World Monetary Crisis. Macmillan, London and St. Martin's Press, New York, 1974.

The External Economic Relations of the EEC. Macmillan, London and St. Martin's Press, New York, 1976.

Europe and Money. Macmillan and St. Martin's Press, New York, 1977.

Economic Policies of the Common Market. Macmillan, London and St. Martin's Press, New York, 1979.

The Common Market and its International Economic Policies. Nuffic, The Hague, 1982.

The Main Economic Policy Areas of the EEC, (editor). Martinus Nijhoff Publishers, The Hague, 1983.

The European Monetary System—Past, Present and Future. Martinus Nijhoff Publishers, Dordrecht, 1984; Second Edition, 1986.

The European Community and Mexico, edited, M. S. Wionczek (co-editor). Martinus Nijhoff Publishers, Dordrecht, 1987.

Towards a European Foreign Policy, edited, R. H. Lauwaars and J. K. De Vree (joint editors). Martinus Nijhoff Publishers, Dordrecht, 1987.

Europe and the Andean Countries, together with Ciro Angarita. Frances Pinter, London, and St. Martin's Press, New York, 1988.

The EEC and Brazil, together with L. A. Corrèa de Lago, Frances Pinter, London and St. Martin's Press, New York, 1988.

The EEC and the Netherlands—Costs and Benefits, together with Menno Wolters. Pinter Publishers, London, 1990.

Main Economic Policy Areas of the EEC—Towards 1992. Kluwer Academic Publishers, Dordrecht, 1990.

THE EC AND THE UNITED STATES

Peter Coffey

St. Martin's Press
New York

First published in the United States of America in 1993

Printed in Great Britain

ISBN 0–312–08568–0

Library of Congress Cataloging-in-Publication Data
Coffey, Peter.
 The EC and the United States/Peter Coffey.   p.   cm.
 Includes index.
 ISBN 0–312–08568–0
 1. European Economic Community—United States.   I. Title.
HC241.25.U5C56   1993
341.24'22—dc20   92–28470
                                                              CIP

**For Leila—My wonderful and loyal
American friend**

Contents

List of figures

List of tables

Acknowledgements

The author wishes to thank the authorities at the University of St. Thomas for providing the financial and logistical help indispensable in the preparation of this book. In particular, he is grateful to James Reid, the former Vice-President for Academic Affairs, who gave such encouragement to this project.

Very special thanks are due to the author's assistant, Patrick Dykhoff, who not only procured much of the documentation necessary for this study but also sent out all the questionnaires to the American corporations which are the subject of Chapter 7—and then assisted in the analysis of the responses received. He also transcribed the manuscript of this book in a most professional manner.

The author also gratefully acknowledges Agence Europe in Brussels for giving permission to reproduce documents appearing in the appendices.

Introduction

At no time since 1945 has it been more appropriate and necessary to examine relations between the European Community and the United States. There are so many changes taking place—at an alarming pace—in Europe and in the world at large which profoundly affect relations between the two partners. Among the most important of these, disarmament and the partial disengagement of the United States from Europe already influence and will continue to affect policies on both sides of the Atlantic. Then, the Community's moves toward the creation of a Single European Market (SEM) have intensified American interest in and apprehension about the future of Western Europe. More recently, the signing of the Treaty on European Union—(this document is reproduced in its entirety at the end of this book) on 7 February 1992—with among its aims the creation of common Community foreign and defence policies and an economic and monetary union with a common currency—will certainly change the balance of power between Europe and America. Similarly, the creation of a great European Economic Area between the Community and the countries of the European Free Trade Association (EFTA) on 1 January 1993 and the subsequent enlargement of the Community will strengthen Europe's position in the world. Last, but by no means least, as on previous occasions in other multilateral trade negotiations, in the present Uruguay Round, the chief protagonists, once again, are the European Community and the United States. Here, the whole future of world trade depends on whether or not these two economic superpowers will be able to reach a compromise over their differences—notably over agriculture and services.

In this work, I have not attempted to examine every aspect of relations between the European Community and the United States; rather I have chosen to concentrate on major areas of past, ongoing and future mutual concern to both parties. Also, I felt it unwise to jump too deeply into areas, even those of great importance, where I did not feel competent enough to undertake a study. Thus, for example, despite the great and legitimate current interest—on both sides of the Atlantic—in defence and security, it was considered wiser not to devote a major chapter to this subject.

The book, then, is divided into a number of subject areas. The first and most important of these is trade. The Community and the United States are each other's most important trading partners—though the Americans continue to enjoy a growing trade surplus with the Europeans. In 1991, this stood at 17 billion dollars. This situation, in my view, is caused by combination of factors which include a greater American concentration on products with a high value added and the declining value of the dollar. Apart from the importance of trade in goods and services, both partners possess fabulous direct investments in each other's territories. In 1990, Community investors owned more than half of the foreign direct investment stocks in the United States while American investors held over two-fifths of their foreign direct investments in the Community.

As just mentioned, apart from bilateral skirmishes like the present 'steel war', the two sides confront each other in the multilateral trade negotiations in the framework of the GATT. Here, the Community is represented by the Commission. Currently, the Uruguay Round talks which should have been completed in March 1991 have been extended into 1992. They have seriously stalled over differences about agriculture and services.

It is agriculture which is the most serious point of profound discord between the two sides. All Western countries give support to their farmers, and both the Americans and the Europeans give a lot of help to agriculture. However, it is the Community's Common Agricultural Policy which is diabolical in its logic and which inevitably generates huge surpluses which must then be dumped on world markets. Happily, Ray MacSharry, the EC Commissioner for Agriculture, made sweeping proposals for reform in February 1991 which are examined in this book. Also, President Bush has put forward important compromise proposals. I am hopeful—but not absolutely certain—that these two sets of proposals will lead to the compromise necessary if the present trade negotiations are to be saved from collapse. This compromise is, however being jeopardized by the beginning of a soya war between the two sides.

In the industrial field, the sector which is of most important current and future interest to both Europeans and Americans, is the aircraft industry and the future of airlines. Here, both sides accuse each other of subsidising their industries. Earlier this year, they nearly reached a compromise on this issue and I am sure that they will reach some agreement. However, the balance of power is changing because not only is the Airbus Industry challenging the Boeing Company, but owing to the expected deregulation in the airlines' industry, effective as from 1993, the negotiating power of the Community will be strengthened.

To my delight, it is in the monetary sphere where, in the long run, the most significant change in the international balance of power between the two economic superpowers could take place. For decades France, deeply antagonistic to the exhorbitant privileges conferred upon the United States because of the use of the American currency as an international reserve asset and the major trading currency, had called for the Community, the world's greatest trading bloc, to be endowed with a 'common international monetary personality'. To the French, the easiest way to achieve this goal would be to create a common European currency. Since the signing of the Treaty on European Union, the creation of just such a currency has come closer to reality since a major part of the Treaty is devoted to just such a goal—together with the creation of a European Central Bank.

Despite my long-standing support for the French view, I would remind readers that plans for a full economic and monetary union (EMU) have been in existence since the late 1960s. Furthermore, in 1970, in adopting the second and definitive Werner Report, the original six Founder Member States of the EEC did agree that a full EMU would be completed by 1980—'provided that the political will to do so exists' and that new Member States would be 'invited' to accept this decision. The Werner Report only provided details for the first stage of an EMU, and, to me, we are still in an extension of that stage.

In view of past experience, I caution against trying to adopt precise time-tables for a full EMU. In fact, I would stress that the date 1999 for entering the final stage of such a union—which all newspapers and journals are busy repeating (without, one assumes, having read the Treaty in the original)—is an oversight since it will only be valid if another date has not been chosen.

For over two decades, I have been convinced that the Community would have its own currency (most probably the present European Currency Unit or ECU) but that, for practical reasons, it would most probably not be the sole currency inside the EC. Nevertheless, the widespread use of the ECU internationally, backed by the prudent fiscal and monetary policies of the Community, would make it a very attractive alternative to the US dollar and the Japanese yen and would, to a large degree, replace existing national European currencies. Consequently, the Community's international role would, finally, become very important indeed.

1992—why, how and to what degree? Threat or challenge? So much has been written on both sides of the Atlantic that it seemed unlikely that anything else remained to be said about this now seemingly magic but realistic date. But, I considered it important to put a few matters right about the implications for both Americans and Europeans of the implementation of the Community's Single European Market (SEM) on, ostensibly, 1 January 1993. But first, the date; is it really all going to happen on the first day of 1993? The answer is clearly no. First, not all the directives will be passed by the Council of Ministers by the end of 1992. Second, despite compromises and progress in parallel fields, it has already been accepted that a SEM for a number of sectors will not come into being until about 1995 or 1996—at the earliest. The most obvious examples here are common levels of value-added tax (VAT) together with the use of the origin principle, common excise duties and a Community corporation tax. Although a common European banking passport will exist as from 1 January 1993, the same will hold good only for certain sectors in insurance and not at all for stockbroking. Similarly, temporary exemptions or 'derogations' will continue to exist well into the mid–1990s—notably concerning common pricing for automobiles. Third, as is seen in the final part of this book, the record of translating Community directives into national legislation varies greatly among Member States.

One area of great potential importance for both Americans and Europeans in the future SEM is the question of standardization. There is an impression, wrongly, prevalent in the United States, that common standards will exist for everything throughout the Community as from 1 January 1993. Alas, nothing could be further from the truth—thus nullifying some of the gains from long production runs and economies of scale which had been anticipated in the SEM. Certainly, where safety is concerned, there will be common standards—in such fields as foods, toys, automobiles and medical products. Indeed, the use of common safety standards does mean that we shall have a common market in pharmaceuticals—a development of considerable importance for the United States.

Unfortunately, the principal way of having common standards is for Member States to accept each other's standards—thus maintaining the existing fragmentation of the market.

But, what do American businesses think about all this? In the research undertaken, it was found that some were apparently well prepared for 1993, and that most were optimistic, rightly or wrongly, about the future.

And, the future, what might it hold for the Community and the United States? Are and will institutional changes take place? Relations between the two sides have now been institutionalized and regular consultations do take place. More recently, on 23 September 1991, Sir Leon Brittan, the Vice-President of the European Commission, signed an agreement, in Washington, between the European Commission and the American Administration for the application of Competition Policy on both sides of the Atlantic. In view of the great importance for the United States of the SEM, and the increasing degree of integration between EC Member States, I believe we can expect to have more such agreements concluded between the two sides.

At a strictly Community level, I do not think there will, in the immediate future, be any major institutional changes. Despite an increase in the consultative and delaying role of the European Parliament, the two principal organs are and will remain the Commission and the Council of Ministers. Also, contrary to the hopes of some federalists, the Treaty on European Union was never intended to be an agreement for a future United States of Europe. In fact, although the Dutch did slyly introduce a rogue clause about 'federation', this move was only supported by the Belgians and was peremptorily thrown out of the conference hall window into the nearest canal by the other ten Member States—not led, surprise, surprise, by the British—so much for that! If, in future, as is expected, the EC Member States integrate still further, I expect to see a 'positive devolution' taking place, leading to the creation of a European Switzerland. But that will be the subject of my next book, 'The Future of Europe'.

The future is much less clear at the military level. Correctly, the United States expects the Europeans to accept a greater degree of responsibility for their own defence—as the British, Greeks and Turks have always done since 1945. In the present unsettled state of European affairs, the role of NATO is likely to be enhanced, while those European countries wishing for a greater purely European defence policy—to complement the aim of a foreign policy laid down in the Treaty—will most probably execute this via the Western European Union (WEU). Before the signing of the Treaty, in February 1992 first Italy and Britain, and then France and Germany, had made different proposals in October 1991 about the precise role of the WEU.

Regarding the Treaty on European Union itself, it should be noted that, in principle, an intergovernmental conference on its application and future will be called in 1996. Thus, until that date, the institutional structure should remain fairly static. The exception to this expectation would be a rapid enlargement of the Community which would most likely lead to an intensification of calls for a reduction in the number of Commissioners. For example, it would be reasonable for the big countries to have one commissioner each and for groups of small countries—such as the Benelux States and the Scandinavian countries—to have one commissioner per bloc. Eventually, also, each Member State should nominate a minister for European Affairs and these representatives should be in semi-permanent session in Brussels. Similarly, a better way of electing the European Parliament and some means of making the Commission more accountable should be found.

Can the Community and the United States learn from each other and are they likely to resemble each other over the coming years? Already, alas, the Community is beginning to emulate the Americans with increasing litigation and bureaucracy—and this trend is likely to be accentuated in future. There are, happily, many excellent customs and qualities which they can adopt from each other—American customer service and the European national health coverage—for example. But, in some ways, the two parties are going in different directions. Thus, while, with some exceptions, the Community is becoming more centralized, the United States is tending to de-centralize as far as government is concerned.

The positive development which is almost certain to take place over the coming years is that the relationship between the Community and the United States is likely to be increasingly a dialogue of equals. Such a development will be in the interest of both parties and of other countries. The one danger I see on the horizon is the temptation for each side to relapse into self-sufficiency and isolationism—if either side acceded to this temptation the outlook for the whole world would be very grave indeed. Since, however, the two partners have so many important interests in each other's territories, I do not believe that this will happen.

Footnote

On 21 May 1992, the Council of Ministers of the European Community, at the end of a four-day marathon session, agreed (with a reservation on milk quotas made by Italy) to accept most of the proposals for the reform of the Common Agricultural Policy, made in February 1991, by Commissioner MacSharry. First estimates suggest that the cuts in the prices of Community agricultural products will be in the order of 30 per cent. In my view, the way is now (thankfully) open for a compromise to be made at the Uruguay Round, and the United States should be able to make concessions in the field of services.

The only possible conflicting issue left is whether the Americans will view the proposed direct subsidies to EC farmers as being trade distorting. Hopefully, they will accept these as being social policy measures.

Amsterdam, Brussels and St. Paul
May and June 1992

1
The trade dimension

The background

Only very recently have the two trading partners, the European Community[1] (EC) and the United States, started to formalize their relationships. Formerly, and even today, their most formal and continuous contacts were and are in the field of trade—most notably in the area of the Multilateral Trade Negotiations (MTN's)—organized in the framework of the GATT (General Agreement of Tariffs and Trade). However, the two partners—which more than any other single nation or group of countries do have such a tremendous influence on world trade and economic development—are quite different entities with very different trading policies. A knowledge of these differences is indispensable to an understanding of the major issues, trading and others, which dominate current international relations.

The former EEC and the present EC

The twelve Community Member States[2] are mainly highly developed countries and they are either open or very open economies (see Table 1.1). They form the most highly integrated regional grouping in the world—conducting some 60 per cent of their trade with each other. Unlike the United States—with the recent exceptions of Britain and the Netherlands with their discoveries of North Sea oil and natural gas (though, it is true that the Netherlands has enjoyed the bonanza of the important Groningen reserves of natural gas for the past thirty years—responsible, in part, for the financing of the lavish Dutch social welfare programme)—the EC Member States do not possess their own resources of energy and raw materials. In this sense, they are more similar to Japan than to the United States.

Table 1.1 EC: degree of 'openness' in national economies in 1991 (as a percentage of GDP)

	Exports	Imports
Belgium	74.4	71.3
Denmark	35.8	29.9
Germany	33.7	27.8
Greece	20.7	30.1
Spain	17.1	20.2
France	22.7	22.4
Ireland	63.5	56.3
Italy	20.3	20.1
Luxembourg	97.8	10.4
Netherlands	56.4	50.7
Portugal	32.0	42.2
United Kingdom	23.8	24.2
EC 12	28.3	27.1
USA	10.0	10.8
Japan	11.8	10.1

Source: European Economy No. 50

Unlike both Japan and the United States, at the end of World War II, four countries of the European Community were major colonial powers. In fact, Portugal remained just such a power until 1974! This fact, as we shall see, later in this chapter, was to have a major influence on the Community's external economic policies and relations that has lasted until the present day.

Then, of course, there is the EC's Common Agricultural Policy (CAP), to which a whole chapter is devoted later in this book. To me, it is this policy that has influenced, negatively, the EC's external economic relations with all countries—except with Thailand, and, currently and temporarily (one hopes), the countries of the former Soviet Union. Nowhere is the influence of the CAP more upsetting and potentially more dangerous than with the United States.

But, in all this, is there any particular logic in the Community's external economic relations? Speaking before representatives of the Commission of the European Communities and of the ASEAN group of countries, in Brussels, in the Autumn of 1987, I reiterated the seven main principles influencing the Community's external economic relations and about I had written some years earlier.[3] These principles, which I still believe to be valid, are the following:

1. The EEC (with the recent exceptions of the Netherlands and the United Kingdom) is not self-sufficient in supplies in energy and raw materials. Therefore, these commodities have been allowed to enter the Community either free of duty or with very low tariffs.
2. At the end of the transitional period, the Common External Tariff (CET) would consist of the average of the existing (1957) tariffs of the Member States. Subsequent participation by the EC in a series of international negotiations have resulted in a rather low average CET.
3. It was agreed that special arrangements would be made for existing overseas territories, dependencies and the like for which Member States exercise responsibility. This policy has evolved over time from the special arrangements made for such countries to the two Yaoundé Agreements and further on the present Fourth Lomé Agreement.
4. At the outset, the Community decided to embark upon the construction of a Common Agricultural Policy (CAP), and until the Common Agricultural Market (CAM) actually came into being the EEC was unwilling to discuss the question of agricultural matters in international trade negotiations. Since the full achievement of the CAM, its existence has tended negatively to influence the Community's trade relations with most parts of the world—especially with Eastern Europe, Australasia, Latin America and the United States.
5. The Community expressed its willingness to enter into international trade negotiations with non-Community countries. Subsequently, the EC has been (together with the United States and more recently Japan) the principal protagonist in point 2, and following the Tokyo Round Negotiations, the average CET is now rather low.
6. Partly, as a consequence of the low CET and partly owing to the increased competitive ability of a growing number of Third World countries (particularly in the fields of clothing and textiles) the EC has, since the 1970s, increasingly resorted to non-tariff barriers of a 'voluntarist' nature which are sometimes described as Orderly Marketing Arrangements (OMAs) or Voluntary Export Restrictions (VERs). Currently, efforts are being made to 'persuade' Japan to restrict exports of cars and electronic products to EC Member States.
7. Since the mid 1970s, the Community has started to move in the direction of attempting to secure its supplies of energy and raw materials. This more recent policy is an obvious reaction to the lack of self-sufficiency in these fields as mentioned in point 1.

Some of these points deserve further examination. Numbers one and seven clearly influence the Community's attitude to a number of less-developed countries since they tend to be the EC's main sources of energy and raw materials. Thus, apart from the special historical links between the Community and the African, Caribbean and Pacific (ACP) countries (to which we shall turn in a few moments), efforts have been made to make special arrangements with specific countries. One such example of this trend had been the Community's involvement with the important Carajás Iron Ore Project in Brazil. As a result of these links, Third World countries which supply the EC with energy and raw materials are vulnerable to the Community's fortunes. Some of these countries are also particularly interested in the possibility of enjoying the privileges conferred upon the 'chosen' Third World countries referred to under point three.

At the meeting of the Council of Ministers held in Venice in 1956, France had threatened not to join the nascent EEC if special arrangements were not made for her African territories. The reaction to this threat and the ensuing policies are still with us. First, special arrangements were made for the African Associate States and Madagascar (AASM). Then, as these countries gained their independence, new arrangements were made (called the Yaoundé ones) which took the form of reciprocal preferential trading agreements as well as the transfer of financial aid (similar arrangements, the ARUSHA ones, were also made for three anglophone African states). Subsequently, when Britain joined the EEC, these arrangements were transformed into the Lomé Accords and extended to many former British colonies (more recently, also to the former Portuguese territories). However, these Lomé Accords—which are the object of criticism and envy by many Latin American countries—are different from their predecessors in that they are *non*-reciprocal and embody two very important arrangements, the STABEX (for traditional tropical products) and SYSMIN (for metals). These arrangements aim, through the transfer of funds to the ACP states to compensate for falls in the prices of their listed exports under the STABEX and SYSMIN schemes, to maintain their export earnings. Furthermore, the lists of products under both these schemes are *non-definitive*.

But, the points which are of immediate consequence to us in this book are numbers two, four, five and to some degree point six. As mentioned earlier, point four, concerning the Community's CAP, the point of greatest contention between the EC and the United States, is examined in detail in the next chapter. Similarly, point number six is brought into part of this chapter but more extensively when examining the EC's policies for the Single Economic Market (SEM).

How, then, does the Community translate these policies into action, and can it be said to have clear preferences for specific individual countries or groups of states? Trade relations between the EC and third-party countries are normally developed in one or a mixture of four ways:

(i) through specific agreements between the EC and individual states or groups of countries. Here, an almost endless list of agreements is possible. These may take the form of association agreements, which may or may not lead to eventual full membership of the Community. Such agreements may have a financial aid package attached to them. Examples of the agreements extend from those made with Greece and Turkey which in the former case led to that country's full membership of the EC, to those recently made with three East European countries. There are preferential and non-preferential trade agreements. Such arrangements are normally reciprocal in nature—though the Lomé Accords are not. In the case of highly developed countries—for example, the European Free Trade Association (EFTA)—the normal arrangement offered would be a reciprocal free-trade agreement. Then, for Third World countries not associated with the coveted Lomé Accords, the most flexible arrangement would be a co-operative arrangement which may or may not be linked with a financial and technical aid package. Such arrangements tend to be favoured for links between the Community and Latin American countries.

(ii) through multilateral trade negotiations (MTNs). As already mentioned, these are examined in detail in the second part of this chapter.

(iii) through the Generalized System of Preferences (GSPs). This arrangement, which is intended for Third World countries, takes the form of non-reciprocal tariff-free quotas for the exports of these countries to the more developed ones. Here, the Community is the most important developed participant and has recently extended the arrangement for a further decade.

(iv) through the Multi-Fibre Agreement (MFA). This agreement was originally intended as a means of increasing, on a regular basis, textile exports of Third World countries to the more developed ones. Unfortunately, it has been transformed into a means of controlling exports of textiles from Third World countries. However, it is now intended to bring textiles back into the GATT fold—where they correctly belong.

Which countries or groups of states are the Community favourites and how are the associate privileges translated in concrete results? If we exclude the EC Member States themselves, I would choose the following list (in descending order of importance):

(i) the EFTA countries,
(ii) the ACP States,

(iii) the Mediterranean countries, notably the Mahgreb States,
(iv) the United States,
 (v) the others—including non-ACP Third World countries—and Japan.

What is most surprising is that despite the privileges conferred on the ACP States (some 76 countries), they do not, as a bloc, constitute the most important trading partner of the EC. Rather, the United States is the Community's number one trading partner. Similarly, the EC is the most important trading partner of the United States. At the end of this chapter I will attempt to give an explanation of this phenomenon.

United States' trading policies

In comparison with the clearly defined trading policies of the European Community, the United States cannot be said to have any clearly defined set of trading policies. Instead, as with American agricultural policies, trade policies are unco-ordinated reactions to lobbies at home and countries abroad. In the case of the latter, the United States has frequently tended to use its award of the MFN treatment to countries for political reasons. This was particularly so in 1974 when the then Soviet Union was reluctant to allow Soviet Jews to migrate.

Like the European Community, the United States does use 'anti-dumping' measures; but it also uses quotas on a substantial scale (at the beginning of 1992, 3,600 such product quotas existed).

Reference has already been made to the American trade practice of using the American Selling Price which so incensed the EC during the course of the Kennedy Round Negotiations. More recently, the United States has had recourse to the notorious Article 301. The use of this article has bitterly upset the Community. This article is in fact Section 301 of the United States Omnibus Trade and Competitiveness Act of 1988 (being a revision of the Trade Act of 1974). In this Act, which is reproduced in full at the end of this book, the Americans are empowered to take action against a country or countries which violates American trading rights in the following manner:

If the United States Trade Representative determines under section 304(a)(1) that—
  (A) the rights of the United States under any trade agreement are being denied; or
  (B) an act, policy, or practice of a foreign country—

(i) violates, or is inconsistent with, the provisions of, or otherwise denies benefits to the United States under any trade agreement, or

(ii) is unjustifiable and burdens or restricts United States commerce; . . .

What particularly infuriates the EC is the practice, consequent to article 301, which leads to the placing of a country or countries by the United States on a so-called 'black list'. The EC, together with, among other countries, South Korea, has been placed on this list regarding telecommunications equipment. This action has made the Commission even more angry since it maintains that the decision was taken in the preparation of the Trade Act in 1986, whereas since the agreement, made by the EC in 1990, to open up public procurement to competitive bidding for the telecommunications market, the situation has completely changed. Furthermore, it is stressed that the United States enjoys overall a balance-of-payments surplus with the EC—and specifically for this item.

The Commission was again particularly incensed when, in April 1991, the EEC was placed on its 'priority watch list' under 301 because of the barriers to entry for American television programmes resulting from EC broadcasting legislation. The United States also began separate action under Title 7 of the Trade Act which could lead to a ban on public procurement from Community sources.

Despite the seemingly disparate and unco-ordinated American trading policies, I do believe that things are changing. In 1989, the United States signed a free trade agreement with Canada. Now, negotiations are in progress between the United States and Mexico to extend the agreement to the latter country, thus creating a North American Free Trade Area (NAFTA). Should this NAFTA materialize, then one could see the United States adopting similar trading policies to those long since practiced by the Europeans in creating regional trading blocs.

Having made this observation, it should be stressed, however, that the clearest direction to American trading policies is seen when the US Congress gives a mandate to the president to undertake international trade negotiations in the framework of the Multilateral Trade Negotiations (MTNs). It is to this critical area of relations between the Community and the United States to which we shall now turn.

The Multilateral Trade Negotiations (MTNs): The Kennedy, Tokyo and Uruguay Rounds

The background

At the outset, it is important to note that the General Agreement on Tariffs and Trade (GATT) constitutes a more or less satisfactory substitute—a kind of arrangement together with a code of conduct for international trade—for the envisaged International Trade Organisation (ITO) which was to have provided the third leg of the United Nations tripod together with the IMF and the World Bank (or International Bank for Reconstruction and Development). Unfortunately, the United States could not accept the strong powers which would have been embodied in the planned ITO, and, consequently, we are left with a set of rules, the GATT, which should have been applied by that organization. Now, attempts are being made to transform this agreement into something which could possibly embody some of the powers with which the ITO would have been endowed.

At this point, it is important to take note of a number of the most important GATT articles, some of which, in my opinion, are responsible for several severe problems currently being encountered in the Uruguay Round. First, however, the most positive achievement of this code of behaviour is the principle which is embodied in the first thirteen articles which requires the Most-Favoured Nation (MFN) treatment to be extended, without exception, to all the signatories.

Turning to present problems, of great importance to the EC is Article XVIII, inserted at the insistence of the United States (!), allowing countries to form customs unions and free trade areas—thus conferring privileges on each other—but under no obligation to share them with the other GATT members. Perhaps of equal importance to the Community are articles XI and XVI which allow quantitative restrictions to be placed on agricultural imports as well as giving subsidies to agricultural exports, respectively. There are also 'escape clauses', notably concerning dumping, to which the EC is sometimes accused of having too frequent recourse.

The GATT achieved considerable success in the immediate postwar decades in influencing the removal of quantitative restrictions. However, trade relations between the Community and the United States assumed great importance during the course of the Kennedy, Tokyo and the current Uruguay Rounds.

The Kennedy Round (1964–7)

Writing some years ago, I observed that it was during the course of the Kennedy Round Negotiations that the EEC really came of age on the international stage. This was the time, when, in the field of international trade, that the Community negotiated as one body. Furthermore, it marked the beginning of the definitive transfer of responsibility for EC trade to the Commission and established the Community and the United States as the chief protagonists in the MTNs.

In examining the background to and in analysing the actual negotiations, I made the following observations.

The United States Congress, with what appeared to be a magnanimous gesture, passed the Trade Expansion Act in October 1962 by which the president was empowered to conclude commercial agreements with foreign countries and to amend the restrictions on imports through tariffs or counter-tariffs for a period of five years. He was furthermore given the possibility of reducing tariffs by as much as 50 per cent with the special possibility of going as far as 100 per cent in the case of the Common Market. This act did in fact extend and replace the commercial legislation enacted in 1934 whereby the American president was empowered to conclude international trade negotiations.

Thus, the United States proposed again what seemed to be a magnanimous gesture, across-the-board tariff reductions of 50 per cent over a period of five years; the reductions should cover both industrial and agricultural goods. Technically speaking, this proposal and the subsequent negotiations did mark a change in international economic relations. Formerly, in the framework of GATT, negotiations had been made product by product with, in the case of the Dillon Round negotiations, the addition of partial linear reductions. Now, the procedure was to be one of a policy of equal linear reductions of tariffs combined with a procedure for harmonizing tariffs.

The reaction of the European Community was conciliatory but firm. The Community declared itself perfectly in agreement with the American proposals for a 50 per cent across-the-board reduction in tariffs but declared that preliminary negotiations would have to take place regarding those products, particularly textiles, chemical products and plastics on which American duties were so high as to render the 50 per cent reduction ineffective.

Also, the Common Market wished to negotiate two American obstacles to free trade, the case of the American selling price and the problem of American anti-dumping legislation.

Regarding the agricultural sector, the Community, which was still in the process of organizing its own agricultural market and policy, wished to negotiate a *montant de soutien* at an international level for agriculture and also wished to conclude international agreements for agricultural products. In the latter case, the Community was really rather *avant-garde* since negotiations about such agreements are only now (1992) at the centre of international trade negotiations.

On the side of the Community, during the Kennedy Round nego-

tiations—as during those leading to the creation of special drawing rights—
the role of France was important. France stimulated the other members
into action. She was particularly interested in getting the highest American
tariffs reduced before negotiating across-the-board tariff reductions, and
she did want to get international recognition for the Community agricultural policy.

In the first case, she suggested that the 50 per cent reduction be applied
to the difference between the present and a hypothetical ideal duty (called
the *écretement* method). This suggestion was accepted by the Community
but not by the United States. Nevertheless, the Americans made a concession when they proposed that there should be special rules of general
and automatic application for tariff reductions where great disparities in
tariffs existed. This concession was a major victory for the Community.

Early in 1964, the Community had presented a new mathematical formula known as the *double écart* (expressed in the form 2:1 + 10). According to this formula, a disparity existed when a high customs duty in a
major country or bloc was at least double the tariff applied by another
country to the same item, and the difference between the two tariffs was
at least ten percentage points. This formula was to be applied only to
finished products and raw materials.

The United States presented a counter-proposal in which the fundamental criterion used was to be the idea of a minimum level which would be
above 40 per cent *ad valorem* with a gap between the two tariffs of ten
percentage points. However, the Americans declared themselves prepared
to accept a modified version of the *double écart* should their own proposal
prove unacceptable to the Common Market.

Subsequently, the Common Market proposed a theoretical tariff
reduction ranging from 15 to 35 per cent, implying an average of 25 per
cent. The Community, nevertheless, also included some fixed elements in
this proposal. This new type of scale was accepted in 1964 by the subcom-
mittee on tariff negotiations as providing an adequate working basis.

Nevertheless, the Community came up once again in 1967 with its
proposal for using the *double écart* against a set list of priorities. It suggested reductions varying from 15 per cent for the lowest tariffs to 35 per
cent for the highest. The EEC did not propose adopting this formula on
a unilateral basis. Also, where the United States clearly demonstrated
that a closer examination of the tariffs on some goods showed that they
were in fact lower than the Community's common external tariff, the
Common Market dropped the items from its list. Thus, by mid–1967, the
Community succeeded in invoking against the United States and Britain
just over 200 tariff items in its common external tariff.

The main negotiations of the Kennedy Round covered the period

1965–7. In 1963 the preparatory conference had taken place, and in December 1964 the different participants had laid their lists of exceptions with the GATT secretariat, where they were then examined and compared and recommendations were made as to whether they could really be defended. By the end of 1965 problems had arisen in a number of areas and it was therefore decided that working groups would be created which would examine six products in 1966. These products were aluminium, chemicals, paper, paper pulp, steel and textiles. In the sector devoted to chemicals, the problem of the American selling price was examined.

In some of these areas, the Common Market and the United States were not the only countries involved. Thus, for example, regarding aluminium, paper and paper pulp, Scandinavian countries were chiefly concerned; for steel, Britain was an important partner; while textiles involved an important part of the Third World. At this point, the vexed question of the American selling price is examined.

The European Economic Community regarded the principle of the American selling price with even more hostility than that shown by the Americans towards the Community's agricultural policy. The American policy had originated in the 1920s in an attempt to protect organic products derived from benzene, produced in the United States. In the 1960s four groups of products were protected of which the most important was benzenoids.

The United States maintained that this protection was not important whereas the Common Market pointed out that in the case of benzenoids at least a tenth of all American chemical production was protected, and it was an area in which the United States enjoyed a considerable trade surplus. Furthermore, the level of protection was very high, in some cases varying between 100 and 172 per cent! Finally, the Community pointed out that thousands of products were potentially liable to this form of protection.

The American selling price works in the following manner: a basis is taken for valuation at the customs which is the price of a similar product manufactured in the United States. The qualitative criterion used by the United States is that the good is 'competitive' with a similar American product. Hence the contention made by the Community that thousands of goods are potentially liable to this form of protection.

The American Synthetic Organic Chemical Manufacturers Association (SOCMA) had already in the summer of 1964 sensed the danger when it proposed administrative changes in this form of protection. However, the Common Market was adamant in its opposition to this practice, and when it placed its list of exceptions with the GATT, late in the same year, it stated that it would accept no tariff reductions for organic chemicals, dyestuffs or chemicals unless changes were made in the practice of the American selling price and in similar practices in related fields. The Community again repeated its demands in 1966. At the end of the same year, the United States proposed a compromise which was rejected by the EEC the following year when the Community nevertheless proposed a global compromise. This compromise had been reinforced by a strong suggestion made by the US Tariff Commission that the American selling price should be abolished. Subsequently, the Community did accept the earlier American proposal of *découpage*, which meant that the negotiations in the field of chemicals should be split into two parts.

In the first part, tariff concessions would be made (where possible by the end of June 1967) for chemical products. In the second part, Congress would be invited to abolish the American selling price in exchange for the removal of some non-tariff barriers by partner countries. Unfortunately, while agreement was reached on the first part, the American Congress refused to abolish the American selling price system.

The negotiations concerning agricultural products fared no better than those concerned with the American selling price. It was perhaps somewhat unrealistic to expect success in this field because the European Economic Community was still in the process of organizing its own internal agricultural market. This meant that delays in the negotiations would be inevitable while the Community itself would be sensitive to American attempts to obtain a special position in the European market. The Americans had already in 1963 retaliated against the imposition by the Common Market of increases in tariffs on imports of frozen chickens. This incident became known as the 'chicken war' and made relations between the Community and the United States somewhat delicate. However, the fact that the EEC was still in the process of organizing its agricultural market really meant that the negotiations in the field of agricultural products were premature.

The United States had from the beginning (1964) been most critical of the proposals made by the Community regarding agricultural policy. In that year, Mansholt had made public his second plan wherein through the use of the *montant de soutien* (which would be the difference between the world price of a product and the price in any particular country) agreements would be made at an international level which would aim at stable prices and a fair return for farmers. A part of this plan which is too easily overlooked was that whereby producer countries would make attempts to avoid surpluses of agricultural produce, any surpluses produced would, however, be used to help less-developed nations. Also, this plan aimed at organizing international agreements for a number of products which included grain, beef and sugar.

A series of heated exchanges occurred between the Community and the

United States before both sides agreed to a proposal made by the Director of the GATT that, with some exceptions, they should negotiate sector by sector—as for industrial products.

The Community suggested a self-sufficiency scheme for cereals in 1966 which was supported by many countries but not by the United States. Finally, in May 1967 the Americans presented a new plan which completely ignored internal agricultural policy, stock levels or suggestions about self-sufficiency. In anger, the Community dropped any idea about a general agreement for cereals, and the final negotiations for a system of international grain prices and for the organization of an international food aid programme took place outside the framework of the GATT.

The Kennedy Round negotiations did not concern exclusively the United States and the European Economic Community, but they were the chief partners at Geneva. In themselves, the negotiations were economically important because they did, as Table 1.2 shows, lead to tariff reductions which might not otherwise have been made. The negotiations and the results achieved were important because they were a precedent for future trade negotiations at which particular attention would have to be paid to the needs of the Third World and to making changes in agriculture policy and non-tariff barriers.

The European Economic Community returned from Geneva with its unity, strength and common personality enhanced. It had succeeded in negotiating with the United States as an equal. It had persuaded the Americans to make special reductions in their highest tariffs. While the Community had not succeeded in persuading Congress to abolish the American selling price system, it had, in turn, not made concessions to the United States which could have damaged its infant common agricultural market. Thus, while it would have been foolish and wrong to describe the two main protagonists as being either winners or losers, it would be correct to describe the negotiations as being a dialogue between equals. This fact was to carry some weight in encouraging the United Kingdom and other countries to persist in their attempts to join the European Economic Community.

From my examination, it is clear that both protagonists, the European Community and the United States, did reach most important compromises in Geneva which had great implications for the rest of the world. What is probably most important at the international level is the real reduction in the higher tariffs which is shown in Table 1.2. Probably no other MTN had led to such clear and positive results for the world.

Table 1.2a Distribution of the tariff rates of the principal industrial countries before the Kennedy Round negotiations

Rate of duty	CET[a]	USA	UK
Duty free	6.2	6.9	8.0
> 0–< 5.0%	5.5	5.4	0.8
> 5.0–<10.0%	26.7	15.0	24.9
>10.0–<15.0%	34.8	17.2	12.7
>15.0–<20.0%	22.2	17.7	26.1
>20.0–<30.0%	4.3	20.4	17.4
>30.0–<50.0%	0.2	15.4	9.8
>50.0%	0.1	2.0	0.3
Total	100	100	100
Modal tariff class[b]	>10.0–<15.0%	>15.0–<20.0%	>15.0–<20.0%

Source: J. Dugimont, 'The Kennedy Round negotiations', *Etudes Economiques* (Mons, Belgium) Nos. 127–8 (April 1966), p. 100.

Table 1.2b Distribution of the tariff rates of the principal industrial countries after the Kennedy Round negotiations

Rates of duty	CET[a]	USA	UK
Duty free	8.2	8.7	12.4
> 0–< 5.0%	23.2	23.1	21.2
> 5.0–<10.0%	55.6	29.9	34.7
>10.0–<15.0%	10.7	14.6	16.1
>15.0–<20.0%	2.0	11.2	12.7
>20.0–<30.0%	0.3	8.6	2.6
>30.0–<50.0%	–	3.4	0.3
>50.0%	–	0.5	–
Total	100	100	100
Modal tariff class[b]	>5.0–<10.0%	>5.0–<10.0%	>5.0–<10.0%

Source: Tariff study by GATT, Summary table No. 2, *Tariff and Trade Profiles by Product Categories* (Geneva, 1970).
[a] Common External Tariff
[b] Modal tariff class is defined as the tariff class below which 50 per cent of the tariff levies lie
Reproduced from Peter Coffey, *The External Economic Relations of the EEC*, Macmillan, London, 1976.

The Tokyo Round (1973–9)

As has already been mentioned, as a result of the Kennedy Round, tariffs no longer played any substantial role in the trade of developed countries. Instead, these countries—and especially the EEC—had increasing recourse to non-tariff barriers. Accordingly, it was expected that the next MTNs would have to tackle this question. Also, the United States, especially the American trade unions, were demanding action for agriculture.

Again, it was the two major protagonists who initiated the next moves. Writing about the developments in 1976, I noted that in February 1972 the EEC, Japan and the United States agreed to undertake a new set of international negotiations. At ministerial meetings, held in Tokyo in 1973, it was agreed that the emphasis should be on non-tariff barriers, although the United States would have liked all tariffs eliminated over a five-to-ten-year period. In contrast, the Common Market would have preferred to harmonize tariffs.

On this occasion, the United States was adamant about obtaining advantages in the agricultural field. However, the Americans preferred to see commodity arrangements (in which the Common Market was interested) organized between producer countries outside the GATT negotiations.

It was hoped that a major part of the negotiations could be undertaken in 1974, but the United States decided to link the granting of most favoured nation treatment to the Soviet Union with Russian flexibility concerning the immigration of Soviet Jews. Until satisfaction was obtained on this point it was not possible to get the negotiations started. The negotiations proper started in Geneva in February 1975, and very soon disagreement arose between the Community and the United States over questions of agricultural protection and non-tariff barriers.

Prior to the opening of negotiations, the Community had agreed to enlarge the generalized system of preferences by 15 per cent and to reduce the number of products in the 'sensitive' category to seven. I would still, however, regard the management of this system as being far too complex.

In anticipation of the opening of the negotiations proper, the Commission, in October 1974, sent a document of some thirty pages to the Council containing suggestions regarding the strategy which should be adopted by the Community at Geneva. The main points set down in this document were:

(1) Tariff reductions on average of between 25 and 50 per cent of existing tariff levels were proposed. Very high tariffs should be cut by at least 50 per cent. Most of the countries taking part in the negotiations should not practise tariffs higher than 20 per cent.
(2) Import barriers should be examined and co-operation be encouraged between suppliers and consumers.
(3) International agreements should be made regarding some essential raw materials in order to stabilize the market for these products.

(4) *Agriculture*: international agreements were proposed for a number of products which would include wheat, maize, rice, sugar, milk powder, butter and perhaps some cheeses (these would represent 25 per cent of the EEC agricultural trade).

The Commission suggested three types of agreements:
  (i)   Price agreements for dairy products, with minimum and maximum price levels.
  (ii) Storage agreements for cereals, managed by the world's main producers.
  (iii) In the case of sugar and rice, a similar policy (as for (ii)) was proposed, with the difference that here management would be the responsibility of the appropriate international organisations.

The Commission considered that for agricultural products which were not subject to international agreements (i.e. 75 per cent of the EEC agricultural trade), a code of conduct should be negotiated between importers and exporters (particularly in the case of meat). In practice, this would imply that importers would agree not suddenly to stop importing products while exporting countries would agree to supply goods on a regular and smooth basis.

The views of the European Economic Community on negotiations about agriculture—and notably those of France—did not, perhaps surprisingly, differ too much from those from the United States. However, the Americans were much less consistent than the EEC. The Community, strongly pressed by France, did, at least at the time of the Tokyo Round, consistently favour negotiations among groups of producer and consumer countries, whereas the United States sometimes favoured negotiations among producers and on other occasions among consumers. Once again, however, agriculture remained outside the MTNs. Similarly, textiles had been moved from the GATT framework to the Multi-Fibre Agreement (MFA).

In contrast with the results of the Kennedy Round, the Tokyo Round conclusions were disappointing. There were some tariff reductions, but these were not important because of the substantial reductions already agreed upon in the previous round. As already mentioned, it had been accepted that something had to be done about non-tariff barriers and the GATT rules themselves. The results were mixed.

A Code on Subsidies and Countervailing Measures was indeed accepted by the Community and the United States. In this respect, some experts think that this code actually weakened the GATT's existing rules. Equally, the very necessary Code on Government Procurement was not comprehensive enough and left out critical areas involving pace-making industries.

Whether the agreement reached on civilian aircraft was necessary is open to discussion. Probably of greater importance were the codes on customs valuation—with the move towards the adoption of internationally accepted standards, import licensing and technical standards. Also, the Anti-Dumping Code, already agreed upon during the previous round, was brought more up-to-date.

Unfortunately, it was felt that the Tokyo Round had not gone far enough and that the GATT itself was becoming less able to deal with changes in trading practices. Consequently, following difficult negotiations between the developed and Third World countries, it was agreed that a new set of Multilateral Trade Negotiations, the Uruguay Round, should be opened.

The Uruguay Round

At the outset, it should be stressed that this is the most comprehensive set of international trade negotiations ever organized, and that, once again, the chief protagonists are the European Community and the United States. However, in contrast with previous MTNs, on this occasion more attention is being paid to the needs of Third World countries.

Once again, the United States has insisted but, this time, successfully, in having agricultural policy included in the negotiations (this policy area is examined in the next chapter). Both protagonists wanted services, intellectual property rights and investment safeguards to be included in the present round. In contrast, a number of Third World countries were opposed to the inclusion of these areas in the negotiations. As a compromise to these countries, the Community and the United States agreed to include tropical products in the round in exchange for the aforementioned matters which are of great interest to them.

To me, the greatest need is to bring into the orbit of the GATT the approximately one-third of world trade not covered by the agreement. Of equal importance is the fact that in 1989 there were 250 'voluntary' trade agreements.

Although, correctly, I assume, the greatest emphasis is, once again, on non-tariff barriers, tariffs are by no means excluded. Indeed, the aim is to achieve an overall reduction of 33 per cent with 1986 as a reference year. Here, the negotiations have mainly returned to the older formula of the 'request and offer' approach. However, the two main protagonists have, together with other developed countries, reached an agreement of principle or made progress for freeing trade in a number of industrial sectors—notably in the field of pharmaceuticals.

If we exclude the controversial area of agriculture (which is examined in the next chapter), where are the Community and the United States in the Uruguay Round? Where do they agree and where do they differ in their approaches?

At the outset, it can be said that if we exclude agriculture and the aircraft industry, the European Community and the United States were, until late in 1991, surprisingly close in a number of areas. In other sectors, they did, with some exceptions (notably telecommunications), agree to reach a compromise. More recently, and somewhat unexpectedly, more profound disagreements have arisen between the two parties. This discord bodes ill for the future of international trade.

As already mentioned, the two parties did agree that something should be done about services. Here, they were in some deep disagreement with Third World countries which feared the financial strength and the sophistication of the Europeans and Americans.

In the field of GATT codes and government procurement, the Community and the United States had reached a compromise in 1988, in Montreal, and had also agreed to extend the codes to all government agencies.

Both sides, but more especially the United States, wished to protect their investments overseas. Here, one could discern the beginning of a joint attitude towards their interests abroad. Again, they both wanted action in the field of intellectual property rights—an area where they were both suffering losses in the countries of the former Soviet Union and Third World countries.

Regarding subsidies and countervailing duties (excluding agriculture), both sides started out by adopting different positions. However, by 1992, they seemed to be on the road to adopting a compromise on industrial subsidies. This has certainly been the case (as we shall see in chapter 3) for the aircraft industry.

Again, concerning the disputes' settlement of the GATT, the issue of 'transparency' in trade and the future functioning of the GATT, both parties started out by adopting similar attitudes.

Thus, if we exclude agriculture, we do have a substantial list of areas where the two sides had adopted similar attitudes or where they had reached or were on the road to reaching a compromise. What, then, is the present state of affairs and why has it developed?

Reference has already been made to the important role of lobbies in the United States and the consequential, somewhat erratic course of American trade policies. Naturally, lobbies have become even more important in a time of recession; and although the economic slowdown in the United States is less severe than that being experienced by the countries of the European Community, it is still a painful experience for a large number of Americans—thus strengthening the lobbies. To this must be added the fears of some American corporations that they may face competitive disadvantages in the Community's Single European Market (SEM) when it comes into being on 1 January 1993. Indeed, in the field of public procurement, inside the Community, now open to competitive bidding in a number of important areas, EC companies have a price advantage of 3 per cent for bids while any Member State which finds that the EC value added of any bid amounts to less than 50 per cent can declare the offer invalid. But the Community has offered to negotiate on this matter in the Uruguay Round. Although the United States does try to keep its own public procurement for American enterprises, they are concerned about the SEM. Nevertheless, it did come as a surprise to me when AT&T, one of the world's very greatest corporations in the field of telecommunications, sought a 'derogation' or exception in the Uruguay Round! This was the beginning of the slide downhill into protectionism which we are now witnessing.

Much more serious was the threat, made in February this year, by the United States Trade Representative, Mrs Carla Hills, of 'sanctions' against the Community unless 'an agreement is reached concerning certain measures relating to public procurement'. I will return to this matter later in the chapter.

Much more sinister in its implications was the threat made by the United States Ambassador to GATT, a month after that made by Mrs Hills, to 'refuse to give access to maritime transport, civil aviation, financial services and basic telecommunications on a MFN basis unless other countries come up with better offers to open their service markets to foreign suppliers'. How on earth have matters reached such an impasse?

The reasons for this impasse are fairly simple. The Uruguay Round, which had started in 1986, in Punta del Este, should, according to the 'fast-track formula' accorded to President Bush by the United States Congress, have been concluded in March 1991. Instead, following a summit meeting, in Brussels, in December 1990, the Community and the United States failed to reach a compromise over their differences on agricultural policy and negotiations broke down.

In the meantime, the mandate of the United States Administration to continue the 'fast-track negotiations' was extended until March 1993. Thus, negotiations between the two sides were resumed, and, following the generous American offer made at the summit in The Hague, in November 1991 (which is examined in greater detail in the next chapter), most observers confidently expected the Europeans and the Americans to reach a compromise.

The following month, Arthur Dunkel, Director-General of GATT,

Table 1.3 The structure of Community trade by major trading partner and product, 1958–90 (current prices)

	Import share (%) Origin				Export share (%) Destination			
	1958	1980	1988	1990	1958	1980	1988	1990
By geographic area								
Other industrialized countries	48	46	62	60	48	50	61	60
of which:								
EFTA	14	17	23	23	20	25	27	27
USA	18	17	18	18	13	13	20	18
Japan	1	5	11	10	1	2	5	5
Eastern Bloc[a]	6	8	8	9	7	9	8	8
Other countries	46	46	30	31	44	41	31	32
of which:								
OPEC	17	27	8	10	12	18	9	8
ASEAN	3	3	3	4	3	3	3	4
Asian NIEs[b]	1	3	6	6	2	3	8	6
Mediterranean basin	7	8	8	9	12	13	10	11
Latin America	10	6	6	6	9	6	4	4
By product								
Primary products:								
Food, beverages, tobacco	30	9	9	8	9	8	7	8
Fuel	16	35	11	15	–	–	–	–
Other raw materials[c]	30	11	10	8	8	7	5	4

Manufactures								
Machinery and transport equipment	6	14	28	29	37	37	39	40
Chemicals	–	–	–	–	9	10	12	12
Other manufactures[d]	17	24	35	35	37	32	31	31
Miscellaneous, etc.	1	7	7	5	0	6	6	5

[a] Includes Albania, Bulgaria, Czechoslovakia, GDR, Hungary, Poland, Romania, the USSR, China, Cuba, Mongolia, North Korea and Vietnam
[b] Includes Hong Kong, Singapore, South Korea and Taiwan
[c] EC exports include fuel products
[d] EC imports include chemicals

Source: Commission Annual Economic Report 1991–92

tabled a compromise package of proposals known as the Final Act. These
proposals were accepted by all the participants except the EC. However,
it should be stated that the Community did not reject them out of hand.
Also, it had been hoped that the negotiations would have been successfully
concluded by Easter (late April) 1992. Unfortunately, despite further
conciliatory proposals made by the Americans, in March 1992, negotiations still dragged on. More dangerously, the United States is now
backtracking in the field of services, and, EC industrialists, painfully aware
of the catastrophic danger of a permanent break in the negotiations, have
urged the Community to compromise.

Clearly, in this impasse the Europeans are not the only ones to blame.
Alas, however, it seems to be their uncompromising attitude in the area of
agriculture that has encouraged the United States to threaten to withdraw
critical service industries from the negotiations.

Structural trade considerations

Before turning to the agricultural issue, it is important to try to ascertain
why the Community and the United States still remain each other's main
trading partners (if we exclude the EFTA countries with which the EC
has a preferential free-trade agreement) and why the Americans have such
a persistently important and increasing trade surplus with the Community.

When we examine Tables 1.3 and 1.4a and b, the consistency of the
relationship between the two partners becomes very apparent. Also, it
reflects a total change in world trading patterns which has become increasingly marked in the past two and a half decades. Thus, while before World
War II there seemed to be an unchanging division of labour whereby
industrialized countries traded with less-developed countries, with the
former exporting manufactures to and importing raw materials from the
latter group of countries, in recent decades all this has changed. This
change has manifested itself by an intensification of trade between highly
industrialized countries producing similar products which have a high value
added. Hence the terms of trade have been very advantageous for these
countries and it was this evolution that led to the oil crisis and the formation of OPEC. It is therefore logical that the Community and the United
States should remain important trading partners. Similarly, the observations about the product content of trade are underlined by the figures
in Table 1.3 which show a major increase in imports by the Community
of machinery, transport equipment and other manufactures. Although the
EC has held its own or slightly increased exports of these products, it has

not been able to match the swifter increase in imports. These developments have been to the advantage of the Americans.

Table 1.4a Direction of US merchandise trade with the world, 1990 (%)

European Community	25
Canada	21
Latin America	14
Japan	12
East Asia NICs	10
Other countries	18

Source: Compiled from official statistics of the US Department of Commerce

Table 1.4b US Exports to the European Community, by SITC, 1991 (%)

Machinery and transport equipment	49.8
Miscellaneous manufactured articles	13.1
Chemicals and related products	11.0
Basic manufactures	6.3
Crude materials excluding fuels	5.7
Food and live animals	3.9
Mineral fuels, lubricants, etc.	3.9
Beverages and tobacco	2.2
Oils and fats	.2
Others	3.9

Source: Compiled from offical statistics of the US Department of Commerce

There are a number of reasons why this should have been so. A most obvious one is the sharp depreciation of the US dollar in recent years which has been to the considerable advantage of the United States. This position had been enhanced by stable or declining American labour costs as compared with the steadily rising ones in the Community.

Finally, it should be stressed that the Community is composed of countries with open or very open economies. Although the EC Member States do conduct some 60 per cent of their trade among themselves, their very great degree of openness when compared with that of the United States and Japan means that the Europeans will continue to conduct much of their trade with non-EC countries.

1. Until February 1992, correctly and legally speaking, one talked of the European Economic Community (EEC). After the signing of the Maastricht Treaty, the organization is known as the European Community (EC).
2. The twelve Member States of the EC are: Belgium, Denmark, France, Ger-

many, Greece, Ireland, Italy, Luxembourg, Netherlands, Spain, Portugal and the United Kingdom.
3. *The External Economic Relations of the EEC*, Macmillan, London, 1976.

2
The agricultural issue

When, in July 1990, at the Houston Summit, the United States strongly repeated its three proposals for the reform of the world's agricultural production and trade,[1] it seemed that the European Economic Community and the Americans had reached the culmination of a long process of confrontation in the field of agriculture. The proposals, which formed one of the main American planks in the Uruguay Round of the Multilateral Trade Negotiations, were:

(i) the conversion, by all the negotiating parties, of all non-tariff barriers to agricultural trade to their equivalence in tariffs, using a means known as 'tariffication'. Subsequently, tariffs would be reduced substantially over a period of ten years.
(ii) Countries would phase out export subsidies over a period of five years.
(iii) Also, nations would phase out measures for internal farm support that distorted trade.

It was the refusal of the Community, later in 1991, to accept these proposals in their unchanged form that led to the breakdown of the Uruguay Round. The EEC had made much more modest counter proposals which were equally quite unacceptable to the United States. The dramatic breakdown of these negotiations might lead observers to believe that the two parties had always been confronting each other over agricultural issues. Although there had been regular disagreements over specific issues such as the 'chicken war' and over quality of products or health standards, the two sides had never before reached such a level of confrontation. In fact, according to the erudite study, 'Disharmonies in EC and US Agricultural Policies', published by the Commission of the European Communities, in 1988, when the Common Agricultural Policy (CAP) had been founded, the two sides had made a deal which removed any possible American objections to the policy. Thus, in exchange for American acceptance of the idea of the variable levy (which, in turn, implied acceptance of export refunds or subsidies), which is one of the king-pins of the CAP, the Community agreed to accept free or low-duty imports of all oilseeds, proteins and grain substitutes. At that time, EEC imports of such products were very low whereas today they are important because they successfully compete with highly protected and expensive feedgrains for cattle and other animals.

The real problem is that since the founding of the CAP, the situation of the world agricultural trade has completely changed. In the late 1950s and early 1960s, the world's most important exporters of agricultural products were the United States, Canada, Argentina, New Zealand and Australia but not the EEC. In fact, at that time, the Community was a net importer of many products. Since then, largely as a result of the EEC's CAP—as well as American support for its own farmers—the two international agricultural 'superpowers' are the EC and the United States. Unfortunately, they are competing in a declining market. As can be seen from Figure 2.1, reproduced from the aforementioned Commission publication, the two superpowers account for over 50 per cent of international trade in butter, cereals and skimmed-milk powder. Equally, they are most important exporters of beef, veal and sugar—as well as holding most of the world's stockpiles of agricultural products.

Before continuing with this examination of the major confrontation between the Community and the United States—which led to the breakdown of the Uruguay Round Negotiations at the end of 1991—it is necessary to examine the basic workings of the two systems.

The systems in action

The Common Agricultural Policy (CAP)

The basic mechanism of the CAP, which is described below, does not cover all the agricultural products of the EEC. Thus, for example, there is no common policy for potatoes while sugar has always had a separate and, more or less, self-financing régime. Also, perishables and Mediterranean products are protected by a mixture of guaranteed prices and quotas. It is the classical temperate products—such as beef, cereals, milk and dairy products—produced mainly in northern European countries which are covered by the basic CAP mechanism.

Here, target prices are negotiated, each year, for all the products cov-

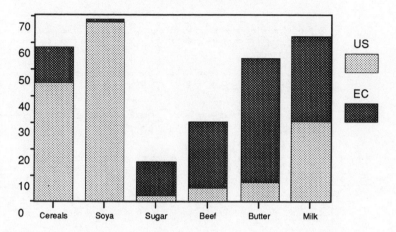

Figure 2.1 Combined EC and US share of world food exports (%)

Sources: Toepfer International, *Grain and Feeding Stuffs Market Statistics 1985/86*, Hamburg; Agricultural Information Bulletin No 467 and 472, USDA, 1985; Eurostat, *Yearbook of Agricultural Statistics*, Luxembourg, various years; Eurostat, *Crop Production*, Luxembourg, various years; Eurostat, *Animal Production*, Luxembourg, various years; *Zenttrale Markt-und Preisberichtstelle fur Erzeugnisse der Land-, Forst-und Ernaehrungswirtschaft, Bilanz, Milch*, Bonn, various years; FAO, Monthly Bulletin of Statistics. Rom, various years; International Sugar Organisation, *Sugar Yearbook*, London, 1983; *Disharmonies in EC and US Agriculturral Policies*, Commission of the European Communities, 1988.

ered by the system. The aim is to attempt to arrive at prices, inside the Community, which will give a decent standard of living to the least efficient farmers. There are then three technical legs to the system. First, when local wholesale prices for the agreed products fall below the intervention price (generally some 10 to 20 per cent below the target prices), the local Intervention Boards must buy up the surpluses, which are put into storage. Then, the second leg is the variable levy (always higher than the target price) which varies with the world price for a product and which is intended to keep out imports from non-Community sources. Finally, there is the export refund (or subsidy) which is the difference between world and intervention prices and which is paid to exporters who sell products outside the EEC.

Inevitably, the big and/or efficient farmers have produced more and more, and huge surpluses have resulted. The United States and the CAIRNS Group of countries have accused the EEC of dumping their surpluses on world markets thus destroying the traditional markets of these countries.

Attempts have been made to reduce these surpluses—notably for milk and cereals—through the use of internal quotas and financial penalties, but still the overall surpluses remain.

Table 2.1 US farm income and expenses, 1970–88 (in US$ billions)

Item	1970	1975	1979	1980	1981	1982	1983	1984	1985	1986	1987	1988
Gross income from farming	58.8	100.6	150.7	149.3	166.3	163.5	153.1	174.9	166.4	160.4	171.6	177.6
Cash income	54.8	90.7	135.1	143.3	146.0	150.6	150.4	155.3	156.9	152.5	162.0	171.6
Marketings cash receipts	50.5	88.9	131.5	139.7	141.6	142.6	136.6	142.4	144.1	135.5	139.5	151.4
Crops[1]	21.0	45.8	62.3	71.7	72.5	72.3	67.1	69.5	74.3	64.0	63.8	72.6
Net CCC loans[2]	-.1	.2	-.9	.5	3.1	9.1	-.7	-.8	11.8	8.3	.2	-5.2
Livestock	29.5	43.1	69.2	68.0	69.2	70.3	69.4	73.0	69.8	71.5	75.7	78.9
Government payments	3.7	.8	1.4	1.3	1.9	3.5	9.3	8.4	7.7	11.8	16.7	14.5
Other farm income[1]	.6	1.0	2.2	2.3	2.5	4.5	4.5	4.4	5.0	5.1	5.8	5.7
Value of home consumption	.8	1.1	1.3	1.2	1.2	1.1	1.1	1.1	.9	.9	.8	.8
Rental value of dwellings	3.3	5.4	9.3	11.0	12.6	13.1	12.5	12.3	10.9	9.7	9.1	9.5
Value of change in inventories[3]	(Z)	3.4	5.0	-6.3	6.5	-1.4	-10.9	6.3	-2.4	-2.7	-.4	-4.3
Expenses of farm production	44.5	75.1	123.3	133.1	139.4	140.0	140.4	142.7	134.0	122.4	124.5	132.0
Intermediate products	25.2	42.5	71.9	76.1	76.6	73.7	75.8	76.0	72.2	65.8	69.4	76.3
Farm origin	13.3	20.0	35.2	34.9	33.3	31.4	33.5	32.8	30.3	28.9	31.8	36.9
Feed purchased	8.0	12.9	19.3	21.0	20.9	18.6	21.7	19.9	18.0	16.2	16.9	21.0
Livestock, poultry purchased	4.3	5.0	13.0	10.7	9.0	9.7	8.8	9.5	9.0	9.7	11.8	12.8
Seed purchased[4]	.9	2.1	2.9	3.2	3.4	3.2	3.0	3.4	3.4	3.0	3.0	3.1
Manufactured inputs	5.4	12.4	17.9	22.4	23.9	22.2	20.9	21.5	21.0	17.0	17.0	18.2
Fertilizer and lime	2.4	6.7	7.4	9.5	9.4	8.0	7.1	7.4	7.3	5.8	5.6	6.4
Pesticides	1.0	1.8	3.4	3.5	4.2	4.3	4.2	4.8	5.0	4.5	4.6	4.7
Fuel and oil	1.7	3.3	5.6	7.9	8.6	7.9	7.5	7.1	6.6	4.8	4.4	4.5
Electricity	.3	.6	1.4	1.5	1.7	2.0	2.1	2.2	2.1	1.9	2.4	2.6
Repairs and maintenance[5]	2.8	4.5	7.3	7.6	7.6	6.4	6.5	6.4	6.4	6.4	6.5	6.9
Other[6]	3.7	5.6	11.5	11.2	11.9	13.6	14.9	15.3	14.5	13.5	14.1	14.3

Interest	3.4	6.4	13.1	16.3	19.9	21.8	21.4	21.1	18.7	16.9	15.5	15.2
Real estate	1.8	3.3	6.2	7.5	9.1	10.5	10.8	10.7	9.9	9.1	8.2	7.9
Non-real estate	1.6	3.1	6.9	8.7	10.7	11.3	10.6	10.4	8.8	7.8	7.3	7.3
Contract, hired labour expenses[7]	4.3	6.6	9.0	9.3	8.9	10.1	9.7	9.7	9.8	9.9	10.8	11.2
Net rent to non-operator landlords	2.1	4.0	6.2	6.1	6.2	6.1	5.1	8.6	8.2	6.7	7.1	7.5
Capital consumption[8]	6.9	12.4	19.3	21.5	23.6	24.3	23.9	23.1	20.8	18.9	17.4	17.4
Property taxes	2.6	3.2	3.9	3.9	4.2	4.0	4.5	4.1	4.2	4.1	4.3	4.4
Net income of farm operators from farming	14.4	25.5	27.4	16.1	26.9	23.5	12.7	32.2	32.4	38.0	47.1	45.7
In constant (1982) dollars	34.2	43.1	34.9	18.8	28.6	23.5	12.2	29.9	29.2	33.4	40.0	37.5

Z Less than $50 million. [1]Forest product sales are included in cash receipts for crops for 1970 and 1975 and in other farm income beginning 1979. [2]Commodity Credit Corporation (CCC) loans made minus loans repaid. [3]Minus sign ($-$) indicates decrease in inventories. [4]Includes bulbs, plants and trees. [5]Expenditures for repairs and maintenance of farm buildings, motor vehicles, and machinery. [6]Includes machine hire and customwork expenses; marketing, storage, and transportation expenses and miscellaneous expenses. Beginning 1979 data not strictly comparable with prior years. [7]Includes Social Security payments and perquisites. [8]Depreciation and accidental damage.

Source: US Department of Agriculture, Economic Research Service, *Economic Indicators of the Farm Sector: National Financial Summary,* annual. Quoted from the *Statistical Abstract of the United States,* 110th edition, 1990.

The American system(s)

It is not possible, as in the case with the CAP, to talk of one American system: instead, we must talk of systems.

Over past decades, the United States has had recourse to a combination of systems—having greater or lesser use of one or others at different times. This combination includes the use of target prices, loans, taking land out of production, export subsidies, direct subsidies to farmers, direct purchases of products by the government from farmers and import quotas. The main criticism of these policies is that they have been badly co-ordinated, resulting in a mixture of high prices and surpluses.

Although the United States (according to the OECD statistics) does seem to spend proportionately less (taken as a whole) on its farmers—when compared with the EEC—the statistics published in the most recent (110th edition, 1990) *Statistical Abstract of the United States* (see Table 2.1) do, over the period 1984 to 1988, indicate an increasing reliance by American farmers on financial support from the government.

Also, as was seen in May 1990, when the US Agriculture Department started to pay off $10 billion on losses on already strongly subsidized loans to farmers made by its Farmers' Home Administration, it is clear that the government is not averse to helping farmers when crises arise. Equally, if the EC were to accept the agricultural trade proposals made by the American administration, then many American farmers—notably the dairy farmers in Wisconsin—would suffer very heavily. Whether or not the American farmers are ready to accept such sacrifices is not at all clear.

Negotiations or confrontations

In an effort to save the Uruguay Round negotiations, the Community did, in November 1990, make a compromise counter-offer to the American proposals. The EEC agreed to cut farm subsidies by 30 per cent over ten years. They did add qualifications which were intended to cushion the impact on smaller producers and to prevent the inflow of cheaper imports. These proposals were rejected by the United States and the members of the CAIRNS Group.

The next steps

It was not possible for the Community to remain indifferent to the accusation that it alone bore the responsibility for the breakdown of these negotiations which, if definitive, would have almost inevitably led to the collapse of the world trading system. Furthermore, at a more immediate practical level, the Commission had pointed out that agricultural budget costs would, in 1991, increase by 20 per cent over 1990. Something had to be done. Thus, at the beginning of February 1991, the Commission adopted a series of guidelines for the reform of the CAP.

In its proposals the Commission set down seven objectives for reforms:

(i) to enable the EEC to retain its competitive position on international markets;

(ii) to control food production in food sectors whose supply exceeds consumer demand;

(iii) to hold the agricultural budget under agreed ceilings;

(iv) to redistribute support by taking into account inequality between different categories of producer;

(v) to break the automatic link that has grown up between price support and the volume of food produced;

(vi) to recognize that farmers are both food and non-food producers and that they play a vital role in rural society as the guardians of the countryside and protectors of the environment; and

(vii) to encourage farmers to respond to public concern for better quality of food by use of less intensive farming methods.

In the summer of 1991, the Commission expanded these proposals in greater depth and detail and succeeded in persuading the Council of Ministers to accept them in principle in anticipation of the resumption of the extended 'fast-track' Uruguay Round Negotiations in the autumn of 1991.

It is necessary to examine the Commission's document: 'The Development and Future of the Common Agricultural Policy: Proposals of the Commission', in greater detail because the proposals cover 75 per cent of the Community's agricultural output in value terms. Particularly important—both for the EC and the rest of the world—are the proposals for cereals, milk and beef—all products which, over time, have been in considerable surplus.

In the case of cereals, using a current reference date, the Commission proposed lower target prices for all cereals (in fact, 35 per cent below present levels). These lower prices will replace the present co-responsibility levies. There is also a dual system of compensatory payments to farmers. The one system is intended for small farmers who will suffer income losses while the other is a set-aside system for more important farmers. These schemes will also apply to the existing arrangements for oilseeds and other proteins.

For milk, where only 15 per cent of farms are responsible for over 50 per cent of the final output and for which output is increasing while butter consumption is diminishing—a severe regime is proposed. The existing quota system will be expanded in scope and reduced in quantity, and there will be price reductions. However, as with cereals, a compensation scheme (a generous one) is planned for farmers whose quotas are reduced and for farmers ceasing production on a voluntary basis.

Similarly, for beef—where output is continuously increasing—intervention prices will be reduced (by 15 per cent). Equally, a generous compensation scheme is proposed for farmers suffering income losses.

Some other areas merit our attention. Thus, a system of deficiency payments which has been in operation for sheepmeat will continue to operate. Here, as in other areas, the number of animals has been increasing and it is therefore planned to introduce limits on the size of the flocks. As before, however, the existing supplementary subsidies for less-favoured regions will continue.

At this point it is important to note that, as in the case of sheepmeat, the Community operates a system of deficiency payments for oilseeds' production. Also, the Community has agreed to reform the present regime following the findings of the GATT 'Oilseeds Panel'. Basically, the reform will take the form of a 'standardized compensatory payment system with per hectare aids paid directly to the producer'.

The Commission's proposals do have implications both for the Community as well as for the rest of the world. At the outset, it should be stressed that the different compensation schemes which are proposed for EC farmers will cost money—a lot of money. The suggested figures in the Delors Budgetary Package Two are shown in Table 2.2. However, the compensation costs will be offset by the lower target and intervention prices. Also, if, as one might expect, the Community's agricultural levels decline, this will be good for world trade and would certainly be welcomed by the Americans and the CAIRNS Group of countries.

Nevertheless, a nagging problem does remain, can the other countries accept the direct compensation subsidies which the Community plans to give its farmers? It seems that the Community is concerned as to whether this form of subsidy will be considered as permitted under the GATT's 'green box'. Some observers seem to think that this issue no longer presents a problem and that the MacSharry Plan—which has just been examined—and the Dunkel proposals are not incompatible. Certainly, if the two sets of proposals could be merged, then agriculture would be brought firmly within the GATT framework, where it really belongs.

Table 2.2 Delors Package II: 1993–7 (billion ECUs 1992)

Commitment Appropriations		1987	1992	1997
I.	Common agricultural policy	32.7	35.3	39.6
II.	Structural operations (including the Cohesion Fund)	9.1	18.6	29.3
III.	Internal policies (other than structural operations)	1.9	4	6.9
IV.	External action	1.4	3.6	6.3
V.	Administrative expenditure (and repayments)	5.9	4	4
VI.	Reserves	0	1	1.4
	Total	51	66.5	87.5
Payment appropriations required		49.4	63.2	83.2
As a percentage of GNP		1.05%	1.15%	1.34%
Own resources ceiling – as percentage of GNP		(none)	1.20%	1.37%
Average annual GNP growth rate 1987–92 (actual) 3.1% 1992–7 (projected) 2.5%				

Source: EC Commission, 1992

Towards a compromise?

At the historic EEC-US summit, held in the Hague, on 9 November 1991, and at which a solemn declaration was issued (this document is reproduced in the appendices at the end of this book), President George Bush made (in my view a generous) compromise to dilute American demands for subsidies and help for agriculture. Thus, he agreed to reduce American demands for cuts in export subsidies to 35 per cent and 30 per cent for other forms of aid. However, the other major difference was that these changes should be put into effect over a period of between five and six years, in comparison with ten years in the earlier proposals.

At this point, it should be noted that the carefully thought out proposals for the reform of the CAP, put forward by the Irish Commissioner for Agricultural Policy, Ray MacSharry (and which are listed above), had already caused the most bitter controversy among the EEC Member States. Indeed, I was astounded to read that my own government—which had always criticized the CAP—found many of MacSharry's proposals to be unacceptable! Certainly, any transformation will cost money, but in my view, in the long run, the costs of encouraging farmers to produce more and then having to pay for the storage of and to subsidize the export of the resulting surpluses will, in every sense of the term, be even costlier.

However, returning to Brussels, where the intensive negotiations between the EEC and the United States were taking place and despite agreement by the two parties in a number of other very important areas—notably concerning services and intellectual property rights—a fundamental obstacle soon appeared in the interpretation of the Bush compromise proposals. The United States insisted that the EEC set ceilings on the tonnage for subsidized farm exports. Thus, in the case of wheat—a most important product, especially for France—the United States proposed a limit of eleven million tonnes at the end of five years, though they were also willing to accept twelve million. In contrast, the EEC proposed fifteen million as a limit but hinted that it might accept thirteen million.

Arthur Dunkel, the Director-General of the GATT, in presenting his 438-page 'final act' of the Uruguay Round on 20 December 1991, pleaded with the governments to accept this last chance of saving the world's trading system. He had also intervened with a compromise proposal for cuts in aid for agricultural products—a 36 per cent cut in budgetary payments and a 24 per cent cut in quantities—but to be spread over a six-year period, starting in 1993 and using the period 1986–90 as the base for reference. Perhaps of even greater importance is Dunkel's aim—in the long run—to convert all trade barriers into customs duties and then to lower them over time. Perhaps this will be the subject of the next MTN?

To the EEC (though I consider that this could be a misinterpretation on the part of the Community) the Dunkel proposals fail to cover much of the American aids to their farmers as deficiency payments and compensation for 'land banks', but should their interpretation be correct, then it would seem to imply that they would also be free to engage in such practices. Since in my opinion the problem of small farmers—notably those in the former West Germany—is a social one, then direct payments to these people would seem to be the best solution but, with a time limit for such compensation, as is done in Sweden.

Alas, alas, on the black Friday, 20 December 1991, the talks between the Community and the United States broke down in Brussels. Like two offended prima donnas, the two sides parted in an atmosphere of thinly veiled (to put it mildly) invective. In its editorial, dated 23 December 1991, the *Financial Times* talked of the world being 'on the brink of disaster'.

It seems that the last chance both sides have of retreating from the edge of the precipice is to reach a commonsense compromise. Although blame cannot be laid exclusively on one side since both the EC and the United States heavily subsidize their farmers, I would find it hard to see the finger of history pointing at the Community as being the party responsible for the breakdown of world trade and a return to the protectionism of the 1930s.

My own views and proposals

It was almost certain that the apparent willingness of the EEC to consider more substantial compromises on agriculture helped President Bush to persuade Congress to accept the exceptional and highly unusual request for a time extension for the 'fast-track' multilateral trade negotiations beyond the mandate for the Uruguay Round which ended in March 1991. Consequently, the Community would not allow itself to bear the responsibility for a further, final and definitive breakdown in negotiations.

Both sides—and the rest of the world—have so much to gain if they reach an agreement on agriculture. Basically, both sides face the same problems. The huge and increasing amounts of money being devoted to agricultural support amount to a scandalous and quite unacceptable squandering and misallocation of resources. Both parties need to channel these resources into high technology to improve their competitiveness *vis-à-vis* Japan.

Then, in both the EEC and the United States, the main beneficiaries are not the small or medium-sized farmers, but the 'big boys' and the major corporations. These people do not need help nor do, for example, the very efficient Dutch and Danish farmers. Instead, income payments should be channelled directly to the small and poorer farmers.

Apart from competing with each other, these two agro superpowers are distorting world trade by damaging traditional markets of other countries, notably those of the CAIRNS Group.

Last, and by no means least, there is the grave problem of over-intensive farming which is destroying the land and producing unappetizing food which is also sometimes dangerous for our health.

But, these are negotiations, so, what could the EEC demand in exchange for accepting American demands for agriculture? There are, in fact, a number of issues where the Community could use its leverage. The United States has placed the EEC on its black list for electronics. This is surely unwarranted, and the EEC must request its removal from this list.

Another area of dispute is steel. Here, the EEC accepted self-imposed exports of steel to the United States hoping, unwisely it seems, that the Americans, like the EEC, would use the breathing space to rationalize, reduce the size of and modernize their steel industry. When, in 1989, the agreement expired, the United States asked the Community to extend it for a number of years. This matter should also be negotiated.

Finally, in the framework of the Uruguay Round, AT&T, the world's most important telecommunications corporation asked (the request was apparently accepted) the United States Administration to support its request for protection. Protection from what or from whom? I am astonished at this extraordinary request and can only assume that this corporation is, alas, following the path downwards already trodden by Philips, the Dutch electronics giant. Here, the Community must surely reject this request if it is to accept American proposals for agriculture.

Unfortunately, in all this imbroglio, one fact remains: time is running out, and, as I have already observed, the Community cannot possibly allow the finger of history to be pointed—blackly and most negatively—in its direction. Future generations would never forgive us.

1. Originally, the proposals took the form of a 75 per cent cut in internal subsidies and border protection, and a 90 per cent reduction in export subsidies to be spread over a period of ten years.

3
The aircraft industry and airlines

The background

Ever since the end of World War II, Europeans have viewed with envy the American aircraft industry. They saw that, assured of a large integrated and wealthy internal market for both civilian and military aircraft, aircraft companies in the United States could use this secure home base to enjoy important economies of scale and to dominate the rest of the world. The importance of this home base has tended to increase with the passage of time because it has been observed that, with the exception of small niches, for example for the production of executive or small regional aircraft, even countries the size of Britain or France were too small to afford an aircraft industry of their own. Quite simply, Europeans would have to organize joint production programmes among themselves.

Similarly, with airlines, the United States has long enjoyed the advantage of having a huge internal and protected market. Further, when negotiating flying and landing rights with European airlines, after World War II, the Americans negotiated on a bilateral basis and were able to gain concessions from the Europeans which they only partially reciprocated.

Clearly, then, the United States has gained major advantages because of its sheer size and the degree of integration of its internal market. It is precisely the desire—and partial success—of the Europeans to emulate the American experience in the two fields of the aircraft industry and airlines that is at the root of the present quarrel between the EC and the United States.

European policies

At the outset, it is important to stress one peculiarity that is expressly European: some aircraft industries and nearly all national airline carriers are either fully or partially owned by European governments. Hence, these companies are expected, in some way, to reflect national identities and to serve their countries' interests. These interests are not always identical with those of European consumers. Thus, for example, the bilateral fixing of air fares between governments—known as 'cabotage'—means that the costs of air travel inside Europe are generally much higher than they should be. Fortunately, following an agreement by the Council of Ministers, on 22 and 23 June 1992, it was agreed to begin liberalising this regime. However, there will not be a fair and completely deregulated market until 1997.

Surprisingly, co-operation between European aircraft industries is not entirely new. The most prestigious and costly (in fact, the real costs of production have never been divulged!) project has been the example of Franco-British co-operation—Concorde. In my view, the Americans (who never made even a whimper about this project) and the Soviets were both only too pleased to have two misguided European nations undertake the astronomical research and development costs in the field of civilian supersonic aircraft, confident perhaps that they themselves would actually share in the spin-off benefits of the project.

But the main and logical areas of co-operation between European countries have been in the field of military aircraft. Following the successful co-operation between Britain, Germany, Italy and Spain in the production of the Tornado Fighter Aircraft, these same countries are now in the very quarrelsome development stage for the successor to the Tornado, called the European Fighter Aircraft. Unfortunately, as I had forecast, the escalating costs of this project—linked with other considerations—have forced Germany to announce its decision to drop out of this project. This places the other partners, Britain, Italy and Spain, in a delicate position. Should they continue with the existing project or should and can they embark upon a less ambitious, and, hopefully, less costly one?

It is notable all these projects—plus the most important project of all, Airbus—have been developed in spite of and not as a result of the European Economic Community.

The motor behind the development of the Airbus has been France. For some time (as in other fields), Britain was apprehensive about the project. Now, however, Britain, like the other partners France, Germany and Spain, would like to increase its share in the project. After a faltering start, Airbus has become very successful—supplying different versions of its aircraft to meet different needs and markets—and supplying about 30 per cent of world orders for civilian aircraft compared with only 13 per cent at the beginning of the 1980s. In fact, Airbus is the only real challenger to the domination of the world's civilian aircraft markets—for decades dominated by American companies—notably Boeing and McDonnell Douglas. At a time when, with some exceptions, the world market for military aircraft is declining, these American companies take the challenge and threat of Airbus very seriously indeed.

The American view

When I came to write this work, I discovered that at least one-third of the materials in my personal research consisted of American criticism of and action against the Airbus Industrie. To me, this is more than adequate proof of the fabulous power of the lobby of American aircraft industries in Washington and of the seriousness with which they view the Airbus challenge.

American concern about Airbus had been simmering for some time when, in September 1990, two events brought the matter to a head. The first was a study commissioned by the US Commerce Department, prepared by the consultants Gellman Research Associates, in which it was calculated that the British, French, German and Italian governments had given 13.5 billion dollars to the different Airbus Programmes since the late 1960s. Furthermore, the study insisted that Airbus would never become economically viable.

The second event was the agreement made by the German government to provide the Daimler-Benz Company (a participant in the programme) with two billion dollars to cover currency exchange risks until 1999 because of losses incurred in the sales of the Airbus aircraft invoiced in dollars instead of ECUs.

The European reaction

The Europeans, in the person of Henri Martre, the Chairman of Aérospatiale, said that American support for its aerospace industry was greater than that given to European aircraft industry by European governments. Martre said that the American aerospace industry received at least three times as much government aid as the European industry.

Despite this strong riposte by the French element in the Airbus programme, the Europeans decided to attempt to negotiate with the Americans. Unfortunately, the United States Administration decided to reject conciliation and, surprisingly, to take the case to the GATT in Geneva. Interestingly, officially, at least, the Americans decided on this course of action because they could not accept the EEC offer to ban all aid in aircraft production and set a 45 per cent limit on the aid for the development of new models without entering into a clear commitment for a second-stage reduction following the successful conclusion of a multilateral agreement in the framework of GATT.

The Europeans are, quite understandably, surprised at the American reaction to their proposals. Amid all the recriminations, it would be wise to return to the main thread of the argument which was laid down in the introduction to this section. The EEC is trying to create something, on the European continent, similar to the great internal market of the United States. One important point which has always been stressed by Europeans is the fact that it is the market for military aircraft, so very important in the United States, which is directly supported by the United States administration. The importance of this market is borne out by the statistics in Tables 3.1–3.3. Also, these figures are reinforced by two fabulous contracts for military aircraft which were published in April 1991 in the United States: first, the Pentagon chose a Boeing-Sikorsky team for the award of a contract for a new generation of combat helicopters for the army, estimated to be worth 34 billion dollars; then the air force chose the Lockheed design for a new fighter plane, the F–22. The estimated cost to the air force, alone, is 95 billion dollars.

Table 3.1 Sales of the aerospace industry, by customer (in millions of dollars)

Aerospace products & services

Year	Total sales	Government Dept. of Defense	NASA & other agencies	[1]Commercial aerospace	Non-aerospace products & services
P 1989	120,643	63,996	8,234	28,306	20,107
R 1988	114,562	61,327	7,899	26,242	19,094
R 1987	110,008	61,817	6,813	23,043	18,335
1986	106,183	59,161	6,236	23,089	17,697
1985	96,571	53,178	6,262	21,036	16,095
1984	83,486	45,969	6,063	17,540	13,914
1983	79,975	51,558	5,910	19,178	13,329
1982	67,756	34,016	4,899	17,451	11,390
1981	63,974	27,244	4,709	21,137	10,884
1980	54,697	22,795	4,106	18,977	8,819

[1]Incl. exports. P—Preliminary   R—Revised

Source: Aerospace Industries Association.

Table 3.2 Sales of the aerospace industry, by product (in millions of dollars)

Aircraft

Year	Total	Military	Civil	Missiles	Space	Non-aero-space
P 1989	120,643	41,805	20,127	11,512	27,092	20,107
1988	114,562	41,867	19,019	10,270	24,312	19,094
R 1987	110,008	43,723	15,465	10,219	22,266	18,335
1986	106,183	40,687	15,718	11,964	20,117	17,697
1985	96,571	36,752	13,730	11,438	18,556	16,095
1984	83,486	31,215	10,690	11,335	16,332	13,914
1983	79,975	30,058	12,373	10,269	13,946	13,329
1982	67,756	24,502	10,982	10,368	10,514	11,390
1981	63,974	19,635	16,427	7,640	9,388	10,884
1980	54,697	15,179	16,285	6,469	7,945	8,819

P—Preliminary   R—Revised

Source: Aerospace Industries Association. Quoted from Industry Surveys, June 21 1990.

Table 3.3 Defense budget authority (DOD only) (In billions of dollars)

Fiscal year	1985	1986	1987	1988	1989	1990	1991[1]
Procurement	96.8	92.5	80.2	80.1	79.4	82.5	77.9
RDT & E	31.3	33.6	35.6	36.5	37.5	36.8	38.0
Operating maintenance	77.8	74.9	79.6	81.6	85.9	86.8	90.1
Military personnel	67.8	67.8	74.0	76.6	78.6	78.5	79.0
Other	13.1	12.6	10.0	8.9	9.0	6.7	10.5
Total[2]	286.8	281.4	279.5	283.8	290.2	291.4	295.1

[1]Proposed in January 1990—subject to revision [2]Sum rounded off

Source: Department of Defense.

Further developments

The Commission was clearly stung by the American decision to take the Airbus case to the GATT since it asked the American law firm Arnold and Porter to undertake an audit of American aid to the commercial aircraft industry. The result of this audit appeared simultaneously in Brussels and Washington in a report, published at the beginning of December 1991, in which Arnold and Porter alleged that owing to the flexibility of the American taxation system and the financing of military contracts with civil impact by both the Department of Defense and NASA, the United States administration does indeed indirectly subsidize the aircraft industry.

Anticipating the American reaction to the report, Mogens Carl, a senior official in the Commission, in Brussels, said that the study, had, in reality understated the case because of the rigorous nature of the calculations undertaken. However, he stressed that the study, which simply examined the facts of the case, did underline the profound links existing between the United States administration and its civil aircraft industry.

The anticipated reaction was not long in coming. Exactly a day later, the Boeing Company contested the results of the audit and questioned the impartiality of the law firm concerned, pointing out that it had been over a number of years a consultant for Airbus Industrie.

The future

It is particularly important to note that Mogens Carl did also hold out an olive branch to the Americans when he stated that the Community was still waiting for the American reply to its suggestion that the two parties resume bilateral consultations. He added that they should begin negotiations aiming at reaching a precise bilateral or multilateral agreement in the field of commercial and civil aircraft.

It is also equally important to note that Airbus Industrie entered the international capital markets for the first time, at the end of June 1991, with the issue of a five-year Eurolira bond for 112 million dollars. This implies that in the future the Airbus programme will be financed partly by governments and partly by the markets. At the same time, sales of the aircraft have increased and the programme will consequently become more viable commercially.

In the dispute between the two parties, it is worth noting (see Table 3.5) that the United States enjoys a substantial surplus for aircraft on its balance-of-payments account. Having said this, it should be stressed that the United States and American aircraft contractors are extremely worried at the present time about the outlook for the aircraft industry. On the one hand, with military *détente* and disarmament a reality, cuts in defence spending are taking place in many parts of the world. As the statistics in Tables 3.3 and 3.4 clearly demonstrate, this is going to hurt American aircraft contractors particularly hard since they have, in the past, relied heavily on the market for military aircraft. Consequently, they are trying to compensate the envisaged losses in the military field by selling more civilian aircraft. Here, however, while some—but only some—airlines are expanding and ordering more aircraft, others are ordering fewer than was originally planned. The hoped-for expansion in passenger traffic, with the exception of special holiday periods such as Thanksgiving and Christmas, is not materializing. Thus, the success of Airbus Industrie is particularly worrying to the Americans.

Table 3.4 Defense Department outlays—aircraft procurement (in millions of dollars)

ªFiscal year	DOD Total	Air Force	Navy	Army
E 1990	26,510	14,678	9,019	2,813
E 1989	28,751	16,536	9,346	2,869
1988	28,246	15,961	9,407	2,878
1987	32,956	20,036	9,614	3,306
1986	30,828	18,919	8,992	2,987
1985	26,587	15,619	8,263	2,705
1984	23,196	12,992	8,040	2,165
1983	21,013	11,799	7,490	1,724
1982	16,793	9,624	5,872	1,297
1981	13,193	7,941	4,397	855
1980	11,124	6,647	3,689	788

E—Estimated ªFiscal years end Sept. 30

Source: Aerospace Industries Association. Quoted from *Industry Surveys*, June 21 1990.

Table 3.5 Aerospace trade balance (in millions of dollars)

Year	Total U.S. trade balance	Aerospace Trade balance	Exports	Imports
P 1989	(112,777)	20,938	31,429	10,491
1988	(118,526)	17,860	26,947	9,087
1987	(158,207)	16,019	23,924	7,905
1986	(162,281)	12,802	20,704	7,902
1985	(136,627)	12,592	18,724	6,132
1984	(110,932)	10,082	15,008	4,926
1983	(60,710)	12,619	16,065	3,446
1982	(35,182)	11,035	15,603	4,568
1981	(30,051)	13,134	17,634	4,500
1980	(27,336)	11,952	15,506	3,554

P—Preliminary

Source: Aerospace Industries Association. Quoted from *Industry Surveys*, June 21 1990.

The position regarding the airlines themselves in Europe is also changing. After 1 January 1993, the market will, to a large degree, have become deregulated. There is also a trend towards bigness as is shown by the proposed merger between British Airways and KLM, and the planned major participation by Air France and Sabena Airlines.

With increasing deregulation (finally) of the EEC internal airline market, the United States will, eventually, have to negotiate with the Community as a whole when new agreements for trans-Atlantic airline rights come up for discussion. A taste of things to come was the agreement made between Britain and the United States when the British extracted major concessions for landing rights in both continental Europe as well as in the United States in exchange for the transfer of PanAm's, and TWA's landing rights at London's Heathrow Airport to United and American Airlines.

The result will be that both the remaining European aircraft contractors and the airlines will improve their negotiating power internationally. If we exclude Japan, then, as in trade, the two economic and commercial superpowers are the United States and the EEC or the members of the future European Economic Area or Space. The two sides will then, as in other fields, be forced to negotiate. If the result is increased competition and, almost inevitably, improved landing rights for European airlines in the United States, then consumers on both sides of the Atlantic will benefit.

The GATT ruling and its consequences

Reference has already been made to the complaint made by the United States to the GATT on the exchange-rate guarantee granted by the Federal German Government to Daimler-Benz when it took over Deutsche Airbus in 1989. According to this agreement, the guarantee would become operational when the dollar dropped below an exchange rate of 1.60 DM The United States alleged that this guarantee subsequently resulted in a subsidy of 2.5 million dollars per Airbus.

In January 1992 the GATT panel ruled in favour of the American complaint because it concluded that the exchange-rate guarantee did not conform with the GATT Code on Subsidies. Despite the disappointment of the Community over this ruling, and its subsequent silence about the matter, the Commission did understand the German action was illegal. Also, the Commission took the wise initiative of proposing a revision of the GATT Code on Subsidies for the Aeronautical Sector. It suggested that advances on future development programmes should not exceed 45 per cent of the cost—with possible reimbursement if successful. This proposal contrasted with an American suggestion for a limit of 25 per cent. This wise initiative led to a series of semi-secret negotiations on these matters between the two sides which almost resulted in tentative agreement at the end of March 1992. Differences between the two sides centered mainly on the Community's criticism of American help for military programmes and American criticism of European governmental help for the development of civilian aircraft.

According to *Europe* 1 April 1992 the tentative agreement between the two sides was thought to have comprised the following points:

(a) subsidies already in existence would not be touched;
(b) production supports would remain totally prohibited;
(c) using pressure on third country governments to convince them to buy aircraft of a certain origin would be prohibited;
(d) aid for the development of new models of over 100 seats would be allowed in the form of repayable advances with well-defined limits: for direct aid, 30 or 35 per cent (the exact figure was not revealed) of the cost of overall development (indirect aid would not be allowed to exceed 5 per cent of the turnover of the beneficiary firm in the civil sector);
(e) detailed provisions would govern the transparency of subsidies and compulsory reciprocal information;
(f) a protection clause would allow the agreement to be suspended in the event of exceptional circumstances due to external events;
(g) both parties would agree to refrain from complaints or attacks against the respective systems.

As for the conclusions already handed down by a GATT panel on a specific aid scheme, the exchange guarantees provided by the German government to the German branch of the Airbus consortium, the European Commission's position is as follows:

— the panel's arguments are unacceptable, particularly because they consider the sale of aircraft from one EC country to another to be 'exports';
— the controversial regime will nevertheless be modified to make it compatible with GATT rules. The German government is currently defining the appropriate measures to this end.

The text of the agreement is obviously far more complex than the brief summary given above and contains detailed provisions as well on interest rates on reimbursable public loans, on the reimbursement period, on the calculation of indirect aid and on application of the safeguard clause, etc.

To me, despite the apparent Community disappointment about a lack of firm agreement about aircraft subsidies by the two parties, the desire of the Commission to have this matter settled in the GATT framework is a wise one because it will then become binding on the participating parties. Also, it should prevent the Europeans and Americans from resorting to 'non-transparent' aids for their aircraft industries. Then, the fact that the two sides are actually negotiating on a bilateral basis is a most positive development. It seems likely that they will reach a compromise on aircraft subsidies.

4
The monetary dimension

In the past, so much was written about the monetary dimension that the present calm seems to be almost unnerving.

Until the Louvre Accord, I was one of the main critics of America's dangerous disregard for the position of the US dollar in the international exchange markets. Indeed, both Presidents Carter and Reagan had openly stated that the position of the US dollar did not bother them. Imagine any European prime minister saying this about his or her national currency! It was America's unacceptable behaviour in the monetary field that, among other considerations, persuaded EEC Member States to launch the European Monetary System (EMS). We shall return to the EMS later in this chapter.

Until the creation of the predecessors of the EMS, the 'Snake in the Tunnel' and the 'Snake Arrangement', international monetary relations between the United States and Europe had taken place almost exclusively in the framework of the IMF, ie the old Bretton Woods Agreement. The kingpin of the system had been the pivotal role of the US dollar and America's agreement to exchange official holdings of its currency for gold. Only France, incidentally, had pushed things so far as to demand gold for its dollars. Because of its key role in this gold exchange standard, other countries in the system intervened in the markets to keep the value of the dollar constant. Also, one other major pillar in the system was convertibility.

During the 1960s, a major controversy had arisen about the adequacy of international liquidity. On the one hand, the Americans and the British insisted that there was not enough liquidity, using the argument that the quantity of international liquidity had not kept pace with the growth of world trade. The French, on the other hand, insisted that the trade deficits of certain Western countries was the proof that there was more than enough liquidity. The French also added that the role of the US dollar as a reserve currency conferred exorbitant privileges on the Americans who were allowed to manufacture more and more dollars—which were taken up by foreign governments, institutions and banks—in order to finance the American budgetary and trade deficits. Continuing in the same view, the French, at the end of the sixties and in the early seventies, gave strong support to the creation of an economic and monetary union (EMU) among the EEC Member States, pointing out that since the Community was the world's largest and most important trading bloc it should therefore have a 'common international monetary personality'. To the French, the most obvious and easiest way of achieving this aim would be to create a common European currency.

Although, with the return to power in France in 1958 of General Charles de Gaulle, France also returned to monetary orthodoxy—helped by Messers Pinay and Rueff—it was, in fact, the West Germans who were the paragons of monetary virtue in their own national economic management. Also, in their obsession with the danger of inflation (a call back to the 1920s and 1930s when astronomical levels of inflation had wiped out the savings of the middle classes and had caused serious social unrest), the West Germans have (and continue) to raise constantly the value of their currency. They were, however, strangely silent in this international monetary argument. The only relevant statement made by the West German Bundesbank was that they did not want the Deutsche Mark to become a reserve currency. In my view, it was a combination of military and political considerations which encouraged the West Germans not to rock the boat. The presence of so many Soviet troops on their borders with East Germany made the presence of American troops in their own country both desirable and necessary.

The outcome of this, at times very heated, argument between the Anglo-Saxons and the French was the inevitable compromise. A slight increase in international monetary liquidity was accepted through the creation of the Special Drawing Rights (SDRs). As a counterpart, through a change in the statutes of the IMF, the EEC Member States did obtain the right of veto, although the United States does maintain its own right of veto.

But, as mentioned earlier, the important moves by the EEC in the monetary field have been internal and have taken the form of the first steps on the road leading to the creation of a full EMU. It is to this exciting development that we should now turn.

The community's moves towards a full Economic and Monetary Union (EMU)

The European Community, in its moves towards achieving a full economic and monetary union (EMU) can, where economic and monetary policies are concerned, serve as an example or model for other countries—including the United States. Equally, the Community has, correctly, looked to the Federal Reserve System of the United States as a possible model, at least, in part, for a future European Central Bank. However, it is necessary, at the outset, first to define an economic and monetary union and then to note the reasons why the Community should have decided, voluntarily, to embark upon the difficult and hazardous task of creating a full EMU.

In numerous works—but notably in *The European Monetary System— Past, Present and Future* (Kluwer, 1987, second and revised edition) I have defined an EMU as follows:

In the case of the members of a customs union, such as the EEC, a full EMU implies the free movement of goods, persons, capital and services within the union—plus the existence of a common external tariff *vis-à-vis* third parties. It implies irrevocably fixed exchange rates plus full convertibility—or a common currency. Also, it implies common economic, fiscal and monetary policies— together with a minimum degree of fiscal integration. In turn, common monetary policies *vis-à-vis* third parties would exist. Finally, these implications would presuppose certain common decision-making organs such as a central bank, among others, for example. Last, but by no means least, all this would imply a transfer of national sovereignty from the participating countries to the centre. Herein lies the real problem when nation states decide, on a voluntay basis, to move along the road to an EMU.

Why then, did the original Six Founder Member States, in The Hague at the end of 1969, agree on such an important transfer of economic and monetary sovereignty to the centre—'provided that the political will to do so exists'—a decision renewed by the present twelve Member States twenty years later? There are, in fact, a number of very logical reasons why these countries should have reached such a momentous decision.

These countries had, by 1968, achieved most of the aims as laid down in the Treaty of Rome. Quite simply, ahead of time, the customs union had been achieved. Consequently, the economies of the Member States had become well integrated and they were conducting about half their trade among themselves. Then, there was the position of the Community's Common Agricultural Policy. The successful functioning of this policy depended on upon stable (preferably fixed) exchange rates. At an international level, the EEC had become the world's most important economic and trading bloc, endowed with the most important reserves of gold and convertible currencies. France had, for a number of years, considered that the Community should consequently be endowed with a 'common international monetary personality'. One of the best ways of demonstrating such a personality would be to create an EMU and a common currency. Also, it should be borne in mind that up to 1968 the Western world had experienced a full decade of relatively stable exchange rates. It was hoped that this situation would continue, and one the best ways of ensuring the continuation of this state of affairs would be to create an EMU. Finally, these countries were either 'open' or 'very open' economies and needed exchange-rate stability. Hence their support for an EMU.

Earlier attempts at EMU

In the late 1960s, two schools of thought had developed, the 'economists' and the 'monetarists'. It was, however, the second and definitive Werner Report, a compromise between the two schools of thought and published in 1970, which was the original blueprint for the Community's EMU. It is also salutary to remind ourselves that, according to this plan, the then EEC was to have created a full EMU by 1980! This fact must be borne in mind when examining the current Treaty on European Union. The Werner Report, nevertheless, laid down the details only for the first stage of the plan. The most important innovation was the idea of an EEC currency snake in a dollar tunnel—hence, the 'Snake in the Tunnel' (see Figures 4.1 and 4.2) After only a year of operation (which came into being two years later than the originally planned date), it became the 'Snake Arrangement'—with a margin of fluctuation of 2.25 per cent around the central parity (the predecessor, in fact of the Grid Arrangement in the present European Monetary System). At the end of its life, in March 1979, this Snake Arrangement took the form of a small Deutsche-mark zone.

There were a number of reasons why it was both desirable and necessary that the Community should create a European Monetary System (EMS)—originally proposed by Roy Jenkins. The EEC Member States had become more integrated and open than before. As a consequence of their already mentioned 'openness' (see Table 1.1), they could not accept the American irresponsibility in international monetary policy and the apparent total disregard by the United States for the international position of the dollar. Then, the Community Member States wished to integrate further implying greater economic and monetary co-operation. Consequently, ex-Chancel-

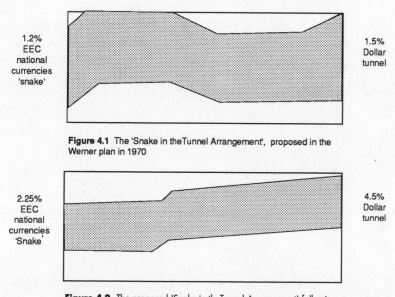

Figure 4.1 The 'Snake in theTunnel Arrangement', proposed in the Werner plan in 1970

Figure 4.2 The proposed 'Snake in theTunnel Arrangement' following the Smithsonian agreements in 1971

Source: P. Coffey, *Main Economic Policy Areas of the EEC*, Nijnoff,Den Haag,1983

lor Schmidt of Germany and ex-President Giscard d'Estaing of France pushed very strongly for an EMS.

The EMS bears some similarity with its predecessor, the Snake Arrangement, but it also embodies fundamentally key differences which could serve as an example for other countries, especially those embarking upon similar forms of economic and monetary union.

Technically speaking, there are two elements to the EMS, the Grid or bilateral national currency mechanism and the more constricting Exchange Rate Mechanism (ERM), ie the national currency to the ECU (European Currency Unit) link (see Figure 4.3). In the former, the same margin of fluctuation, 2.25 per cent, is operated as under the Snake Arrangement. However, in the earlier case, Italy and in the more recent cases of Britain and Spain, a wider margin of 6 per cent is in operation.

In the case of the ERM, the Commission has individualized the margins of fluctuation *vis-à-vis* the ECU (see Table 4.1). The ECU itself is a basket of the twelve currencies of the EC Member States as shown below.

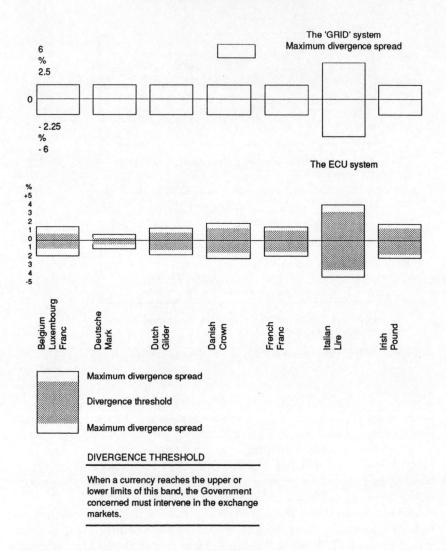

Figure 4.3 The 'Grid' and ECU systems of the EMS

Source: P. Coffey, 'The European Monetary System - Six months Later', *Three Banks Review,* December 1979, London.

New Composition of the ECU as on 21 September 1989

Deutsche Mark	30.10%
French Franc	19.00%
Pound Sterling	13.00%
Italian Lira	10.15%
Dutch Guilder	9.40%
*Belgian Franc	7.90%
Danish Crown	2.45%
Irish Punt	1.10%
Greek Drachma	.80%
Spanish Peseta	5.30%
Portuguese Escudo	.80%

*Includes the Luxembourg Franc

The narrow, in some cases extremely narrow, margins of fluctuation *vis-à-vis* the ECU (all Member States except Greece participate in the ERM) are a constraint on the members of the ERM. Even more constrictive are the four commitments that Member States accept on joining this active part of the EMS whenever their currencies come under pressure.

Thus, the responsibilities of the country concerned when the Divergence Indicator is reached *vis-à-vis* the ECU by its currency are clearly laid down by the Resolution of the Council of Ministers on 5 December 1978. They are:

1. diversified intervention;
2. monetary measures;
3. drawing on credit facilities;
4. external and domestic policy measures.

These commitments are indeed a salutary lesson for other countries, notably the United States. In detail, they imply that when a participating country's currency comes under pressure on the exchange markets that country—and the other countries whose currencies are concerned—will intervene on the markets in an attempt to remedy the situation. If this action fails, then the country concerned will raise or lower interest rates. Then, it may have recourse to the generous short- and medium-term credits available under the EMS. Fourth, if all these three sets of action are of no avail, then the country concerned will be obliged to take internal and external economic action, normally of a fiscal nature. Finally, if all these still fail to improve the position of the currency which is under pressure, a swift and discreet exchange-rate re-alignment may have to be operated. All in all, these are indeed major commitments which have been voluntarily accepted by these countries.

To underline the role of the ECU, all twelve Member States exchanged 20 per cent of their reserves of gold and US dollars for official ECUs.

In comparison with its predecessor, the EMS has been successful. No participant has left the system while three new countries, Britain, Spain and Portugal, have joined the ERM. Although no further allocations of official ECUs have been created and the EMS did not move on to a second stage—as had been planned—in March 1981, the unplanned creation and expansion of the commercial ECU market has been very successful. This expansion is clearly shown by the statistics in Table 4.2. Here, a number of EC governments have made major issues of ECU-denominated treasury bills, securities and bonds. It is possible also to buy ECU-denominated travellers' cheques and to open up ECU-denominated private bank accounts. In these countries, ECU coins are accepted as legal tender. Most important of all, the ECU has remained more stable than other units of account or currencies and the EMS has constituted an important zone of monetary stability. Now, with the signing of the Treaty on European Union, it seems that the EC Member States have really committed themselves actively to creating a full economic and monetary union.

The new moves towards an EMU

Once again (!) the Community decided to embark upon a full EMU and they agreed that the first stage would begin in July 1990. Many countries had hoped that the second stage would begin in 1993, but the opposition of some EC Member States led to the adoption of a compromise whereby the second stage will begin on 1 January 1994. In the meantime, the EMS continues to operate. Concerning the future of the EMU, further details— both precise and imprecise in nature—are laid down in the Treaty on European Union. Most important of all, it is imperative to get the dates right regarding the final stage of the union. Regarding this matter, I have detailed a kind of conspiracy of inattention—shared and adopted by many journalists and experts alike. If we refer to article 109 J, sections 3–5, of the Treaty, we read the following:

3. Taking due account of the reports referred to in paragraph 1 and the opinion of the European Parliament referred to in paragraph 2, the Council, meeting in the composition of Heads of State or of Government, shall, acting by a qualified majority, not later than 31 December 1996:
—decide, on the basis of the recommendations of the Council referred to in

Table 4.1 The Commission's 'individualization' of Maximum Divergence Spreads and Divergence Thresholds (%)

Currencies	Maximum Divergence Spread *vis-à-vis* the ECU	Divergence Threshold *vis-à-vis* the ECU (until 16 Sept. 1984)	Divergence Threshold after 16 Sept. 1984
Belgian/ Luxembourg Franc	2.03	1.52	1.543
Deutsche Mark	1.51	1.13	1.146
Dutch Guilder	2.01	1.51	1.516
Danish Crown	2.18	1.64	1.642
French Franc	1.80	1.35	1.366
Italian Lira	5.43	4.07	4.051
Irish Punt	2.22	1.67	1.667
Pound Sterling	—	—	—

Source: EC Commission.

Table 4.2 The private ECU market in billions of US dollars

	1985	1986	1987	1988	1989	1990	Stocks at end 1990
Total bank lending[1]							
Gross	17.2	6.2	11.1	23.4	24.6	23.7	194.6
Net[2]	9.0	5.0	8.0	12.0	10.0	18.0	65.0
International bond issues							
Gross completed	7.3	6.3	8.4	10.9	12.0	17.6	
Net	7.2	5.9	7.5	9.8	6.7	11.2	74.6
Net Euro-note placements						4.9	8.4
Domestic bond issues							
Gross completed	2.0	1.7	2.0	8.4	10.3	15.0	
Net	2.0	1.7	2.0	8.4	8.7	13.9	47.8
Short-term domestic treasury bills and notes							
Gross	0.0	0.0	2.0	8.3	19.5	20.2	
Net	0.0	0.0	2.0	6.5	3.7	− 2.4	11.4
Memorandum item: Official reserve holdings of private ECUs[1]	0.8	1.1	1.4	8.1	7.3	13.7	36.9

[1] At constant end-of-period exchange rates [2] Minus double-counting due to re-depositing among the reporting banks

Source: Bank for International Settlements 61st Annual Report

paragraph 2, whether a majority of the Member States fulfil the necessary conditions for the adoption of a single currency;
—decide whether it is appropriate for the Community to enter the third stage, and if so,
—set the date for the beginning of the third stage.
4. If by the end 1997 the date for the beginning of the third stage has not been set, the third stage shall start on 1 January 1999. Before 1 July 1998, the Council, meeting in the composition of Heads of State or of Government, after a repetition of the procedure provided for in paragraphs 1 and 2, with the exception of the second indent of paragraph 2, taking into account the reports referred to in paragraph 1 and the opinion of the European Parliament, shall, acting by a qualified majority and on the basis of the recommendations of the Council referred to in paragraph 2, confirm which Member States fulfil the necessary conditions for the adoption of a single currency.

Thus, it is only if the date for the beginning of the final phase has not been agreed upon by the end of 1997 that it shall start on 1 January 1999; but the ministers could decide on 1 July 2015, for example. Certainly, if as at present, only two countries, France and Luxembourg, fulfil the strict criteria for moving on to the final phase, there would be absolutely no point in so doing. These strict criteria, set down in the protocol on the Excessive Deficit Procedure and on the Convergence Criteria are as follows:

  (i) government deficit spending (the national budget) shall not exceed 3 per cent of gross domestic product (GDP) at market prices;
 (ii) government debt shall not exceed 60 per cent of GDP at market prices;
(iii) inflation for a country over one year before examination shall not exceed by more than 1.5 per cent 'that of at most the three best performing Member States in terms of price stability';
 (iv) a country must be a member of the ERM and must not have experienced serious upheavals in the two preceding years; and
  (v) in the preceding year, a Member State shall have had an average nominal long-term interest rate that does not exceed by more than 2 per cent 'that of, at most, the three best performing Member States of price stability'.

These are indeed strict conditions that must make any American politician green with envy or simply filled with total disbelief. Whether or not the EC Member States are capable of fulfilling such conditions is open to discussion. According to Table 4.2, only two countries do so at the present time.

Table 4.3 Economic and Monetary Union—1991: economic convergence

Country	Criteria						
	1	2	3	4	5	6	7
Germany	4.2	3.2	46.2	yes	8.6	3	4
Belgium	2.8	6.3	129.4	yes	9.3	3	3
Denmark	2.3	1.7	67.2	yes	10.1	4	5
Spain	5.5	3.9	45.6	no	12.4	1	1
France	3.1	1.5	47.2	yes	9.0	5	5
Britain	4.5	1.9	43.8	no	9.9	3	3
Greece	17.8	17.9	96.4	no	19.5	0	0
Ireland	3.6	4.1	102.8	no	9.2	3	3
Italy	6.2	9.9	101.2	yes	12.9	1	1
Luxembourg	2.6	2.0	6.9	yes	8.2	5	5
Netherlands	4.9	4.4	78.4	yes	8.9	2	2
Portugal	9.6	5.4	64.7	no	17.1	0	1

Criteria:

1. Inflation (%)
2. Public deficit (% of GDP)
3. Public debt (% of GDP)
4. Participation in the Exchange Rate Mechanism
5. Long-term interest rates (%)
6. Total criteria (Strict)
7. Total criteria (Loose)

Source: Commission of the European Community, *Annual Economic Report 1991–92*

A European Central Bank—the example of the United States

Rightly or wrongly, many European observers have held up the Federal Reserve System of the United States as being a model which the Community, in its moves towards the creation of a European Central Bank, should emulate. Personally, I believe that the examples of the Dutch and German Central Banks are more relevant for Europe. But first, it is interesting to note that while the United States has had its own currency since independence, its central bank, the Federal Reserve System, was not created until the eve of World War I. Until that moment, the country had used the London capital market for many of its needs.

Most observers praise the independence of the Federal Reserve, but what exactly is its autonomy? In my view and that of my friend, Jean Victor Louis, it takes three forms. First, the Federal Reserve is financially independent of Congress and it is not required to submit its accounts to that body. This fact will come as a complete and salutory surprise to many Europeans. Second, it has supremacy in internal monetary matters and the Board fixes the rates of interest and liquidity reserves. Third, the Board has considerable powers which are reinforced by the fact that its members (not the chairman) are selected for a period of fourteen years and they cannot be removed from office; this is indeed very important.

Although so many observers talk about the monetary supremacy of the Federal Reserve, it does, as Jean Victor Louis has observed, have to share these powers with other organs. Thus, it is the Treasury that enjoys supremacy in international monetary matters, but it cannot force the Federal Reserve to intervene in the currency markets 'against its will'. There is, nevertheless, a considerable amount of contact between the Federal Reserve and the Treasury.

There is, however, another body with which the Federal Reserve must share its power, the Federal Open Market Committee. It is this organ which fixes the criteria for recourse to open market operations.

Finally, there are certain aspects of the Federal Reserve System which will seem curious to the Europeans. Most important of all is the position and personality of the chairman of the board. This person is appointed by the president for a period of four years and is renewable. The appointment must then be confirmed by the Senate. It is very much, as has been proven by the example of Paul Volcker, the personality of the incumbent which moulds the position. Would the Europeans desire or accept such a personality as the head of the future European Central Bank? This must remain a matter for speculation.

A peculiarity which would certainly be unacceptable to Europeans is the division of that huge country into twelve completely disparate Federal Reserve Districts. Here, while Missouri has two Federal Reserve Banks, in Kansas City and St. Louis, the one in San Francisco has to serve the whole of the West Coast of the United States—from Seattle to San Diego!

European moves toward the creation of a Central Bank

For years, I have observed that the choice for Europe lies somewhere between the German preference for a totally independent European Central Bank (à la Bundesbank) and the British preference for a kind of European Monetary Fund. In the Treaty on European Union, the proposals come closer to the German preference, though, I think, they leave open too many ends, with the result that the division of responsibilities is not really clear. In contrast, however, one thing that is abundantly clear is that the aim of economic and monetary policy is price stability, and to that end the European Central Bank (ECB) will be unable to grant overdraft facilities to the Central Banks of EC Member States in favour of 'Community institutions or bodies, central governments, regional, local or other public authorities, other bodies governed by public law . . . public undertakings of Member States'.

Tasks of the European Central Bank

In article 105A of the Treaty, the ECB is empowered with the 'exclusive right to authorize the issue of bank notes within their Community'. However, interestingly enough, both the ECB and the national central banks share the right to issue these notes. But it is the ECB which shall have the exclusive right to determine the volume of such notes which, incidentally, will alone have the status of legal tender in the Community.

The sharing of tasks between the future ECB and the existing national central banks is underlined by the fact that they will, together, make up the European System of Central Banks (ESCB), which, in turn, shall be governed by the Governing Council and the Executive Board. According to article 107 of the Treaty, both the future ECB and the existing national central banks are expected to be totally independent of the Community and the governments of the Member States! This implies a change in the status of some of the present national central banks. In the following article, Member States are expected to change their national legislation in order to be able to conform with this stipulation. *Voilà!* It is, however, the ECB alone that is empowered to issue regulations which will be binding on the whole Community. But, in article 109, it is the Council which, acting unanimously, has the right to 'conclude formal arrangements on an exchange rate system for the ECU in relation to non-community currencies'. I hope that the implication here is that the ministers concerned will be those in charge of finance. In contrast, the Council only needs to act by a qualified majority to 'adopt, adjust or abandon the central rates of the ECU within the exchange rate system'. Although in both cases the Council is expected to consult with the ECB—though not necessarily to agree with it—it is quite clear that the ministers will have a tremendous degree of authority within the ESCB, and, in a number of other areas of exchange-rate policy and in relations with international institutions, they only need a qualified majority in order to arrive at their decisions. However, surprisingly perhaps, acting within the EMU framework, 'Member States may negotiate in international bodies and conclude international agreements'.

Article 109A of the Treaty lays down the institutional provisions (see below) for the ECB. In contrast with the Federal Reserve Board of the United States, their terms of office are relatively short.

Article 109a
1. The Governing Council of the ECB shall comprise the members of the Executive Board of the ECB and the Governors of the national central banks.
2. (a) The Executive Board shall comprise the President, the Vice-President and four other members.
(b) The President, the Vice-President and the other members of the Executive Board shall be appointed from among persons of recognized standing and professional experience in monetary or banking matters by common accord of the Governments of the Member States at the level of Heads of State or of Government, on a recommendation from the Council, after it has consulted the European Parliament and the Governing Council of the ECB. Their term of office shall be eight years and shall not be renewable. Only nationals of Member States may be members of the Executive Board.

A body which will almost certainly have an important advisory role is the future Economic and Financial Committee to be created at the beginning of the third stage of the EMU. This body will replace the Monetary Committee, which will have been created in the second stage and which will have given advice to the European Monetary Institute (EMI) whose main role will be to create the ESCB, and which will have replaced the present Committee of the Governors of Central Banks and the embryonic European Monetary Co-operation Fund.

The single European currency

Apart from the creation of the ESCB and the future European Central Bank, the most important aim in the monetary field—for the Community, the United States and other countries—is the creation of a single European currency. At the outset, it should be stressed that it is not clear as to whether there will be one unique currency (I myself, think not), nor when exactly this currency will be in general use throughout the Community. However, one thing is clear, and that is that this currency, despite strong German objections, will almost certainly be the present European Currency Unit (ECU) which is a basket of the national currencies of the twelve Member States of the Community. Also, according to the Treaty on European Union (article 109G), the currency composition of the ECU shall not be changed and its value shall be 'irreversibly' fixed from the start of the final stage of the EMU.

On many occasions, I have listed five basic roles which a sound currency should play. These, are:

 (i) a unit of account;
 (ii) a medium of exchange (between individuals);
(iii) a means of settlement (between institutes, central banks, governments and similar bodies);
(iv) a store of value; and
 (v) a refuge from economic and/or political instability. In this last case, individuals and/or institutes may be willing to forego (at least partially and/or temporarily) the attractiveness of the role of the currency or asset as a store value (iv) in exchange for enhanced security.

Compared with most currencies—and particularly when compared with the special drawing rights (SDRs) of the IMF—the ECU performs these roles very well. Most especially, it is noted for its stability which it draws from its composition. It is thus a 'risk spreader' and should be an excellent vehicle for trade but not for speculation. So, why is it so little used for trade whereas its use in international fixed bond issues has increased (see Table 4.3). The answer is very simple: it is not—with some small exceptions—legal tender inside the Community, nor anywhere else either. Consequently, although the use of the US dollar in international trade has declined in recent years, it is still the pre-eminent currency used in trade and is still the number one international reserve asset. All this is almost certain to change when the ECU becomes the single European currency. But before examining the possible implications for the Community and the United States of such a development, it is useful first to examine the practicalities of this move—inside the Community.

I do not believe for one moment that the ECU, at least not in the immediate future, will be the sole currency inside the Community. At the most practical level, not enough ECU coins and notes could be minted in time. Then, since the exchange rates (with full convertibility) between the ECU and the national currencies of the Community Member States would be irrevocably fixed as from the beginning of the third stage of the EMU, they would be interchangeable. Furthermore, at a local level, citizens would be more familiar with their own national currencies and would most likely prefer to use them for their local needs. However, there would now be nothing to prevent the Community from using the ECU for its own internal trade, and it could also invoice its sales of goods to third-party countries in the Community currency.

Table 4.4 Share of the ECU in commercial trade and current account

Country	Period	Goods Exports		Imports		Current Account Receipts		Expenditures	
		XEU mn.	%	XEU mn.	%	XEU mn.	%	XEU mn.	%
BLEU (1)	1986	248	0.4	50	0.1	2461	2.4	1459	1.5
	1987	132	0.2	53	0.1	2197	2.1	1391	1.3
	1988	189	0.4	71	0.1	2699	2.0	1492	1.2
	1989	247	0.3	180	0.2	3422	2.4	2309	1.7
	01–06/90	170	0.4	109	0.3	2354	3.1	1864	2.5
DK	1987	9	0.0	9	0.1	89	0.3	245	0.7
	1988	18	0.1	12	0.1	134	0.3	338	1.0
	1989	23	0.1	11	0.1	154	0.4	401	1.0
	01–08/90	33	0.2	11	0.1	143	0.5	404	1.3
DE	1986	NA	NA	39	0.0	NA	NA	NA	NA
	1987	NA	NA	65	0.0	NA	NA	NA	NA
	1988	NA	NA	133	0.1	NA	NA	NA	NA
	1989	NA	NA	216	0.1	NA	NA	NA	NA
	01–06/90	NA	NA	99	0.1	NA	NA	NA	NA
GR	01–06/90	NA	NA	NA	NA	NA	NA	NA	NA
ES	1987	25	0.1	5	0.0	65	0.1	135	0.3
	1988	115	0.3	43	0.1	226	0.4	203	0.3
	1989	367	1.0	345	0.6	1001	1.3	729	0.9
	01–09/90	346	1.2	478	1.0	1378	2.4	1050	1.6
FR	1986	480	0.4	1220	1.0	2139	1.0	3164	1.5
	1987	420	0.4	730	0.6	2070	1.0	2620	1.2
	1988	540	0.4	570	0.4	2110	0.9	2610	1.1
	1989	685	0.4	1190	0.6	2385	0.9	3287	1.2
	01–07/90	375	0.4	710	0.7	1654	1.2	2001	1.3

IE		NA	NA	NA	NA	NA	NA	NA	NA
IT	1986	721	0.9	312	0.4	NA	NA	NA	NA
	1987	998	1.1	305	0.3	NA	NA	NA	NA
	1988	659	0.8	359	0.4	NA	NA	NA	NA
	1989	854	0.8	485	0.4	NA	NA	NA	NA
NL	1986	1025	1.3	5	–	1500	1.5	238	0.2
	1987	405	0.5	19	0.0	854	0.8	207	0.2
	1988	468	0.6	52	0.1	972	0.8	232	0.2
	1989	859	0.9	517	0.6	1607	1.3	902	0.7
	01–10/90	525	0.7	441	0.6	1296	1.2	624	0.8
PT	1986	33	0.4	11	0.1	56	0.4	100	0.9
	1987	58	0.7	18	0.2	107	0.7	97	0.8
	1988	285	2.6	70	0.5	397	2.1	177	1.0
	1989	532	3.0	356	1.7	782	2.9	523	2.5
GB		NA	NA	NA	NA	NA	NA	NA	NA

(1) ECU-denominated current account flows mainly consist of interest receipts and payments.
Source: EC central banks. Reproduced from CEPREM documentation, Lyon, France 1992.

Possible implications for the Community and the United States

All this will have the most profound implications for both parties, and for other countries. It will most certainly mean that the Community will, finally, find itself endowed with an 'international monetary personality' which France has so long desired. Consequently, it will have to assume greater responsibilities internationally.

Over time, we can assume that the ECU will gradually, at least partially, replace European currencies such as the pound sterling and the Deutsche Mark in international trade. Thus, countries, for example in Latin America, will have the choice of another major international reserve asset when invoicing the sales of their products to Europe (their main customer) and when taking up international loans. All this will have at least two sets of consequences for the United States.

First, as has just been explained, the position of the dollar, internationally, will be less important than it is at the present time. Thus, the Americans will have less freedom, for example, to run up budgetary deficits than has hitherto been the case because other countries will have the choice of another reserve asset—this time, a really important one, the ECU—at their disposal. Second, as a positive counterpart to this consideration, the American currency could be less volatile internationally since there would, in future, be three major international currencies—the dollar, the yen and the ECU—of somewhat similar importance.

Final observations

The potential importance of the creation of a full EMU, ESCB and a ECB are enormous both for the Community as well as for the United States and other countries. Yet some issues still remain unclear and there are areas where both parties could learn from each other.

When we look at the American Federal Reserve System we observe a very clear division of powers between the Federal Reserve, the Federal Open Market Committee and the Treasury. When examining the Treaty on European Union, there is not the same clarity. While the future European Central Bank will, apparently, be independent—and Member States are also required to grant their own central banks independence where they do not yet enjoy it—the Council of Ministers does seem to enjoy an important degree of power *vis-à-vis* the ECB and in the ESCB. There is also (astonishingly) discussion (already!) about grounds for the removal of the members of the Board of the ECB although their non-renewable terms of office are relatively short. However, there is not even a mention of the role of the national ministries of finance in the future EMU. Will we, for example, have a super-European Ministry of Finance or Treasury? It is not clear what will happen in this field. Similarly, there is no proposal, surely necessary in the capital markets, for the creation of either a capital issues' committee or an open-market committee. These matters will most certainly have to be cleared up before the creation of the ESCB.

On the other side, the United States could certainly follow the example of the Community where careful fiscal management, present or future, is concerned. The world will have little to fear from the use of the ECU as a major reserve asset if it is backed by such rigorous budgetary and monetary policies.

Finally, if the Community does succeed in creating a full EMU with a European currency, it will then be forced to assume a major role in international monetary affairs.

5
1992—The European view

The background

Why 1992? Why should it be so important? In reality, the answer is frighteningly simple. 1992 is simply a date—31 December 1992, to be precise—when the European Economic Community (finally!) hopes to achieve all the aims (plus a few others thought up in the intervening years) which were laid down in the Treaty of Rome as early as 1957. Here, however, the simplicity ends because, at this point, it is necessary to turn to theoretical considerations which sometimes underpin economic reality.

Some economic considerations and the EEC

When we examine the case of the EEC with its aims as laid down in the Treaty of Rome we see that one of the aims leads to the creation of a customs union and the remainder, if achieved, would lead to the setting-up of a common market. While the Community has found it relatively easy to remove tariffs and quantitative restrictions on the internal movement of goods, the creation of a common external tariff (CET) and the introduction of rules of competition and the same type of sales tax (the value added or VAT) throughout the EEC—thus creating a customs union—it has found it very difficult to create a common market. The latter implies not only the free internal movement of goods—plus the CET—but also freedom of internal movement for persons and capital plus the freedom of establishment for services. Although nationals of EEC Member States have been free to take up employment throughout the Community since 1968, this freedom can only be fully used by members of the liberal professions if national diplomas, degrees and professional qualifications are mutually recognized by all Member States. This mutual recognition

THE EUROPEAN VIEW

73

of qualifications is also a precondition for introducing freedom of establishment for services. Here, also, in the case of the financial sector, the same basic rules must apply throughout a common market.

In the case of freedom of capital movements, in the bad old days, before the EEC achieved its present degree of exchange-rate stability, any moves towards freeing capital movements tended to lead to a surge of capital from France, Italy and Britain into the then West Germany, the Benelux countries and Switzerland, which is not even a member of the EC. Here, however, there is a fundamental theoretical and practical precondition which must be met. A common market must introduce a corporation or business income tax which will ensure capital neutrality so that one country does not, through tax concessions, lure capital, unfairly, away from partner countries. Similarly, if a common market wishes to have a VAT using the *origin* principle—taxing a product where it is produced—it is imperative that neutrality of location of production be respected through ensuring that the rates of taxation for the same products do not vary too much. Here, the Commission believes that a 6 per cent divergence is acceptable.

But where does this lead us at both the theoretical and practical levels? In the case of a customs union, the gains from changes in trade will be once-and-for-all or static. It is hoped that trade creation will outweigh trade diversion. In the case of the EEC, most observers have agreed that, with the exception of the wasteful CAP, the Community did more of the former than the latter. Indeed, with the persistently exceptional levels of economic growth in the early years of the Community's life, there was a real positive effect on world trade, including trade with the United States. Sooner or later, however, these effects wear themselves out. It is therefore important to profit from dynamic effects; this is where the common market theory comes into play.

Even before the World War II, Europeans were mesmerized by the economic power of the United States. At the end of the war, a group of British economists, led by Graham Hutton, came to the United States to try to discover the magic secret of America's economic success. On their return to Britain, they published their findings in a book called, *We Too Can Prosper*. In this readable work, it was explained that apart from America's rich natural endowment with natural resources, it had become wealthy through the use of dynamic concepts—chiefly the use of long production runs, economies of scale and standardization—which can only be enjoyed from the existence of a large internal home market unfettered by trade barriers and similar obstacles. This, then, is what the common market and 1992 are all about. Until now, the EEC has not, because of the existence of these internal barriers, been able to profit from these potential dynamic concepts although the aims are clearly laid down in the Treaty of Rome.

The main thread of the argument

At this point, it is necessary to leave theoretical considerations and return to the main thread of the argument.

So, the aims are all (with some exceptions) there in the Treaty of Rome and have all been legally accepted by the Member States. However, there seemed to be no urgency to go too much further than the creation of a customs union. Then, in the late 1970s and the early 1980s, there was increasing talk of 'Euro-sclerosis'. Business leaders, officials and experts expressed concern that if the Europeans did not do something dramatic—*together*—then, economically and technologically, they would be eclipsed by the Americans and Japanese.

In 1985, the Commission published its white paper on the Single European Market (SEM) in which it laid down the aims and conditions for the creation of a real common market. A year later, the Single European Act (SEA) was signed by the twelve Member States, and, when in July 1987 the Republic of Ireland, in a national referendum, accepted the SEA, it became law.

In my opinion, had most of the Member States understood what they were letting themselves in for when they accepted the document, they would have never signed it. But, it is important to note that while this dreary document does bring on-stream an increased use of decision-making in the Council of Ministers by a qualified majority, it does NOT state as an aim the creation of a full economic and monetary union (EMU). It does give a greater consultative role to the European Parliament and it does make more official the European Monetary System (EMS). But, the rule unanimity in the Council of Ministers is still maintained for questions concerning the admission of new members to the Community, changes in the Treaty of Rome, fiscal and monetary policies and those parts of social policy concerning labour laws. Finally, it is stressed that while the date December 31 1992, is the goal (or 1 January 1993) for the achievement of the SEM, it is not definitive. Last, it was established that if this goal was to be reached, then 282 directives concerning policies would have to be adopted. After that, they would have to be translated into national legislation, but that's quite a different story!

But, no one, positively no one, could raise a shred of enthusiasm for this dreary, boring and wearisome document, the SEA. Then, Paolo Cecchini, who was about to retire from the European Commission, in

Brussels, had a brainwave which he succeeded in selling to Jacques Delors, the president of the Commission. Why not put together the most fabulous research project in the Commission's history with lots and lots of experts and estimate, analyse etc. the costs of not getting to 1992 or the 'Costs of Non-Europe'? Jacques Delors was delighted with the proposal and Cecchini was entrusted with carrying out the project. Experts were brought together and outside institutions were consulted. Work proceeded apace and still no one seemed to be able to summon up any enthusiasm what so ever for 1992. Then, literally from one day to the next, 1992 became the buzzword, and everyone wanted to get their hands on the twenty or so volumes of working papers which all the experts had produced.

Eventually, the Commission reduced these findings into an important work, *The Economics of 1992*. This erudite work was further reduced in size into a popular work accessible to the general public. So, finally, whether or not they understood anything at all of the implications of the future SEM, everyone, positively everyone—some with enthusiasm—the others with fear and trepidation—started talking about the magic date of 1992.

Progress and disappointments

At the outset, it is important to stress, yet again, the old platitude that when the SEM is created on 1 January 1993, the Europeans will represent the world's most important single market. It will, in the case of the EC alone, consist of a market of over 320 million persons, who, for the most part, enjoy high and rising standards of living. If, however, we extend this market to include the EFTA countries with which an agreement was signed in 1991 to create a European Economic Space or Area (EES or EEA) on 1 January 1993, then this trading bloc assumes an even greater importance because the EFTA countries are very rich countries with a high standard of living. Quite simply, the SEM or EES or EEA will, whatever happens, constitute a challenge and or a threat to other countries—most notably the United States. But, before tackling this question, it is first necessary to ascertain to what degree the SEM will have been completed by the end of 1992 and what its implications might be, first of all, for the local producers and consumers.

Will they have achieved the SEM by the end of this year? The answer is no, most definitely not. If we wish to examine basic facts and statistics, then, of the 282 directives which the Community set out to enact, only 69 remained outstanding in September 1991. However, these concerned the most difficult issues notably fiscal, monetary and social (relating to labour law) questions. Equally, no European Company Law had seen the light of day, while integration for some important services had, by common agreement, been postponed. So, what are the achievements, where have we postponed the application of directives and where have we failed? Finally, what does all this mean, first for the Europeans and then for the Americans?

There are, indeed, considerable achievements to the Community's credit. These successes, are mainly the following:

The free internal movement of goods

Following the commonsense compromise for the VAT agreed upon by the Council of Ministers in June 1991, which complemented earlier agreements not to raise or lower the existing top and lowest VAT levels, the internal movement of goods will be facilitated. This compromise is discussed in greater detail below.

Public procurement

To everyone's surprise, in February 1990 agreement was reached in the Council of Ministers on establishing open bidding for public procurement between ten of the Member States by 1 January 1993 in the four major areas of water, energy, transport and telecommunications. Greece and Portugal were allowed to open up their markets in 1996. In July of the same year, it was agreed to create a Community-wide telecommunications market in 1991. Here, unfortunately, in comparison with Britain, which has already opened up its telecommunications market to others, Germany is opposed to opening up its PTT Bundespost to its Community partners. If, however, German reticence can be overcome, the savings which can be made in this lucrative market—plus the potential for profiting from economies of scale—are quite fabulous. Also, the European market is particularly tempting to Americans who have very much a comparative advantage in all the fields of public procurement. Alas, the Community does give EC companies a 3 per cent price advantage for bids. Then, any Member State which finds that the Community value added or local content does not reach 50 per cent may declare a bid invalid.

Freedom of establishment

Here, we shall go much further than the United States. Thus, having achieved the mutual recognition of each other's qualifications, diplomas and degrees inside the EC, it is now possible for a lawyer, for example, qualifying in London, to practice in the other eleven Member States. Similarly, a doctor or dentist, qualifying, for example in Paris, may practice in the other eleven Member States. With some exceptions, this situation has existed since early 1991. In the United States, each of the fifty states proscribes the qualifications for the professions. Even a driving license is not transferable from one state to another.

Financial services

Banking
In the field of banking, common standards for liquidity ratios have been in operation since 1991. This is the basis on which the next step is built. Thus, as from 1 January 1993, a bank operating in one Member State and legally recognized by the authorities of that country will be given the European Banking Passport allowing it to set up branches throughout the EC.

Insurance
Since 1990, following the acceptance of the Second Directive, non-life insurance for big industrial risks have been freed in all EEC countries — except in Greece, Portugal and Ireland. Also, a reciprocal agreement was made with Switzerland. The opening-up of the market has led to an increase in competition and a slump in fire-risk rates in France and Germany.

At the end of 1992, the Council of Ministers reached an agreement in principal on the Third Directive for Non-Life Insurance which will lead to the issuing, under specific conditions, of a European Non-Life Insurance Passport which will come into operation in July 1994. In the case of Spain, this has been delayed until 1996 and for Portugal and Greece until 1998.

Freedom of capital movements

Already since 1989, it has been possible to sell unit-trust-fund shares throughout the EC. This, in itself, was an important move in the opening-up of capital and financial markets to Europe's citizens.

Then, in July 1990, capital movements were freed among the eight most developed EEC Member States. In January of that same year, France, after maintaining controls for over forty years, freed capital movements—and nothing happened.

Merger's legislation

At the same time of the freeing of capital movements, and after discussions lasting nearly twenty years, the Community's Mergers' Legislation became effective. However, I consider that the threshold of five billion ECUs combined turnover for two merger candidates for examination by the Commission is far too high and simply encourages bigness while at the same time discourages competition. Also, mergers below this threshold will be the domain of the Member States, but they do not all have monopolies' institutions.

Fiscal compromises

As mentioned earlier, in June 1991 a commonsense compromise was reached for the VAT. First, however, it should be stressed that the Commission has always wanted an origin principle (i.e. goods should be taxed at the point of production) for the VAT as against the present destination principle (ie goods and services are taxed at the point of consumption). The Commission's reason for this preference is that it believes, rightly or wrongly, that the adoption of the origin principle will lead to the removal of fiscal frontiers. For the forseeable future, the Community will, nevertheless, maintain the use of the destination principle, but there will be regular exchanges of information between major enterprises and finance ministeries regarding sales.

Regarding the VAT rates, as from 1 January 1993 there will be a minimum VAT rate of 15 per cent while the extreme rates on luxury goods will disappear. At the bottom, countries will be able to choose between rates with a difference of around 5 per cent, while Britain will be allowed to maintain a zero rating on certain items.

At the same time, in the very controversial field of excise duties, a modest compromise was reached whereby a minimum excise duty on cigarettes would be applied equivalent to 57 per cent of the final retail price. In the case of beer, the duty will be 1.87 ECUs for every degree of alcohol per 100 litres while wines would be zero rated. The minimum duty on leaded petrol would be 337 ECUs per tonne but only 50 ECUs per tonne for the unleaded variety.

The question of excise duties has always been controversial because two countries, Denmark and the Republic of Ireland, rely heavily on these taxes for their government revenue. If duties were harmonized downwards, which body would make good the differences in revenue?

Finally, we did not get a Corporation Tax; this is indeed a disappointment after decades of discussion and in spite of the Commission's preference for an Imputation System. Instead, there is a parent-subsidiary directive which will come into force in 1992 but which will take until 1996 to become fully operational. At the time of writing, however, the Commission is again talking of a common 'Imputation' tax.

Despite this last disappointment, which must eventually be made good if we are to achieve the necessary capital neutrality in the common market, great progress has been made after the relative inaction of earlier years and, in some cases, the EEC will, at the beginning of 1993, go further ahead than the United States has succeeded in doing. But, the picture is not complete because there have been disappointments and delays. It is precisely these setbacks—plus the tendency towards bigness—which may well prevent the Europeans from enjoying the dynamics of integration which their American cousins have long since taken for granted.

Standardization

No, there will definitely not be common EEC or EEA or EES standards for products on 1 January 1993. In fact, we shall not get them—if at all—before the next century.

Many, many times, to my absolute consternation, I have heard American academics say that there will be common standards inside the EEC as from 1 January 1993. Even some major American corporations believe in this dangerous myth and are very unwisely gearing their policies in Europe accordingly.

No, the tragedy is that with the exception of situations where common security must prevail, the Community's Member States have agreed to accept or recognize each other's standards.

This means that in most cases, we shall still continue to produce for different national markets and shall consequently not be able to enjoy the benefits of economies of scale which our American cousins have long since enjoyed.

This is indeed a dramatic state of affairs, which has been emphasized in the Commission's *Green Paper on the Development of Standardisation*, published in October 1991. Our foolishness will diminish our competitiveness internationally.

Road haulage or trucking

Although the Commission has succeeded in increasing the number of pan-EEC road haulage or trucking permits on a provisional and experimental basis, visceral German opposition to any further loosening of its quasi-monopoly of carrying German products destined for other countries in German lorries or trucks means that we shall not have freedom of road haulage on 1 January 1993. This is economic suicide and means that the EEC will continue to waste its precious assets. The present policy for road haulage is even more ludicrous than the CAP.

Social policy

This is also an area of great controversy. At the present time, nationals of one EEC Member State who work in another Community country automatically enjoy the full social security benefits of the receiving and host country. This pragmatic policy has worked well over the years. Unfortunately, Jacques Delors, in his desire to change the impression that the SEM will be a community of producers, launched his Social Charter. This is a most notable document with laudable aims. The fears of the British— whether correctly founded or not—were that apart from introducing worker participation in industry, which is anathema to the Conservative Party, the acceptance of the Social Charter would eventually lead to the introduction of a European minimum wage. On this last point, the British feared, correctly in my view, that it would cause difficulties for low-wage countries such as Portugal and Spain making them less attractive to foreign investors.

Already in December 1990, eleven Member States had, in principle, accepted the Social Charter. Then, a year later, they repeated their acceptance but allowed Britain to desist. The story does not end there since there remain legal problems about the applicability of such a fundamentally important policy which does fall under the rule of unanimity in the Council of Ministers. With the signing of the Treaty on European Union, in February, 1992 Britain again opted out of the social part.

And after Maastricht?

We are still digesting the aftermath of the European Summit. Apart from the problem of the Social Charter policy, it seems, as has been mentioned earlier, that at the present time hardly any countries at all would manage to fulfil the criteria for membership of a full EMU.

Everyone agreed to co-operate in the field of foreign affairs, and those who wish to will also co-operate in the field of defence. Political co-operation is another aim—without any clear definition of its precise form. The Council of Ministers remains supreme, the European Parliament gets a bit more power and, as ever, the Commission remains responsible to no one. Finally, I imagined I saw a nod in the direction of the European Consumers' Bureau. I will return to the Treaty on European Union in Chapter Seven of this book.

Possible implications for EEC producers and consumers

The Merger's Legislation and the trend towards bigness will benefit EEC producers. In the long run, however, their greed and blindness in not accepting common European standards will remove all their short-term benefits from national protection because they will not be able to enjoy economies of scale. Those who are flexible may be able to enjoy the benefits of this huge European market.

As better basic social and working conditions are adopted for workers, their lot will improve. However, where the costs of such benefits prove to be too heavy for some industries, their companies may have to close down forcing the workers to migrate to other regions or countries.

Despite the scandalous disregard by the Council and the Commission for Europe's consumers—and notably the European Consumers' Bureau—citizens will gain from the opening up of markets. Already the choice of goods is very great, and it will probably become larger. In the field of some financial services—notably insurance—costs are being and will continue to be reduced, thus benefiting the consumer. In contrast, the trend in banking is towards bigness, and I do not believe that the consumer will gain any real benefits in this field.

Of course, much will depend on the degree of competition which will emanate from outside the SEM, EEA or EES. Here, I have in mind mainly, though not exclusively, competition from the United States.

Possible implications for the United States—a European view

Many Americans do view the prospects of 1 January 1993 and the imminent SEM, EEA or EES with great anticipation since, rightly or wrongly, they believe that they will enjoy a basic competitive advantage in a huge integrated European market having already had many decades of experience with their own integrated market. But, as has already been explained in the previous section, this market—certainly as regards standards—will continue to be fragmented, and if we exclude banking, the markets for financial services will not be fully integrated until well into the mid 1990s. Furthermore, the Europeans have already adopted, or plan to adopt, a host of non-tariff restrictions which, while not always aimed specifically at the United States, will nevertheless affect the Americans. But, first, we have to be clear about the four different categories into which United States businessmen might belong. I distinguish four basic categories:

(1) Americans who wish to invest directly inside the EEC or the extended area through purchases of shares in existing European companies.
(2) American companies which are already manufacturing inside the EEC and who consider themselves to be European companies, for example Ford of Britain.
(3) American enterprises who wish to set up (i) a manufacturing plant or (ii) to open up a branch of a bank or financial service inside the EEC.
(4) American companies which are based inside the United States and wish simply to export directly to the EEC.

(1) Americans investing directly inside the EEC

The upsurge in American investment inside the EEC in recent years is an eloquent testimony to the faith which American businessmen have in the future of the SEM. This direct investment is probably the most simple way of enjoying all the benefits of the SEM without getting directly involved in such hassles as labour relations and the vexed and unresolved question of value added or local content to which we shall turn in a moment. Furthermore, since European countries do welcome American investment and place no restrictions on the repatriation of profits, then their investments are very safe.

(2) American companies already established inside the EEC

A number of American companies have been established inside Europe for decades. In the case of Honeywell, for example, the company has been established over there since the mid–1930s. These companies respect the local national laws of the countries in which they do business, and, legally speaking, they are considered to be European companies—though we do not yet have a pan-EEC European Company Law, but the products themselves may not be considered 'European'. France, for example, does not wish to recognize automobiles produced by Japanese companies established in Britain as British or European products. This, then, does conjure up future problems of nightmarish dimensions. For the time being, it is recognized by the EEC that **a product is 'European' if 60 per cent of the value added or local content takes place inside the EEC**. Unfortunately, this could change since the French would like to raise this level to 80 per cent or more! I do not, however, consider this development to be a realistic possibility.

At the present time, I consider that the failure by the EEC to adopt common standards is a much greater deterrent to business to both American companies already established inside the EEC as well as to those wishing to export directly from the United States. Furthermore, the accelerated trend towards bigness among European companies does not bode well for increased competition inside the future SEM. This development would tend, therefore, to diminish any degree of comparative advantage which American companies enjoy.

(3) American enterprises wishing to set up business inside the EEC

Here American enterprises have, basically speaking, two options: they can buy up an existing European company or they can set up a manufacturing plant or branch of their business (for example a bank or a financial institution) in the EEC.

Where goodwill is at a premium, for example in banking, and where they do not wish to face the question of 'reciprocity' (which we shall examine a little later) or the uncertainty of value added or local content, then the easiest option is probably to buy up an existing European company. Specifically in the banking field, the Europeans themselves have set the example by buying small or medium-sized but very well established local banks in other EEC Member States in order, quickly and surely, to gain a strong foothold in the region(s) or country(ies) concerned.

If Americans wish to set up a manufacturing plant inside the EEC, they

will discover, if they do their homework correctly, that in many countries—notably in Ireland and Spain—owing to a mixture of local, national
and Community regional incentives—they will have many of their construction and other costs heavily subsidized. Thus, provided that they can
meet the rules, present and potential, of value added or local content,
this could be a really excellent option for them.

(4) American companies, based in the United States, and wishing to
export directly to the EEC

Here, American companies really have to do their homework. Depending
on the sector involved, the Community uses one of three types of controls,
quantitative restrictions, reciprocity or EEC preferences. Before examining the areas which are of great interest to the United States and the
controls used by the EEC, it should be stressed that the Community's
average common external tariff is really quite low although it can be above
average for a few specific products.

Telecommunications and semi-conductors
The EEC imposes quantitative restrictions on imports of semi-conductors.
In the field of telecommunications, it is seeking reciprocity with the United
States, ie that the Americans should open up their market for European
products in exchange for which the Europeans will open up their markets
to American products.

In both these areas, as well as in other fields of electronics, the EEC is
currently negotiating with the United States, Japan and other countries
for the opening up of all their markets to imports of each other's products.
In contrast with the disagreement over agricultural products, it is highly
possible that they will reach an agreement in the different fields of electronics.

Financial services
The EEC and the United States have already reached an agreement for
banking where they have accepted the principle of 'soft' reciprocity. It is
also almost certain that the same principle will be used for insurance and
stockbroking once agreement has been reached among EEC Member
States for the creation of European Insurance and Stockbroking Passports.
But what are the implications for American banks and financial institutions?

At the outset, it is necessary to understand the meaning of 'hard' as well as 'soft' reciprocity since the Commission in Brussels has not dropped the former weapon from its negotiating armoury.

In the specific case of banking, the Commission strongly favoured 'hard' reciprocity. This would have meant that in return for the granting of the European Banking Passport to American banks and financial institutions, based in the United States but wishing to open up branches throughout the EEC, the United States should likewise grant the right to European banks and financial institutions to set up branches throughout the United States. Unfortunately, this would have given to European banks privileges which their American counterparts do not enjoy, since banking in the United States is state-based unlike banking in European countries (except Italy) which is national (in Germany, savings banks are also regionally based). Both Italy and Germany will have to change either in 1993 or shortly afterwards.

Fortunately, thanks to the pressure of Lord Cockfield, wiser counsels prevailed and the option of 'soft' reciprocity was adopted. Here, in exchange for the granting of the European Banking Passport to American banks and financial institutions, the United States agreed to accord the same rights inside the country as are enjoyed by American banks, ie state-based but not inter-state banking.

Certainly, the opening up of the large and lucrative SEM or rather the EEA/EES is extremely tempting to American banks and they could make big profits where they can offer their excellent personalized services to the Europeans.

At a different level, it is highly likely that the opening up of the European banking and insurance sectors will encourage the Americans to change their own banking and insurance laws, since, in both sectors, activities are at present state-based.

Cultural affairs

When the Community made its first moves towards formulating and adopting a common cultural policy, no one but no one imagined this would be the area which would cause the greatest controversy between the two sides. At first, on either side of the Atlantic no eyebrows were raised when the Europeans talked about a European cultural identity and moved towards intensifying cultural exchanges among themselves. But when, under pressure from France, it was decided that 50 per cent or more of the programmes shown on European television and 50 per cent of the films shown in European cinemas should be 'European', it raised a huge outcry among American television and film producers. Some went so far as to say that most American films would be excluded from the European continent. Furthermore, the United States Administration placed the EEC on its 'priority watch list' under the Special 301 provision of its Trade Act.

Now that the initial uproar would seem to have subsided somewhat, I would make the following mitigating observation. A reading of the relevant Community legislation which came into effect on 3 October 1991, suggests it as implying that the productions should be made in Europe, but it does not stipulate who should make them. Also, this legislation is only intended as a guideline.

Some of the more wily American producers have also come to the same conclusion as my own and are busy teaming up with European colleagues and companies. Thus, the outlook for American film and television producers inside the EEC could still be positive.

Manufacturing

The EEC does impose quota restrictions (and also above-average tariffs on some of the products) mainly in three important sectors: textiles, automobiles and electronics.

In the first case, they are aimed at Third World countries. Where American manufacturers are producing high-quality products—together with the advantage of the weaker dollar—they will not be affected by these restrictions.

The quotas on automobiles are aimed expressly at the Japanese. Some countries, notably the United Kingdom, are more favourably disposed to imports of Japanese cars. However, other countries, notably France and Italy, are bitterly opposed to such imports and wish to keep the present import ceilings in place for as long as possible.

These restrictions should not affect American exports of automobiles to the EEC except where the component parts are, to an unacceptably high level, of Japanese origin.

Restrictions on imports of electronics are aimed first at Japan, then at South East Asia and last at the United States. However, in the case of semi-conductors, they are aimed equally at Japan and the United States. Here, apart from quota restrictions, the EEC asked the Japanese and Americans substantially to increase the prices of this product exported to the Community. These producers had difficulty in concealing their astonishment and glee.

The fear that Europeans have that they are being eclipsed by the Americans and the Japanese in the field of electronics is leading to the formulation and adoption of two different kinds of industrial policies. On the one hand, the French, who have just announced the creation of a monster conglomerate under state control and ownership, want to see the adoption of a strong, interventionist and protectionist European industrial policy. It is unlikely, however, that the British and the Germans would accept this at a Community level. Then, on the other hand, there are co-operation agreements between European and American enterprises in the field of electronics and also between European and Japanese companies.

Public procurement

This is a most important and lucrative market on both sides of the Atlantic. In both cases, preferences are given to local producers and contractors. Mention has already been made of the major developments made inside the EEC in opening up public procurement to competitive bidding in four major areas but with certain preferences given to European enterprises.

Since this is such an important market for both parties, and as American enterprises do enjoy a comparative advantage in a number of fields, it is almost certain that both parties will negotiate an agreement to open up their markets to each other.

Overview

The large number of areas of activity for which the EEC had formulated specific policies *vis-à-vis* third parties is really important. Although these policies are only occasionally (notably in banking and financial services, cultural affairs and semi-conductors) specifically aimed at the United States, most of them do, in some way or other, affect American enterprises. While the Americans do not face anything vaguely comparable with the difficulties encountered in getting into the Japanese market, I would warn them that 1992 (or rather 1993) and the SEM are more complicated than was at first imagined. Furthermore, all these developments imply that after 1 January 1993 the international negotiating power of the EEC in economic and commercial affairs will have been greatly strengthened.

6

1992—Possible implications for the United States: official and general American views

Some three to five years ago, there was general talk in the United States of a threat of 'Fortress Europe'. This fear was shared by officials of the United States Administration, business leaders and members of the general public. Now, things seemed to have changed.

First, at the most official level, the observation has been made by Eugene McAllister, Assistant Secretary of State for Economic and Business Affairs, that 'transparency and openness characterize the Europe 1992 Programme'. McAllister, who on 20 February 1990 testified in front of three subcommittees of the House of Representatives' Foreign Affairs Committee, concluded that he believed that the 'EC 1992 Program will benefit US business'. The full text of this speech is reproduced in the appendices at the end of this book, in *Europe Documents*, no. 1599.

This positive view, is understandably, not shared by all American officials. Certainly, Carla Hills, the United States' chief negotiator in the Uruguay Round of Multinational Trade Negotiations, does not share McAllister's enthusiasm. Some of her colleagues, who are of her own generation, are likewise somewhat more sceptical of the EEC's behaviour after 1 January 1993.

In contrast, I have gained the impression when talking with business leaders and students among younger age groups that they, on the whole, do not think that a 'Fortress Europe' will emerge and, in contrast, hope that the Europeans will form some kind of political union. On this point, I have found that when talking to different groups in the United States, members of my audiences invariably express disappointment at the slow rate of progress made by Western Europe in establishing some form of political union or even a United States of Europe.

Since the views about the possible future emergence of a 'Fortress Europe' do appear to be mixed, I decided to send a questionnaire to a number of important American enterprises currently doing business in or with Europe. It is to the results of this research to which we shall now turn.

7

The American views – results of our research

In view of the mixed reactions received by me and my assistant when asking friends, colleagues and students about Europe 1992, it was decided to send a questionnaire to a selection of important American corporations which do business in or with the EEC. In selecting the areas of activity to be examined, two criteria were used. First, the corporations should be in an area where it is considered that the United States has a comparative advantage and should, where possible, already be international in character. Second, for local reasons, where possible, the corporations should be identified (preferably having their corporate headquarters here) with the state of Minnesota. This preference was made because of our geographical location here and because of the unusually high concentration of multinationals in Minneapolis and St. Paul. Thus, the following areas of business activity were chosen:

agribusinesses,
airlines,
automobiles,
banks,
computers,
law firms,
medical aids/biotechnology, and
pharmaceuticals.

In the questionnaire, which was sent to 101 corporations, after asking each company to describe its operations, the following questions were asked:

1. (a) Are you currently doing business in or with Europe?
   (b) If your answer is in the affirmative, please supply the following information:
      (i) do you manufacture in the United States and export your products directly to Western Europe?

> (ii) do you manufacture in or are your services already in Western Europe?
2. Do you view the development of the Single European Market by 31 December 1993 as:
    (i) positive for your corporation?
    (ii) negative for your corporation?
    (iii) uncertain for your corporation?
3. Is there any action which you consider should be taken in anticipation of 1992:
    (i) by your corporation?
    (ii) by the United States in general?

Quantitatively, the responses varied considerably. In the case of both agribusinesses and airlines, they were very good. In contrast, the response from the automobile manufacturers was so bad it was decided not include them in this overview since there was no point, statistically speaking, in so doing. Interestingly, the response by law firms and members of the pharmaceuticals industry was encouraging, We had expected a bigger response from the banks which, in fact, was only modest. Then, the response from two very important sectors, the computer industry and medical aids/biotechnology was disappointingly very modest.

Qualitatively, the responses were always interesting and useful—sometimes quite fascinating. Nearly all the responses could be used with some profit by the United States administration. It is therefore useful to examine these sectors—and the responses received—in some depth and detail.

Agribusinesses

Here, as has already been mentioned, the response, quantitatively speaking, was very good. Out of five corporations we questioned, four sent us responses. We were particularly pleased with this high rate of response since this business activity is very important for Minnesota.

Among the four replying, two said that they already had operations in Europe. Interestingly, all four viewed the development of the SEM positively.

What action should be taken? One corporation said that they had already undertaken the necessary preparations for 1992, while another thought they should make an acquisition in Europe or enter into a joint venture.

Regarding action by the American administration, two thought that the administration should keep market barriers from forming and two thought that the United States should sign the GATT Treaty.

Airlines

Again, a very heartening response. Out of the seven airlines questioned, six replied.

In contrast with the representatives of agribusinesses, they seemed (interestingly) to be more apprehensive about 1992. Only one corporation viewed it positively, none viewed it negatively, but five viewed it with uncertainty. I believe that this apprehension may be due to the planned deregulation of the European airline industry and to the expected increase in the negotiating strength of the Europeans.

A number of airlines had perfectly clear ideas of what policies should be adopted in advance of 1992. Four airlines thought that they should expand their presence in Europe by becoming 'insiders'. Regarding action by the administration, the responses were similar to those given by the agribusiness corporations: three thought that the United States should ensure 'fair access' to the European market and ensure that there will be a 'level playing field'.

Banks

We were surprised by the moderate response from the banks since they are the institutions which are almost always influenced by events outside the United States. We sent questionnaires to the largest seventeen banks but only seven chose to reply.

Among those seven, six were already doing business with Europe, among which three had already established operations over there.

Interestingly enough, no bank viewed 1992 negatively, no one was uncertain, but five viewed the SEM positively.

None was willing to say what had been done in anticipation of 1992, whereas one thought that the United States should keep market barriers from forming, one wanted the administration to provide information to American business while two didn't think anything should be done.

Computers

Once again, we were disappointed by the low rate of response, especially since this is an important area where the United States does clearly enjoy a comparative advantage *vis-à-vis* Europe. In the event, we wrote to twenty-one corporations and received replies from only seven. Of these seven, however, five were already doing business with Europe, and, of these, four already had operations over there.

Six of the seven viewed the creation of the SEM positively and none was negative or uncertain about this development.

One corporation had already undertaken the necessary action in advance of 1992. One planned on expanding its presence in Europe and becoming an 'insider', while another was creating a '1992' task force.

In contrast with earlier responses, one corporation (this was a novelty and seemed more European than American in its nature) thought that the administration should provide American businesses with financial incentives. Like the reply from one bank, two computer corporations thought that the administration should provide current and complete information to American businesses.

Law firms

As we had anticipated, the response from the law firms was quite good. We wrote to fifteen firms and eight replied. All the eight firms are currently doing business with Europe, and two have offices over there.

Five firms viewed the development of the SEM positively, no one was negative, but two were uncertain about it.

All replied that they will and must keep abreast of all changes that may affect their clients.

The replies concerning possible action to be taken by the United States did, in large part, correspond to the views of the banks, the airlines and the agribusiness corporations. Four thought that the administration should keep market barriers from forming. In contrast, and of particular interest to us, two thought that the United States should influence EEC moves towards standardization.

Medical aids/biotechnology

We had expected a much greater response from corporations in this very important sector of the international economy where the United States enjoys a particularly strong comparative advantage. Having overcome our disappointment, we found the responses to be particularly interesting.

We wrote to twenty-seven corporations but only nine replied. However, all the nine were doing business with Europe, of which, as many as five do have operations over there.

Four viewed the development of the SEM positively, no one was negative, but five were uncertain.

One corporation had already taken the necessary action in advance of 1992. One was staying informed, another planned to establish distribution agreements inside the SEM, while two others planned to expand their presence by becoming 'insiders'.

As with companies in four other areas, so four of these corporations thought that the United States should ensure 'fair access' to the EC, an 'open market' and a 'level playing field'. One corporation thought that the American administration should provide current and complete information to American businesses while another, interestingly, called for tax incentives for expatriate placement in Europe and American nationals and the acquisition of foreign-language skills by Americans.

Pharmaceuticals

We had quite a good response from the corporations questioned in this really important area. Out of sixteen companies to which we sent our questionnaire, exactly half replied. Of these eight companies, six said they were already doing business with Europe, and, of these, five affirmed that they also had operations established there.

Six corporations viewed the developments of the SEM positively, no one was negative and one corporation was uncertain.

Two corporations had already completed their plans for 1992 while another was pursuing the establishment of a European manufacturing facility.

We were very surprised to receive only one response concerning possible action by the United States in general, but it is a fairly novel one. One corporation thought the United States should use the creation of a North American Free Trade Zone as a counterweight to the SEM.

What surprised us here is that no pharmaceutical company suggested that the United States should actively influence the moves towards adopting common standards and legislation for patents inside the EC. This really is strange because it is almost exclusively concerning safety standards and pharmaceuticals where the EC is really discussing the adoption of common standards.

The Overview

As we had gathered in discussions with friends, students and colleagues, according to the replies to our questionnaire most corporations do view the development of the SEM positively and no one views it negatively, but quite a substantial minority viewed this development with uncertainty.

We had expected more corporations to tell us, and in greater detail, about their plans for 1992. But despite our promise not to divulge names to anyone, state secrets must obviously remain state secrets. Where they did choose to reply, most planned on becoming 'insiders' in the future SEM.

Where corporations chose to give their views about United States' action in general, most expected the administration to prevent the development of obstacles to trade, to ensure fairness, openness and the proverbial 'level playing field'. A few did, however, call for the provision of information for American businesses.

Having looked at these responses several times and having noted the positive attitudes towards the future SEM shown by the majority of corporations which replied, I wonder if they might not be just a little optimistic about the future—maybe.

8
Institutional developments

The Treaty on European Union and parallel developments have important implications for future relations between the European Community and the United States.

Turning to the preamble of the Treaty itself, there are calls for the adoption of a common foreign policy and, hopefully, common defence. Should these calls be heeded, they would complement the Community's common trading and commercial policies which have been in existence for over two decades.

At the trans-Atlantic level, relations between the two sides have recently been institutionalized in the form of twice-yearly summit meetings and co-operation in the field of competition policy. Consultations and co-operation also exist in other fields. The precise nature of this framework, in the Declaration on EC-United States Relations, made in November 1990 (this document is reproduced in the appendices at the end of this book), is as follows:

Both sides agree that a framework is required for regular and intensive consultation. They will make full use of and further strengthen existing procedures, including those established by the President of the European Council and the President of the United States on 27th February 1990, namely:
- bi-annual consultations to be arranged in the United States and in Europe between, on the one side, the President of the European Council and the President of the Commission, and on the other side, the President of the United States;
- bi-annual consultations between the European Community Foreign Ministers, with the Commission, and the US Secretary of State, alternately on either side of the Atlantic;
- ad hoc consultations between the Presidency Foreign Minister or the Troika and the US Secretary of State;
- bi-annual consultations between the Commission and the US Government at Cabinet level;

- briefings, as currently exist, by the Presidency to US Representatives at European Political Cooperation (EPC) meetings at Ministerial level.

Both sides are resolved to develop and deepen these procedures for consultation so as to reflect the evolution of the European Community and its relationship with the United States.

They welcome the actions taken by the European Parliament and the Congress of the United States in order to improve their dialogue and thereby bring closer together the peoples on both sides of the Atlantic.

More recent developments

At a more elevated level, some observers had, wrongly, tried to compare the meetings of Community leaders in December 1991 with the series of meetings of the Federal Convention, held in Philadelphia in 1787, by the Founding Fathers of the United States. Alas, alas, no comparison could have been further from the truth. At best, with few exceptions, the European leaders are technocrats (when we are lucky!) and/or party apparatchiks, dressed in their uniform undertakers' suits, lacking in vision and about as stimulating as rice pudding! Usually, they are engaged in horse-trading of the basest political kind and are not an inspiring bunch. Perhaps, wisely, there is, with occasional exceptions, no grand design for the future of Europe on the side of Europeans. Consequently, those of us who do want a greater degree of co-operation in Europe do occasionally get a pleasant surprise because, usually either unintentionally or through some compromise, Europe does take a giant leap into the future. Nevertheless, at no time has a meeting of European leaders had as its mandate and mission the drawing up of a constitution for a United States of Europe.

It is clear that Philadelphia fell into a completely different category than any of the aforementioned European meetings. First, the delegates were there for a special and specific purpose: the drawing up of a federal constitution for the nascent United States of America. Then, for the most part, they were highly educated persons; in some cases, they were intellectuals and/or enlightened universalists (one observer even talked of demi-gods!). Finally, they were in Philadelphia for an indeterminate period of time—not for a few days. Hence, they had the time to create a constitution, which, together with subsequent amendments, serves the United States until the present day. Thus, the difference between the two sets of meetings could not be more glaring. Where then are we, at the institutional level, at this moment?

On the side of the United States, foreign governments deal directly with the administration in the persons of the president himself, his ministers or immediate subordinates. The president must, however, seek the approval of Congress on a number of important issues, especially where trade and multilateral trade negotiations are concerned.

On the side of the Community, power is shared between institutions and countries. Regarding the latter, despite some of the aims laid down in the Treaty on European Union, individual Member States still maintain their independence in the fields of defence, foreign affairs, research and development, cultural affairs, capital investment flows and, with the exception of money transferred to the European Development Fund, transfers of development aid to other countries. Furthermore, in the future, even if the Community does create an EMU with a European Central Bank, individual countries will still be able to take part in bilateral monetary negotiations with other countries and institutions. The Member States, then, do still retain quite a degree of sovereignty.

Turning to the Community institutions themselves, the Treaty has given extended powers of consultation and delay to the European Parliament, but if we exclude the European Court of Justice, the Court of Auditors and the Committee of Permanent Representatives, the two most powerful bodies are the Council of Ministers and the Commission. Although the Council must increasingly consult and co-operate with the Commission and the Parliament, it still wields considerable decision-making powers. Also, although more decisions are now taken on the basis of weighted majority voting, unanimity is still required for the taking of decisions in the following areas: fiscal and monetary policies, changes in the Treaty, social policy where labour law and/or finances are involved and the admission of new members—though the last requires the approval of the Parliament by an absolute majority of all the registered members. It is, however, the Commission which is responsible for initiating legislation and for the daily management of Community agricultural, competition and industrial, regional, social and trade policies, and which manages (with the co-operation of the Central Banks of the Member States and the Bank for International Settlements) the EMS. It is also the Commission which negotiates on behalf of the Community in multinational trade negotiations. Consequently, at the much-heralded and subsequently disappointing summit between the two sides, held in Washington, DC on 22 April 1992, the crucial meeting took place between President George Bush and President Jacques Delors of the Commission of the European Community.

At a general international level, however, it is the Community's individual Member States—and not the European Community—which are members of the Council of Europe (not to be confused with the EC Council of Ministers), the Western European Union (WEU), NATO, the

OECD, GATT, the IMF and the World Bank—to give just the most important examples.

All these facts do give cause for considerable reflection when attempting to judge the feasibility of the Community's attempts to formulate a common foreign policy and common defence. Also, it is absolutely necessary to take into account the international political complexion of prospective candidates for Community membership.

As has been examined earlier in this book, the Community has, since its inception, consistently developed and maintained special relations with Africa and, more recently, with the Caribbean and Pacific states (ACP states). It has and is increasing its association and co-operation agreements with countries in all parts of the world. However, these are essentially trading and co-operation agreements, frequently involving financial and technological transfers. They can, therefore, only be seen as part of an EC foreign policy in the purest sense of the expression. Generally speaking, foreign policy also implies the possible use of military power when this should be considered necessary; herein lies the problem. At present, the Republic of Ireland is neutral while Greece and Denmark show no enthusiasm for military operations. Of the immediate potential future Member States of the EC all four—Austria, Finland, Sweden and Switzerland—are neutral! The way out of this dilemma would be for countries which are willing to commit forces for a common military action to be allowed to do so. Then, in the long run, as is suggested in the Treaty on European Union, a common defence would be organized through the WEU.

To date, alas, the Community's attempts, in the case of Yugoslavia, at organizing a common policy—whether foreign and/or defence—have been nothing short of scandalous. The relative lack of Community action in the face of the killing of all the innocent civilians and the destruction of parts of Europe's priceless architectural heritage has been nothing less than criminal.

Even where the Community does not wish to use military force when formulating a common foreign policy, it has redoubtable diplomatic, economic and financial weapons at its disposal. Thus, in a strictly European context, it can call for the suspension of a country from the Council of Europe. Similarly, it can ask for the suspension of aid and/or loans from the EIB, the IMF, the World Bank and the EBRD. The Community can also—and with relative ease—suspend trade and financial links with a recalcitrant nation.

Despite the author's unusual and relative pessimism right now, he nevertheless believes that as the EC becomes more and more integrated and as it moves along the road to the full creation of an EMU, it will be forced to adopt common attitudes in the field of foreign affairs.

In the field of defence a common policy is likely to be developed because of the disengagement by the United States and the former Soviet Union from Europe. Correctly, the Americans do and will expect the Europeans to assume a greater degree of responsibility for their own defence. Both the Americans and the Europeans do, however, apart from their links through NATO, have a joint and important role to play in the Conference on Security and Co-operation in Europe (CSCE) which both Czecho-slovakia and Germany would like to see playing a more active role.

Another institutional development of the most considerable importance for the Community and the United States was the signing in Porto, Portugal, in May 1992, of agreements between the European Community and the European Free Trade Association (EFTA) creating, on 1 January 1993, a European Economic Area (EEA). We shall return to this development in the next chapter.

9

The Single European Market—progress and problems

There continues to be—on both sides of the Atlantic—so much misunderstanding about the Single European Market (SEM). At the time of writing it seems that the Council will get through all the necessary directives by the end of 1992. On 16 March the Council had adopted 219 out of the required 282, but the rate of transposition into the national legislation of the individual Member States has been very varied indeed, as Table 9.1 indicates. Thus, while Denmark and France lead as the 'good' boys, Germany and the Benelux countries have been lagging seriously behind.

Table 9.1 EC Directives transposed into national legislation as at 16 March 1992

	Measures transposed	Derogations	Measures not transposed	Not relevant
Belgium	99	0	54	6
Denmark	133	0	19	7
Germany	107	0	46	6
Greece	111	5	38	5
Spain	107	3	46	3
France	123	0	31	5
Ireland	109	1	43	6
Italy	113	0	41	5
Luxembourg	93	0	58	8
Netherlands	104	0	49	6
Portugal	111	4	42	2
United Kingdom	116	1	36	6

Source: EC Commission Reproduced from *Europe* (16 April 1992)

Consequently, even if, as is expected, the Council does get through all the required directives by the end of this year, they could not possibly be transposed, as is required, into national legislation by 1 January 1993.

Turning to the economic realities, while border controls on the movement of goods—aided by the agreements on the transmission of information about VAT and excise duties—are set to disappear by 1 January 1993, disparities will remain. The dispensation allowed by the Commission to automobile dealers for exclusive dealing arrangements is set to continue until the mid–1990s. Thus, car prices will continue to vary considerably throughout the Community. Then, as has already been examined, we shall not, with the exception of banking (which will come into force on 1 January 1993), have a SEM for financial services until the mid–1990s.

For non-Community countries, the creation of the EEA, on 1 January 1993, implies that there will be, with some exceptions, a much larger SEM than was originally anticipated. Thus, we shall have the largest and most important integrated economic area in the world with 380 million people, responsible for 40 per cent of world trade. It should also be noted that the EFTA countries enjoy a high standard of living. Apart from opening up their markets to each other, the two regional groupings will also apply similar competition rules and will co-operate in social, consumer and environmental policies. In the field of consumer protection, standardization is an important factor. It is also an area in which some EFTA countries have a good record. Similarly, it is a question of mutual interest to Europeans and Americans alike.

Standardization

This is still a very controversial issue about which there is considerable misunderstanding. Earlier in this work I stressed that there are three moves which can be adopted by Member States in this field. These are as follows:

 (i) absolute standardization;
 (ii) the recognition of each other's standards, ie each Member State recognizes and accepts the standards of every other Member State; and
(iii) information.

It is obvious and logical that where safety is the criterion—as in medicine, veterinary products and safety standards for vehicles—absolutely the same norms will and are being adopted. However, the tendency is, where safety considerations are not involved, for the Community to use the second approach. This development was bitterly criticized by Jacques Repussard, the new Secretary-General of the CEN, the European Committee for Standardization, in April 1992, where he spoke of a 'rampant re-nationalization' of standardization procedures. Furthermore, he strongly rejected the Commission's call for the creation of a European Standards Institute and a Community logo, pointing out that his own institution— plus the CENELEC for the electronics sector and the ETSI for telecommunications—worked very well. Also, in June 1992, the CEN will have concluded an agreement with the ISO, the International Standardization Organization, which will aim at authorizing the presence of ISO observers at CEN committees and vice versa. In my view this will be an important international development which will certainly be to the benefit of the Community and the United States.

At an immediate practical level, according to the aims of the Commission, the CEN was expected, by the end of this year, to have set 4,500 standards—mainly in the areas of safety: for example, some seven hundred in the fields of construction, food and machine safety. According to Jacques Repussard, his organization will not be able to meet this deadline.

Returning to his fierce denunciation of the EC Directive based on mutual recognition, Jacques Repussard pointed out that this misnamed (it seems to me) new approach only contained general provisions and that surprisingly (again, my own reaction) 'it was intended that the details would be worked out by private European standardization bodies'. The unbelievable finale to this saga is that the national public authorities (correctly) will not let these bodies take over responsibility for these duties! Hence, lawyers (again!) are, among other national experts, being called in to 'interpret' this directive. God save us from lawyers!

Where safety is involved, I am decidedly of the opinion that the Community must have common standards. Certainly, the Commission's call, also made in April 1992 for common 'regulations and procedures for navigability' and the implementation of 'Joint Airworthiness Requirements (or JARs)' by mid–1993, is desirable and would give the Community a strong negotiating card *vis-à-vis* the United States.

Although I have always stressed that we shall not have an internal SEM like the internal market of the United States on 1 January 1993, whereby most spare parts would be interchangeable and all equipment will be able to be used throughout the European Economic Area (EEA)—thus depriving us from benefiting from economies of scale and long production runs on a European-wide stage—there are sectors where the adoption of common safety standards will lead to the creation of a real SEM. Probably the most important of these is the pharmaceutical sector. When in April, 1992, the Council adopted four important directives in medicine, they did, in effect, pave the way for the creation of a SEM in pharmaceuticals. These directives concerned (i) the wholesale distribution of medicinal products for human use, (ii) the classification with regard to supply of medicinal products for human use, (iii) the labelling and information on medicinal products for human use and (iv) the advertising of medicinal products for human use.

Complementing these four very important directives, the Commission also submitted four proposals to the Council for the future system of authorization of medicines for human and veterinary use in Europe. The Commission also proposed the creation of a European agency for the evaluation of medicines.

Whether or not a special agency for this purpose will be created, it is certain that we shall have a real SEM for pharmaceuticals as from 1 January 1993 year. This development is of the most crucial interest to the United States since the Americans enjoy an important comparative advantage in this field.

10
And . . . the environment

Many Europeans are rightly deeply concerned with the environment. In the densely populated parts of Western Europe, any disaster like the Chernobyl one, can have catastrophic consequences. This vulnerability intensifies concern about pollution of all kinds.

Although Americans—and notably in the state of Minnesota—are increasingly aware of the dangers of pollution, Europeans are always shocked by the tendency in the United States to waste everything—especially energy—and by the apparent American disregard of the effects of their own pollution on other countries.

The European Community's Attitude towards the Environment

As in the United States, where different states have different attitudes towards the environment, so, in the European Community, different countries also support policies of differing degrees of intensity regarding the environment. It is the Netherlands, with its congested land area and its great vulnerability to the quality of water in the River Rhine, which is in the forefront of environmental legislation and is pushing and pulling its partners to adopt more energetic policies—notably in the field of pollution from car exhausts.

Before the 1972 Stockholm Convention on the Environment, the Community did not have a common environmental policy. However, in Paris, in that same year, it laid down its environmental goals as follows:

1. Pollution should be restrained at the source.
2. Pollution abatement should be integrated in European economic and social development.

3. EC environmental policy should be based on a 'the polluter pays' principle.
4. Scientific research in environmental problems should be extended and improved.
5. Border-exceeding pollution should be prevented.
6. International discussion of the pollution topic should be stimulated.
7. European citizens should be informed about pollution problems and their interest in the environment stimulated.
8. Co-operation on environmental topics should be stimulated among Member States.
9. Last but not least, improving the EC environmental standards should stimulate co-operation between Member States and harmonize national policies but not restrict national developments.

Although the Community subsequently adopted over 200 pieces of legislation (mainly directives) and several action programmes, it should be said that no piece of Community legislation is as far-reaching as the US Clean Air Act of 1990. Most recently, the EC has adopted its 5th Action Programme on the Environment. Its current philosophy on the environment is laid down in the declaration made by the Council of Ministers, in Dublin, in June 1990:

We recognise our special responsibility for the environment both to our own citizens and to the wider world. We undertake to intensify our efforts to protect and enhance the natural environment of the Community itself and of the wider world of which it is a part. We intend that action by the Community and its Member States will be developed on a co-ordinated basis and on the principles of sustainable development and preventative and precautionary action . . . The objective of such action must be to guarantee citizens the right to a clean and healthy environment . . . The full achievement of this must be a shared objective.

Also, it should be pointed out that Environmental Policy is now part of the Single European Act and the Treaty on European Union.

When, in May 1992 the Council of Ministers adopted the Fifth Action Programme for the Environment, it also agreed, in principle, to advance the date for the total removal of substances which impoverish the ozone level to 1 July 1995. Furthermore, it agreed to sign the framework convention on climatic change at the Rio Earth Summit.

In calling for a global strategy for the limitation of CO_2, the Council confirmed the Community's commitment to stabilizing, by the year 2000, the emission of CO_2 at the level of 1990. This last confirmation is extremely important, and, as we shall see, placed the Community in a policy position diametrically opposed to that adopted by the United States at the Rio Earth Summit on the Environment, in June 1992. On the eve of the most important conference of the Earth Summit, the Council met several times and adopted a rather revolutionary common position. They agreed that they would sign, together, the conventions on bio-diversity and on climatic change. It should be added here that the Commission has, on several occasions, made proposals for the imposition of a Community energy/CO_2 tax. These proposals will almost certainly be adopted by the Council.

The United States policy for the environment

Basically speaking, the United States has two sets of laws for the environment. In the 1980 Superfund legislation, America adopted the internationally accepted principle, 'polluter pays'. Thus, the main aim here is to pin the blame—and consequently, the costs for the pollution—on some company or polluter which caused it in the first place. This is not, unfortunately, a particularly strong law for the promotion of public health because it simply places the blame for an act on some body.

Of much greater importance is the Clean Air Act of November 1990, which, in principle, does control every form of air pollution and is far more comprehensive than any EC Directive. Unfortunately, under the negative influence of Vice-President Dan Quayle and the President's Council on Competitiveness, a rule was issued on 25 June 1992, giving manufacturers broad authority to vastly increase their emissions of pollution in the mid–1990s. According to the New York Times of 26 June 1992, the following results can be expected from this decision:

Under the rule, a company can increase the amount of pollution it emits into the atmosphere by up to 245 tons a year without public notice or hearings if it is forced to do so by a change in production methods. They can do this by applying for an increase; while the application is pending, the company may go ahead with its plans.

A giant refinery typically emits millions of pounds of pollutants into the air in its normal operations over a year, but small manufacturing plants generally discharge only a fraction of that amount.

The Environmental Protection Agency has 45 days to reject the application, and states have 90 days to approve or disapprove.

Just before this disappointing decision was taken, President Bush, at the Rio Earth Summit, refused not only to sign the Bio-Diversity Convention, but also declined to give a firm date for the stabilization of CO_2

emissions by the United States. In the case of the latter, he said he could not put the jobs of Americans at risk by giving such undertakings.

Economic Considerations

The reason given by President Bush for not giving an undertaking for the stabilisation of CO_2 emissions naturally leads us to economic considerations. Certainly, in the short run, a degree of freedom for industries will give them some room for manoeuvre, but, as in the case of the American steel and European shipbuilding industries, years of protectionism have failed to make them strong.

In contrast, the country with probably the strictest laws on pollution in the world, the former West Germany, is, economically, the strongest country in the world because that country has always aimed at quality. Not only do they have the most draconian pollution controls in the world, but also the highest labour costs and ever-increasing holidays! Yet, they still enjoy important balance-of-payments surpluses — quality pays.

Indeed, if all Western countries were to adopt the policy proposed by the EC Commissioner for the Environment, Carlo Ripa di Meana, of having car-free cities, life would be both cleaner and cheaper. Also, if the United States, after the 1992 presidential election, was to emulate the Community and adopt energy and CO_2 taxes, the Administration would, in one sweep, reduce the budget deficit and pollution and improve its relations with all countries in the world — except Turkey.

The Community and the United States

The Commissioner, Carlo Ripa di Meana, to his eternal credit, did not go to the Rio Earth Summit since he believed, rightly, that the Community had been browbeaten by the United States at a preparatory meeting held earlier in New York, and that the policy stance of the EC was too weak. Certainly, in view of the gravity of the danger facing the world, the Europeans were weak while the Americans were just irresponsible.

The gravity of the situation had been underlined on several occasions in 1991. Thus, in June, Britain, like its European partners, deeply concerned about the greenhouse gas effects, tried to bridge the gap between the Community and the United States by proposing a 'phased, comprehensive programme' allowing countries to make 'national commitments' to reductions in a range of greenhouse gases — not only CO_2.

In August, the Association for the Conservation of Energy was appalled when the US Government forecast major increases in American CO_2 emissions over the next 20 years—cancelling out, in effect, the reductions or stabilisation in/of CO_2 emissions to be made by EC countries.

The following month, Tim Hermach, President of the Native Forest Council, estimated that with the excessive logging which is supported by the Bush Administration, American native forests could disappear by the end of the century!

At this point, the question facing the Community and the United States, is, what can be done? Will the United States, hopefully, adopt a more responsible policy following the November 1992 elections, or, will Americans continue blindly wasting everything under the sun? Can the Community bring pressure to bear on the Americans, if so, how?

I believe that little can be done before the presidential election. However, once the new President is elected, the Europeans must bring pressure to bear upon the United States to change their behaviour and policies. Certainly, it is neither desirable nor useful to try to isolate the United States. But, the question of the environment is too grave to be ignored. One approach would be to repeat the British offer of a phased reduction in emissions on both sides of the Atlantic. However, Britain seems to have progressed further than its 1991 position.

Under the 1992 British presidency of the Community Council of Ministers, I sense a greater sense of urgency on the side of the EC. Thus, on the eve of taking over the presidency, the British Prime Minister, John Major, had written not only to the heads of government of the European Community, but also to those of the Group of Seven countries. The British aim is to set the end of 1993 as the deadline for implementing many of the decisions taken at the Rio Earth Summit. The principal decisions on which the Community has reached agreement are:

1. the implementation of the convention on climate change,
2. the implementation of the second Rio Treaty on bio-diversity—which the United States has refused to sign, and,
3. an explanation by industrial nations of the implementation of Agenda 21, the Rio action programme, and the provision of financial means for poorer nations, thus enabling them to implement it.

Britain is therefore seeking a commitment from Western industrialised nations to apply decisions one and two, and an explanation of the means of implementation—together with the provision of the necessary financial means—the third one.

Rightly or wrongly, despite the protectionist tendencies currently rearing their heads in the United States, I believe that the Americans could not afford to find themselves isolated in the western world.

11
What might happen

In this chapter, I attempt to look into the future and to assess what might happen on both sides of the Atlantic, and then, what the Community and the United States might learn from each other.

First, let us look at the positive developments which are already beginning and which will most probably be intensified over the coming years. The two partners are consulting each other more than ever before about many important issues. They now have a formal institutional framework in which regular consultations take place. Equally, with the developments in trade standardization, security and defence, there are bound to be more and more consultations. Furthermore, in future, these will increasingly take the form of a dialogue between equals. This equality will clearly be intensified by the Community's increasing strength and size, and, as the Member States become, inevitably, ever more integrated among themselves, so their negotiating power will grow.

Equally, the Community's insistence on reciprocity in such important areas as financial services, intellectual property rights and public procurement means that not only will there be more dialogue between the two partners, but that they are likely to influence each other. In particular, the Community is already influencing and will continue to affect the moves of the United States to make its banking and insurance sectors more national than state-based in character. There could also be, though this is by no means certain, a move by the Americans to emulate the Europeans by states giving mutual recognition to professional qualifications as the European Community has done (with some exceptions) for its own Member States since January 1991. Certainly, in its present form, American medical practitioners, dentists and lawyers, working inside their own country, must feel themselves to be at a disadvantage when compared with their European counterparts working inside the Community.

The greater degree of negotiating equality between the two partners could, one hopes, mean that both sides, in public procurement, for example, will open their markets to each other. However, at least on occasions, they could be tempted to do exactly the opposite. Thus, the Community fears, with some justification, that the Americans may undertake unilateral action and go it alone in the field of trade instead of ironing out differences in the GATT framework.

Trade is obviously an area where so much is at stake, and, each year, both partners issue studies about trade which concern (exclusively or heavily) each other; 1992 is no exception to the rule. Thus, within two weeks of each other, first the United States published its *1992 National Trade Estimate Report on Foreign Trade Barriers*; then the Community published its *Report on United States Trade and Investment Barriers, 1992*, the eighth such report.

Without wishing to repeat verbatim the contents of these reports, I think it wise to highlight the main issues examined in both publications since they do indicate the future trend of differences between the two partners. In the case of the American report, the vast majority of grievances are much the same as those of the previous year. Thus, once again, pride of place goes to agriculture. Since a whole chapter has already been devoted to this sector, I will say no more about it at this stage.

The other main grievances cover a variety of topics. Interestingly, the Americans are angry about the EC Broadcasting Directive and have consequently placed the Community on their 'special 301 priority watch list'. But, for the future, they are at least equally concerned about the Standards, Testing, Labelling and Certification Procedure. Here, as I do, they stress the problem created by the mutual recognition of national standards among EC Member States and the basic lack of common standards. Other important areas of current and future concern are EC government procurement with the trend of 'buying European', intellectual property rights access to the telecommunications market and, as expected, government support for Airbus and for the shipbuilding industry.

The Community, while acknowledging that the United States is basically an open country where trade is concerned, does, however, stress the difficulties encountered by European exporters when faced with the bewildering nature of different American federal, state and local regulations and standards. Equally, much irritation and apprehension is expressed at the increasing tendency of the United States to resort to unilateral action when having trade grievances rather than to discuss them in the framework of the GATT and/or the OECD. As has already been observed, earlier in this work, the Community is particularly incensed by American use of article 301—and more especially at being placed on the 'special 301 priority watch list'—in effect, the blacklist or, as the EC Report notes, a 'super 301'.

The Community is also concerned about a trend in the United States to 'buy American' and the use of the Americans to cite national security considerations—'through petitions of the US industry under section 232 of the Trade Expansion Act of 1962'—as a justification for trade restrictions.

Interestingly and surprisingly—in my opinion—this report stresses the importance of high tariffs—some as high as a range of 30–40 per cent! Equally surprising, citing the Jones Act, American quota restrictions are criticized in this study.

Again, without wishing to enter into a verbatim repetition of the Commission's long and detailed report, I believe that certain areas do merit further examination. But first, if we exclude fisheries legislation, there is only the slightest passing reference to agriculture, ie to agricultural and food import quotas and to the United States Export Enhancement Programme, which to me, looks surprisingly similar to the export refunds of the Community's CAP.

One area of American trade legislation which I view as arrogant and colonialist in nature and totally unacceptable to any allied nation is the incredible extra-territorial aspects of American laws. If we exclude the participation by EC Member States in the COCOM (Co-ordinating Committee on Multilateral Export Controls), then neither the United States— nor any other country or group of countries—has any right in international law to impose its commercial law on other countries. Such is the potential danger of this legislation for the Community and other countries that I would like to quote, verbatim (exceptionally) the Commission's observations (page 13 of the Report):

Extraterritorial reach affects inter alia:
- Importers and exporters based outside the US, who have to comply with US export and re-export control requirements and prohibitions;
- US owned or controlled businesses in Europe which have to comply with US foreign policy trade sanctions (Cuban Assets Control Regulation);
- manufacturers, which have to keep track of end-users or potential mis-users of sensitive items;

The typical case of extraterritoriality is to be found in the Export Control Regulations Issued under the IEEPA(1) and the EAA(2). These regulations require companies created under the law of the Member States and operating in the Community to comply with US export and re-export regulations. This includes compliance with US prohibitions on re-exports for reasons of US national security and foreign policy. Even when goods have left US territory, they are still regarded as being subject to US jurisdiction. These regulations have been criticized many times already by the Community and its Member States, notably during the Siberian pipeline dispute of 1982, but they continue to be applied.

Furthermore, serious extraterritorial concerns have also been raised by the US Trade Act of 1988 amendment to section II of the EAA which provides for sanctions against foreign companies which have violated their own countries' national export controls, if such violations are determined by the President to have had detrimental effect on US national security. Moreover, these sanctions are of such a nature (prohibition on contracting/procurement by US entities and the banning of imports of all products manufactured by the foreign violator) that they are contrary to the GATT and its Public Procurement Code.

The quicker that this legislation is repealed the safer will be international trading climate.

The Commission Report devotes pages and pages to public procurement *per se*, to national security considerations on procurement and to public procurement linked with the Department of Defense. All this will obviously be a field day for the armies of trade and other under-employed lawyers lined up on both sides of the Atlantic! However, the message is clear, except where mutual/reciprocal deals (which have been undertaken) are made between the United States and its military allies (of 'good' standing only); and except for cases where the Americans themselves cannot manufacture the desired equipment, it is very difficult for Europeans to break into the American military market.

In the field of public procurement, the Commission insists that under the Buy American Act, with four slight exceptions, it is not possible for European bidders to enter federally financed markets. The report points to a 10–30 per cent price preference on American offers/bids in important fields (a far cry from the 3 per cent in the EC!) and the provision of a 50 per cent price correction on foreign offers when compared with American ones.

In the very important area of telecommunications, the Commission also insists that 'foreigners are virtually precluded from offering common carrier (telephone, telex, etc.) services in the US using radio communications by the ownership restrictions imposed on common carriers'.

The Commission also strongly complains about American use (section 337 of the Tariff Act of 1930) of a procedure whereby American complainants may petition the International Trade Commission 'for the issuance of an order excluding entry into the US of products which allegedly violate US intellectual property rights'.

Finally, the Commission complains about American barriers (despite President Bush's desire for foreign investment) to foreign investment in the United States.

What do all these complaints made by the European Community and the United States imply for the future? The answer is quite clear. If we exclude agriculture, there are major growth areas in fields of innovation services and public spending where the two sides will be forced to negotiate. The areas which are most obvious are telecommunications, intellectual property rights, financial services and public procurement. In the case of financial services, the Community did, in November 1990, in Geneva, at the GATT, present a clear notion of reciprocity. It did, on other occasions, express the hope that most of the other aforementioned issues — as well as investment flows — could be negotiated in the Uruguay Round. Where this is not possible, the two partners will be forced to negotiate on a bilateral basis because so much is at stake. For both the Community and the United States, the telecommunications markets are huge and they are growing. Similarly, public procurement accounts for a major part of the gross domestic product.

But are there also possible geographical consequences for the future? The answer is 'yes'. Just as the European Community is expanding, so the United States is expanding its regional links. Following the signing and implementation of a free-trade agreement with Canada, the United States plans to extend it to Mexico. It will then almost certainly be extended to Latin American countries. In a decade from now, two giants, on each side of the Atlantic, will face each other.

Leaving trade considerations and turning to other areas of concern to the Community, the question of most constant and persistent interest to the Europeans is the possibility of a much greater degree of military disengagement from Europe by the United States. European worries were certainly intensified, when, in May 1992, Russia vetoed a proposal to exclude Yugoslavia (temporarily) from the CSCE. This move underlined the lack of flexibility inherent in this organization and its apparent lack of usefulness. Consequently, the roles of smaller but more dynamic organizations, specifically the WEU and NATO, are likely to be reinforced. Already two years ago, in public lectures, I stressed that the role of NATO could be reinforced because it would be the only reliable body left in Europe, at least, in a military sense. But in a more specific European military sense, where operations are undertaken on a smaller, voluntary, European scale, then the role of the WEU could be reinforced.

But will the United States repeat its dreadful error of the inter-war years and become isolationist? Certainly, in a presidential election year, there were enough calls to bring the troops home. I do not think that these calls will be heeded to any great degree because the Americans have too much at stake in Western Europe. As was shown in the introduction to this book, not only are the Community and the United States each other's most important trading partners, they also have fabulous levels of capital investment in each other's territories. To both partners—but especially to the United States at the present time—these investments are of the most critical economic and strategic importance and they must be defended. Thus, I am sure that the United States will, at least until the situation in the countries of the former Soviet Union has become stable, be forced, in its own interest, to maintain a military presence in Europe.

NATO itself will almost certainly change its role. It is likely that more countries will join, at least in an associate capacity. In fact, it will almost be necessary to offer a range of types of membership in the future, particularly if the organization agrees to accept members from Eastern Europe. Also, it is already starting to be a kind of bridging body between Eastern and Western Europe, and this role will almost certainly be intensified in future years.

Learning from each other

There is so much each partner can learn from the other, just as there is much which should be avoided—like the plague. To try to make this very subjective topic better structured, it has been divided into two parts: Europeans emulating the Americans and Americans emulating the Europeans.

Europeans emulating the Americans

Despite the exceptional dynamism and wonderful qualities inherent in the American character and society, there are two growth industries—both damagingly unproductive for the economy of the country. These two horrors are litigation, and bureaucracy. The Europeans are already embracing litigation and bureaucracy with sick enthusiasm. The very fact that governments are not sure what many Community Directives mean implies more jobs for the lawyers. Then, the fact that the national bureaucracy is being duplicated by Community and regional bureaucracies means that the Europeans are already, alas, emulating their American cousins in the growth of litigation and bureaucracy.

This terrifying development has to be offset by the adoption of American qualities.

The only way the Americans can possibly afford all this litigation and wastage of resources on lawyers and bureaucrats is that they have so much money. Apart from being fabulously well endowed with natural resources, and stealing huge areas of land from the Indians, they possess extraordinary qualities. They are dynamic, enthusiastic and well-organized. Although they are obsessed with the Japanese threat, they are much more productive than the Europeans.

Again, although they worry about educational levels, once they really get down to studying, they are usually more flexible than the Europeans, certainly much more than the British and Irish. They specialize later than the Europeans, and they can start studying later in life than is the case in Europe. Consequently, if they wish, people do have a chance to fulfil themselves.

Then, of course, there are the personal services—without servility—for customers. To Europeans visiting the United States, this is wonderful. And the flexible (frequently around the clock) opening hours of shops and supermarkets. It all makes life so much easier, especially for people who work. When do the British, Germans and Dutch, for example, get their shopping done if they are working all day and everyday? The marvel of the arrangement in the United States is that these long opening hours allow shops and other enterprises to engage many, many students as part-time employees who are working their way through college and university.

Americans emulating the Europeans

What should the Americans avoid when emulating the Europeans? While possibly enlarging the basic welfare support nationwide for really ill people, they should certainly try to avoid the over-generous social security welfare system in some European countries which is a disincentive to work. Thus, for example, in the Netherlands, one in six of the active workforce has been prematurely retired—on benefits amounting to 70 per cent of their last salary—on a pension paid for by the state.

In contrast, they would be well advised to adopt a British or European-style national health service. These are nation-wide systems which are much less expensive than the present impartial American coverage.

Also, regarding the quality of life, reduction in television advertising and more respect for the private lives of public figures—as is the case in continental European countries—would vastly improve the human quality of life.

One European practice which is already being adopted by a number of major American cities, and which should be further expanded, is an expansion in the size and quality of the public transport systems. The easiest way of accelerating this would be to impose a substantial tax on energy consumption. To Europeans, the greedy waste of energy in the United States is frightening.

Overview

I would like to close on a positive note because despite quarrels that always take place between friends, there is and will be much more contact between Europeans and Americans than has previously been the case. The most positive development, in my opinion, is that the dialogue, now taking place on a much more frequent basis, is more and more one of equals. Similarly, at a much more basic and individual level, whereas in the past it tended to be mainly American tourists who visited Europe, now Europeans visit the United States in ever increasing numbers.

Finally, there is only one really big question on the horizon. In the coming years, does the possibility exist that the Community, through its constant enlargement, will become less interested in other parts of the world? Similarly, the United States, in its moves to create a North and Latin American Free Trade Area, may be tempted into an American continental isolationism. The message is clear: Europeans and Americans need to be vigilant about the future.

Appendix 1

The following documents are reproduced with the kind permission of Agence Europe.

TEXT IN FULL
OF THE
'TREATY ON EUROPEAN UNION'

Here is the text in full of the 'Treaty on European Union', its annexes and the 'Final Act', as signed in Maastricht in the afternoon of 7 February 1992. These texts are the results of negotiations undertaken within the Intergovernmental Conferences on EMU and Political Union, opened in Rome in the afternoon of 15 December 1990, and ended in Maastricht in the evening of 11 December 1991.
This text includes all the modifications brought to the Treaty in force.

* * * * *

TREATY
ON EUROPEAN UNION

HIS MAJESTY THE KING OF THE BELGIANS,
HER MAJESTY THE QUEEN OF DENMARK,
THE PRESIDENT OF THE FEDERAL REPUBLIC OF GERMANY,
THE PRESIDENT OF THE HELLENIC REPUBLIC,
HIS MAJESTY THE KING OF SPAIN,
THE PRESIDENT OF THE FRENCH REPUBLIC,
THE PRESIDENT OF IRELAND,
THE PRESIDENT OF THE ITALIAN REPUBLIC,
HIS ROYAL HIGHNESS THE GRAND DUKE OF LUXEMBOURG,
HER MAJESTY THE QUEEN OF THE NETHERLANDS,
THE PRESIDENT OF THE PORTUGUESE REPUBLIC,
HER MAJESTY THE QUEEN OF THE UNITED KINGDOM OF GREAT BRITAIN AND NORTHERN IRELAND.

RESOLVED to mark a new stage in the process of European integration undertaken with the establishment of the European Communites,

RECALLING the historic importance of the ending of the division of the European continent and the need to create firm bases for the construction of the future Europe,

CONFIRMING their attachment to the principles of liberty, democracy and respect for human rights and fundamental freedoms and of the rule of law,

DESIRING to deepen the solidarity between their peoples while respecting their history, their culture and their traditions,

DESIRING to enhance further the democratic and efficient functioning of the institutions so as to enable them better to carry out, within a single institutional framework, the tasks entrusted to them,

RESOLVED to achieve the strengthening and the convergence of their economies and to establish an economic and monetary union including, in accordance with the provision of this Treaty, a single and stable currency,

DETERMINED to promote economic and social progress for their peoples, within the context of the accomplishment of the internal market and of reinforced cohesion and environmental protection, and to implement policies ensuring that advances in economic integration are accompanied by parallel progress in other fields,

RESOLVED to establish a citizenship common to nationals of their countries,

RESOLVED to implement a common foreign and security policy including the eventual framing of a common defence policy, which might in time lead to a common defence, thereby reinforcing the European identity and its independence in order to promote peace, security and progress in Europe and in the world,

REAFFIRMING their objective to facilitate the free movement of persons, while ensuring the safety and security of their peoples, by including provisions on justice and home affairs in this Treaty,

RESOLVED to continue the process of creating an ever closer union among the peoples of Europe, in which decisions are taken as closely as possible to the citizen in accordance with the principle of subsidiarity,

IN VIEW of further steps to be taken in order to advance European integration,

HAVE DECIDED to establish a European Union and to this end have designated as their plenipotentiaries:

HIS MAJESTY THE KING OF THE BELGIANS:
HER MAJESTY THE QUEEN OF DENMARK:
THE PRESIDENT OF THE FEDERAL REPUBLIC OF GERMANY:
THE PRESIDENT OF THE HELLENIC REPUBLIC:
HIS MAJESTY THE KING OF SPAIN:
THE PRESIDENT OF THE FRENCH REPUBLIC:
THE PRESIDENT OF IRELAND:
THE PRESIDENT OF THE ITALIAN REPUBLIC:
HIS ROYAL HIGHNESS THE GRAND DUKE OF LUXEMBOURG:
HER MAJESTY THE QUEEN OF THE NETHERLANDS:
THE PRESIDENT OF THE PORTUGUESE REPUBLIC:

HER MAJESTY THE QUEEN OF THE UNITED KINGDOM OF GREAT BRITAIN AND NORTHERN IRELAND:

WHO, having exchanged their full powers, found in good and due form, have agreed as follows:

TITLE I
COMMON PROVISIONS

ARTICLE A
By this Treaty, the High Contracting Parties establish among themselves a European Union, hereinafter called 'the Union'. This Treaty marks a new stage in the process of creating an ever closer union among the peoples of Europe, in which decisions are taken as closely as possible to the citizen.
The Union shall be founded on the European Communities, supplemented by the policies and forms of cooperation established by this Treaty. Its task shall be to organize, in a manner demonstrating consistency and solidarity, relations between the Member States and between their peoples.

ARTICLE B
The Union shall set itself the following objectives:
— to promote economic and social progress which is balanced and sustainable, in particular through the creation of an area without internal frontiers, through the strengthening of economic and social cohesion and through the establishment of economic and monetary union, ultimately including a single currency in accordance with the provisions of this Treaty;
— to assert its identity on the international scene, in particular through the implementation of a common foreign and security policy including the eventual framing of a common defence policy, which might in time lead to a common defence;
— to strengthen the protection of the rights and interests of the nationals of its Member States through the introduction of a citizenship of the Union;
— to develop close cooperation on justice and home affairs;
— to maintain in full the 'acquis communautaire' and build on it with a view to considering, through the procedure referred to in Article N(2), to what extent the policies and forms of cooperation introduced by this Treaty may need to be revised with the aim of ensuring the effectiveness of the mechanisms and the institutions of the Community.
The objectives of the Union shall be achieved as provided in this Treaty and in accordance with the conditions and the timetable set out therein while respecting the principle of subsidiarity as defined in Article 3b of the Treaty establishing the European Community.

ARTICLE C
The Union shall be served by a single institutional framework which shall ensure the consistency and the continuity of the activities carried out in order to attain its objectives while respecting and building upon the 'acquis communautaire'.
The Union shall in particular ensure the consistency of its external activities as a whole in the context of its external relations, security, economic and development

policies. The Council and the Commission shall be responsible for ensuring such consistency. They shall ensure the implementation of these policies, each in accordance with its respective powers.

ARTICLE D
The European Council shall provide the Union with the necessary impetus for its development and shall define the general political guidelines thereof.
The European Council shall bring together, the Heads of State or of Government of the Member States and the President of the Commission.
They shall be assisted by the Ministers for Foreign Affairs of the Member States and by a Member of the Commission. The European Council shall meet at least twice a year, under the chairmanship of the Head of State or of Government of the Member State which holds the Presidency of the Council.
The European Council shall submit to the European Parliament a report after each of its meetings and a yearly written report on the progress achieved by the Union.

ARTICLE E
The European Parliament, the Council, the Commission and the Court of Justice shall exercise their powers under the conditions and for the purposes provided for, on the one hand, by the provisions of the Treaties establishing the European Communities and of the subsequent Treaties and Acts modifying and supplementing them and, on the other hand, by the other provisions of this Treaty.

ARTICLE F
1. The Union shall respect the national identities of its Members States, whose systems of government are founded on the principles of democracy.
2. The Union shall respect fundamental rights, as guaranteed by the European Convention for the Protection of Human Rights and Fundamental Freedoms signed in Rome on 4 November 1950 and as they result from the constitutional traditions common to the Member States, as general principles of Community law.
3. The Union shall provide itself with the means necessary to attain its objectives and carry through its policies.

TITLE II
PROVISIONS AMENDING THE TREATY
ESTABLISHING THE EUROPEAN ECONOMIC COMMUNITY
WITH A VIEW TO ESTABLISHING
THE EUROPEAN COMMUNITY

ARTICLE G
The Treaty establishing the European Economic Community shall be amended in accordance with the provisions of this Article, in order to establish a European Community.

A. Throughout the Treaty:
1) The term 'European Economic Community' shall be replaced by the term 'European Community'.
B. In Part One 'Principles':

2) Article 2 shall be replaced by the following:

'ARTICLE 2
The Community shall have as its task, by establishing a common market and an economic and monetary union and by implementing the common policies or activities referred to in Articles 3 and 3a, to promote throughout the Community a harmonious and balanced development of economic activities, sustainable and non-inflationary growth respecting the environment, a high degree of convergence of economic performance, a high level of employment and of social protection, the raising of the standard of living and quality of life, and economic and social cohesion and solidarity among Member States.'

3) Article 3 shall be replaced by the following:

'ARTICLE 3
For the purposes set out in Article 2, the activities of the Community shall include, as provided in this Treaty and in accordance with the timetable set out therein:
(a) the elimination, as between Member States, of customs duties and quantitative restrictions on the import and export of goods, and of all other measures having equivalent effect;
(b) a common commercial policy;
(c) an internal market characterized by the abolition, as between Member States, of obstacles to the free movement of goods, persons, services and capital;
(d) measures concerning the entry and movement of persons in the internal market as provided for in Article 100c;
(e) a common policy in the sphere of agriculture and fisheries;
(f) a common policy in the sphere of transport;
(g) a system ensuring that competition in the internal market is not distorted;
(h) the approximation of the laws of Member States to the extent required for the functioning of the common market;
(i) a policy in the social sphere comprising a European Social Fund;
(j) the strengthening of economic and social cohesion;
(k) a policy in the sphere of the environment;
(l) the strengthening of the competitiveness of Community industry;
(m) the promotion of research and technological development;
(n) encouragement for the establishment and development of trans-European networks; (o) a contribution to the attainment of a high level of health protection;
(p) a contribution to education and training of quality and to the flowering of the cultures of the Member States;
(q) a policy in the sphere of development cooperation;
(r) the association of the overseas countries and territories in order to increase trade and promote jointly economic and social development;
(s) a contribution to the strengthening of consumer protection;
(t) measures in the spheres of energy, civil protection and tourism.'

4) The following Article shall be inserted:

'ARTICLE 3a
1. For the purposes set out in Article 2, the activities of the Member States and the Community shall include, as provided in this Treaty and in accordance with

the timetable set out therein, the adoption of an economic policy which is based on the close coordination of Member States' economic policies, on the internal market and on the definition of common objectives, and conducted in accordance with the principle of an open market economy with free competition.

2. Concurrently with the foregoing, and as provided in this Treaty and in accordance with the timetable and the procedures set out therein, these activities shall include the irrevocable fixing of exchange rates leading to the introduction of a single currency, the ECU, and the definition and conduct of a single monetary policy and exchange rate policy the primary objective of both of which shall be to maintain price stability and, without prejudice to this objective, to support the general economic policies in the Community, in accordance with the principle of an open market economy with free competition.

3. These activities of the Member States and the Community shall entail compliance with the following guiding principles: stable prices, sound public finances and monetary conditions and a sustainable balance of payments.'

5) The following Article shall be inserted:

'ARTICLE 3b
The Community shall act within the limits of the powers conferred upon it by this Treaty and of the objectives assigned to it therein.

In areas which do not fall within its exclusive competence, the Community shall take action, in accordance with the principle of subsidiarity, only if and in so far as the objectives of the proposed action cannot be sufficiently achieved by the Member States and can therefore, by reason of the scale or effects of the proposed action, be better achieved by the Community.

Any action by the Community shall not go beyond what is necessary to achieve the objectives of this Treaty.'

6) Article 4 shall be replaced by the following:

'ARTICLE 4
1. The tasks entrusted to the Community shall be carried out by the following institutions:

— a EUROPEAN PARLIAMENT,
— a COUNCIL,
— a COMMISSION,
— a COURT OF JUSTICE,
— a COURT OF AUDITORS.

Each institution shall act within the limits of the powers conferred upon it by this Treaty.

2. The Council and the Commission shall be assisted by an Economic and Social Committee and a Committee of the Regions acting in an advisory capacity.'

7) The following Articles shall be inserted:

'ARTICLE 4a

A European System of Central Banks (hereinafter referred to as 'ESCB') and a European Central Bank (hereinafter referred to as 'ECB') shall be established in accordance with the procedures laid down in this Treaty; they shall act within the limits of the powers conferred upon them by this Treaty and by the Statute of the ESCB and of the ECB (hereinafter referred to as 'Statute of the ESCB') annexed thereto.

ARTICLE 4b

A European Investment Bank is hereby established, which shall act within the limits of the powers conferred upon it by this Treaty and the Statute annexed thereto.'

8) Article 6 shall be deleted and Article 7 shall become Article 6. Its second paragraph shall be replaced by the following:
'The Council, acting in accordance with the procedure referred to in Article 189c, may adopt rules designed to prohibit such discrimination.'
9) Articles 8, 8a, 8b and 8c shall become respectively Articles 7, 7a, 7b and 7c.
C. The following Part shall be inserted:

'PART TWO
CITIZENSHIP OF THE UNION

ARTICLE 8

1. Citizenship of the Union is hereby established.
Every person holding the nationality of a Member State shall be a citizen of the Union.
2. Citizens of the Union shall enjoy the rights conferred by this Treaty and shall be subject to the duties imposed thereby.

ARTICLE 8a

1. Every citizen of the Union shall have the right to move and reside freely within the territory of the Member States, subject to the limitations and conditions laid down in this Treaty and by the measures adopted to give it effect.
2. The Council may adopt provisions with a view to facilitating the exercise of the rights referred to in paragraph 1; save as otherwise provided in this Treaty, the Council shall act unanimously on a proposal from the Commission and after obtaining the assent of the European Parliament.

ARTICLE 8b

1. Every citizen of the Union residing in a Member State of which he is not a national shall have the right to vote and to stand as a candidate at municipal elections in the Member State in which he resides, under the same conditions as nationals of that State. This right shall be exercised subject to detailed arrangements to be adopted before 31 December 1994 by the Council, acting unanimously on a proposal from the Commission and after consulting the European Parliament; these arrangements may provide for derogations where warranted by problems specific to a Member State.
2. Without prejudice to Article 138(3) and to the provisions adopted for its implementation, every citizen of the Union residing in a Member State of which

he is not a national shall have the right to vote and to stand as a candidate in elections to the European Parliament in the Member State in which he resides, under the same conditions as nationals of that State. This right shall be exercised subject to detailed arrangements to be adopted before 31 December 1993 by the Council, acting unanimously on a proposal from the Commission and after consulting the European Parliament; these arrangements may provide for derogations where warranted by problems specific to a Member State.

ARTICLE 8c

Every citizen of the Union shall, in the territory of a third country in which the Member State of which he is a national is not represented, be entitled to protection by the diplomatic or consular authorities of any Member State, on the same conditions as the nationals of that State.

Before 31 December 1993, Member States shall establish the necessary rules among themselves and start the international negotiations required to secure this protection.

ARTICLE 8d

Every citizen of the Union shall have the right to petition the European Parliament in accordance with Article 138d.

Every citizen of the Union may apply to the Ombudsman established in accordance with Article 138e.

ARTICLE 8e

The Commission shall report to the European Parliament, to the Council and to the Economic and Social Committee before 31 December 1993 and then every three years on the application of the provisions of this Part. This report shall take account of the development of the Union. On this basis, and without prejudice to the other provisions of this Treaty, the Council, acting unanimously on a proposal from the Commission and after consulting the European Parliament, may adopt provisions to strengthen or to add to the rights laid down in this Part, which it shall recommend to the Member States for adoption in accordance with their respective constitutional requirements.'

D. Parts Two and Three shall be grouped under the following Title:
'PART THREE
COMMUNITY POLICIES'
and in this Part:

10) The first sentence of Article 49 shall be replaced by the following:
'As soon as this Treaty enters into force, the Council shall, acting in accordance with the procedure referred to in Article 189b and after consulting the Economic and Social Committee, issue directives or make regulations setting out the measures required to bring about, by progressive stages, freedom of movement for workers, as defined in Article 48, in particular.'

11) Article 54(2) shall be replaced by the following:
'2. In order to implement this general programme or, in the absence of such programme, in order to achieve a stage in attaining freedom of establishment as regards a particular activity, the Council, acting in accordance with the procedure

referred to in Article 189b and after consulting the Economic and Social Committee, shall act by means of directives.'

12) Article 56(2) shall be replaced by the following:
'2. Before the end of the transitional period, the Council shall, acting unanimously on a proposal from the Commission and after consulting the European Parliament, issue directives for the coordination of the abovementioned provisions laid down by law, regulation or administrative action. After the end of the second stage, however, the Council shall, acting in accordance with the procedure referred to in Article 189b, issue directives for the coordination of such provisions as, in each Member State, are a matter for regulation or administrative action.'

13) Article 57 shall be replaced by the following:

'ARTICLE 57
1. In order to make it easier for persons to take up and pursue activities as self-employed persons, the Council shall, acting in accordance with the procedure referred to in Article 189b, issue directives for the mutual recognition of diplomas, certificates and other evidence of formal qualifications.
2. For the same purpose, the Council shall, before the end of the transitional period, issue directives for the coordination of the provisions laid down by law, regulation or administrative action in Member States concerning the taking up and pursuit of activities as self-employed persons. The Council, acting unanimously on a proposal from the Commission and after consulting the European Parliament, shall decide on directives the implementation of which involves in at least one Member State amendment of the existing principles laid down by law governing the professions with respect to training and conditions of access for natural persons. In other cases the Council shall act in accordance with the procedure referred to in Article 189b.
3. In the case of the medical and allied and pharmaceutical professions, the progressive abolition of restrictions shall be dependent upon coordination of the conditions for their exercise in the various Member States.'

14) The title of Chapter 4 shall be replaced by the following:

'CHAPTER 4
CAPITAL AND PAYMENTS'
15) The following Articles shall be inserted:

'ARTICLE 73a
As from 1 January 1994, Articles 67 to 73 shall be replaced by Articles 73b, c, d, e, f and g.

ARTICLE 73b
1. Within the framework of the provisions set out in this Chapter, all restrictions on the movement of capital between Member States and between Member States and third countries shall be prohibited.
2. Within the framework of the provisions set out in this Chapter, all restrictions

on payments between Member States and between Member States and third countries shall be prohibited.

ARTICLE 73c

1. The provisions of Article 73b shall be without prejudice to the application to third countries of any restrictions which exist on 31 December 1993 under national or Community law adopted in respect of the movement of capital to or from third countries involving direct investment – including investment in real estate — establishment, the provision of financial services or the admission of securities to capital markets.

2. Whilst endeavouring to achieve the objective of free movement of capital between Member States and third countries to the greatest extent possible and without prejudice to the other Chapters of this Treaty, the Council may, acting by a qualified majority on a proposal from the Commission, adopt measures on the movement of capital to or from third countries involving direct investment — including investment in real estate —, establishment, the provision of financial services or the admission of securities to capital markets.

Unanimity shall be required for measures under this paragraph which constitute a step back in Community law as regards the liberalization of the movement of capital to or from third countries.

ARTICLE 73d

1. The provisions of Article 73b shall be without prejudice to the right of Member States:

(a) to apply the relevant provisions of their tax law which distinguish between tax-payers who are not in the same situation with regard to their place of residence or with regard to the place where their capital is invested;

(b) to take all requisite measures to prevent infringements of national law and regulations, in particular in the field of taxation and the prudential supervision of financial institutions, or to lay down procedures for the declaration of capital movements for purposes of administrative or statistical information, or to take measures which are justified on grounds of public policy or public security.

2. The provisions of this Chapter shall be without prejudice to the applicability of restrictions on the right of establishment which are compatible with this Treaty.

3. The measures and procedures referred to in paragraphs 1 and 2 shall not constitute a means of arbitrary discrimination or a disguised restriction on the free movement of capital and payments as defined in Article 73b.

ARTICLE 73e

By way of derogation from Article 73b, Member States which, on 31 December 1993, enjoy a derogation on the basis of existing Community law, shall be entitled to maintain, until 31 December 1995 at the latest, restrictions on movements of capital authorized by such derogations as exist on that date.

ARTICLE 73f

Where, in exceptional circumstances, movements of capital to or from third countries cause, or threaten to cause, serious difficulties for the operation of economic and monetary union, the Council, acting by a qualified majority on a proposal from the Commission and after consulting the ECB, may take safeguard measures with regard to third countries for a period not exceeding six months if such measures are strictly necessary.

ARTICLE 73g

1. If, in the case envisaged in Article 228a, action by the Community is deemed necessary, the Council may, in accordance with the procedure provided for in Article 228a, take the necessary urgent measures on the movement of capital and on payments as regards the third countries concerned.

2. Without prejudice to Article 224 and as long as the Council has not taken measures pursuant to paragraph 1, a Member State may, for serious political reasons and on grounds of urgency, take unilateral measures against a third country with regard to capital movements and payments. The Commission and the other Member States shall be informed of such measures by the date of their entry into force at the latest.

The Council may, acting by a qualified majority on a proposal from the Commission, decide that the Member State concerned shall amend or abolish such measures. The President of the Council shall inform the European Parliament of any such decision taken by the Council.

ARTICLE 73h

Until January 1994, the following provisions shall be applicable:

1) Each Member State undertakes to authorize, in the currency of the Member State in which the creditor or the beneficiary resides, any payments connected with the movement of goods, services or capital, and any transfers of capital and earnings, to the extent that the movement of goods, services, capital and persons between Member States has been liberalized pursuant to this Treaty.

The Member States declare their readiness to undertake the liberalization of payments beyond the extent provided in the preceding subparagraph, in so far as their economic situation in general and the state of their balance of payments in particular so permit.

2) In so far as movement of goods, services and capital are limited only by restrictions on payments connected therewith, these restrictions shall be progressively abolished by applying, mutatis mutandis, the provisions of this Chapter and the Chapters relating to the abolition of quantitative restrictions and to the liberalization of services.

3) Member States undertake not to introduce between themselves any new restrictions on transfers connected with the invisible transactions listed in Annex III to this Treaty.

The progressive abolition of existing restrictions shall be effected in accordance with the provisions of Articles 63 to 65, in so far as such abolition is not governed by the provisions contained in paragraphs 1 and 2 or by the other provisions of this Chapter.

4) If need be, Member States shall consult each other on the measures to be taken to enable the payments and transfers mentioned in this Article to be effected; such measures shall not prejudice the attainment of the objectives set out in this Treaty.'

16) Article 75 shall be replaced by the following:

'ARTICLE 75

1. For the purpose of implementing Article 74, and taking into account the distinctive features of transport, the Council shall, acting in accordance with the procedure referred to in Article 189c and after consulting the Economic and Social Committee, lay down:

(a) common rules applicable to international transport to or from the territory of a Member State or passing across the territory of one or more Member States;

(b) the conditions under which non-resident carriers may operate transport services within a Member State;

(c) measures to improve transport safety;

(d) any other appropriate provisions.

2. The provisions referred to in (a) and (b) of paragraph 1 shall be laid down during the transitional period.

3. By way of derogation from the procedure provided for in paragraph 1, where the application of provisions concerning the principles of the regulatory system for transport would be liable to have a serious effect on the standard of living and on employment in certain areas and on the operation of transport facilities, they shall be laid down by the Council acting unanimously on a proposal from the Commission, after consulting the European Parliament and the Economic and Social Committee.

In so doing, the Council shall take into account the need for adaptation to the economic development which will result from establishing the common market.'

17) The title of Title I in Part Three shall be replaced by the following:

'TITLE V

Common rules on
competition, taxation
and approximation of laws'.

18) In Article 92(3):

— the following point shall be inserted:

'(d) aid to promote culture and heritage conservation where such aid does not affect trading conditions and competition in the Community to an extent that is contrary to the common interest.'

— the present point (d) shall become (e).

19) Article 94 shall be replaced by the following:

'ARTICLE 94

The Council, acting by a qualified majority on a proposal from the Commission and after consulting the European Parliament, may make any appropriate regulations for the application of Articles 92 and 93 and may in particular determine the conditions in which Article 93(3) shall apply and the categories of aid exempted from this procedure.'

20) Article 99 shall be replaced by the following:

'ARTICLE 99

The Council shall, acting unanimously on a proposal from the Commission and after consulting the European Parliament and the Economic and Social Committee, adopt provisions for the harmonization of legislation concerning turnover taxes, excise duties and other forms of indirect taxation to the extent that such harmonization is necessary to ensure the establishment and the functioning of the internal market within the time limit laid down in Article 7a',

21) Article 100 shall be replaced by the following:

'ARTICLE 100
The Council shall, acting unanimously on a proposal from the Commission and after consulting the European Parliament and the Economic and Social Committee, issue directives for the approximation of such laws, regulations or administrative provisions of the Member States as directly affect the establishment or functioning of the common market.'

22) Article 100a(1) shall be replaced by the following:
'1. By way of derogation from Article 100 and save where otherwise provided in this Treaty, the following provisions shall apply for the achievement of the objectives set out in Article 7a. The Council shall, acting in accordance with the procedure referred to in Article 189b and after consulting the Economic and Social Committee, adopt the measures for the approximation of the provisions laid down by law, regulation or administrative action in Member States which have as their object the establishment and functioning of the internal market.'

23) The following Article shall be inserted:

'ARTICLE 100c
1. The Council, acting unanimously on a proposal from the Commission and after consulting the European Parliament, shall determine the third countries whose nationals must be in possession of a visa when crossing the external borders of the Member States.
2. However, in the event of an emergency situation in a third country posing a threat of a sudden inflow of nationals from that country into the Community, the Council, acting by a qualified majority on a recommendation from the Commission, may introduce, for a period not exceeding six months, a visa requirement for nationals from the country in question. The visa requirement established under this paragraph may be extended in accordance with the procedure referred to in paragraph 1.
3. From 1 January 1996, the Council shall act by a qualified majority on the decisions referred to in paragraph 1. The Council shall, before that date, acting by a qualified majority on a proposal from the Commission and after consulting the European Parliament, adopt measures relating to a uniform format for visas.
4. In the matters referred to in this Article, the Commission shall examine any request made by a Member State that it submit a proposal to the Council.
5. This Article shall be without prejudice to the exercise of the responsibilities incumbent upon the Member States with regard to the maintenance of law and order and the safeguarding of internal security.
6. This Article shall apply to other matters if so decided pursuant to Article K.9 of the provisions of the Treaty on European Union which relate to cooperation in the fields of justice and home affairs, subject to the voting conditions determined at the same time.
7. The provisions of the conventions in force between the Member States governing

matters covered by this Article shall remain in force until their content has been replaced by directives or measures adopted pursuant to this Article.'

24) The following Article shall be inserted:

'ARTICLE 100d
The Coordinating Committee consisting of senior officials set up by Article K.4 of the Treaty on European Union shall contribute, without prejudice to the provisions of Article 151, to the preparation of the proceedings of the Council in the fields referred to in Article 100c.'

25) Title II, Chapters 1, 2 and 3 in Part Three shall be replaced by the following:
'TITLE VI
ECONOMIC AND MONETARY POLICY

CHAPTER 1
ECONOMIC POLICY

ARTICLE 102a
Member States shall conduct their economic policies with a view to contributing to the achievement of the objectives of the Community, as defined in Article 2, and in the context of the broad guidelines referred to in Article 103(2).
The Member States and the Community shall act in accordance with the principle of an open market economy with free competition, favouring an efficient allocation of resources, and in compliance with the principles set out in Article 3a.

ARTICLE 103
1. Member States shall regard their economic policies as a matter of common concern and shall coordinate them within the Council, in accordance with the provisions of Article 102a.
2. The Council shall, acting by a qualified majority on a recommendation from the Commission, formulate a draft for the broad guidelines of the economic policies of the Member States and of the Community, and shall report its findings to the European Council.
The European Council shall, acting on the basis of this report from the Council, discuss a conclusion on the broad guidelines of the economic policies of the Member States and of the community.
On the basis of this conclusion, the Council shall, acting by a qualified majority, adopt a recommendation setting out these broad guidelines. The Council shall inform the European Parliament of its recommendation.
3. In order to ensure closer coordination of economic policies and sustained convergence of the economic performances of the Member States, the Council shall, on the basis of reports submitted by the Commission, monitor economic developments in each of the Member States and in the Community as well as the consistency of economic policies with the broad guidelines referred to in paragraph 2, and regularly carry out an overall assessment.
For the purpose of this multilateral surveillance, Member States shall forward information to the Commission about important measures taken by them in the field of their economic policy and such other information as they deem necessary.
4. Where it is established, under the procedure referred to in paragraph 3, that

the economic policies of a Member State are not consistent with the broad guidelines referred to in paragraph 2 or that they risk jeopardizing the proper functioning of economic and monetary union, the Council may, acting by a qualified majority on a recommendation from the Commission, make the necessary recommendations to the Member State concerned.

The Council may, acting by a qualified majority on a proposal from the Commission, decide to make its recommendations public.

The President of the Council and the Commission shall report to the European Parliament on the results of multilateral surveillance. The President of the Council may be invited to appear before the competent Committee of the European Parliament if the Council has made its recommendations public.

5. The Council, acting in accordance with the procedure referred to in Article 189c, may adopt detailed rules for the multilateral surveillance procedure referred to in paragraphs 3 and 4 of this Article.

ARTICLE 103a

1. Without prejudice to any other procedures provided for in this Treaty, the Council may, acting unanimously on a proposal from the Commission, decide upon the measures appropriate to the economic situation, in particular if severe difficulties arise in the supply of certain products.

2. Where a Member State is in difficulties or is seriously threatened with severe difficulties caused by exceptional occurrences beyond its control, the Council may, acting unanimously on a proposal from the Commission, grant, under certain conditions, Community financial assistance to the Member State concerned. Where the severe difficulties are caused by natural disasters, the Council shall act by qualified majority. The President of the Council shall inform the European Parliament of the decision taken.

ARTICLE 104

1. Overdraft facilities or any other type of credit facility with the ECB or with the central banks of the Member States (hereinafter referred to as 'national central banks') in favour of Community institutions or bodies, central governments, regional, local or other public authorities, other bodies governed by public law or public undertakings of Member States shall be prohibited, as shall the purchase directly from them by the ECB or national central banks of debt instruments.

2. The provisions of paragraph 1 shall not apply to publicly-owned credit institutions, which in the context of the supply of reserves by central banks shall be given the same treatment by national central banks and the ECB as private credit institutions.

ARTICLE 104a

1. Any measure, not based on prudential considerations, establishing privileged access by Community institutions or bodies, central governments, regional, local or other public authorities, other bodies governed by public law or public undertakings of Member States to financial institutions shall be prohibited.

2. The Council, acting in accordance with the procedure referred to in Article 189c, shall, before 1 January 1994, specify definitions for the application of the prohibition referred to in paragraph 1.

ARTICLE 104b

1. The Community shall not be liable for or assume the commitments of central governments, regional, local or other public authorities, other bodies governed by public law, or public undertakings of any Member State, without prejudice to mutual financial guarantees for the joint execution of a specific project. A Member State shall not be liable for or assume the commitments of central governments, regional, local or other public authorities, other bodies governed by public law or public undertakings of another Member State, without prejudice to mutual financial guarantees for the joint execution of a specific project.

2. If necessary, the Council, acting in accordance with the procedure referred to in Article 189c, may specify definitions for the application of the prohibitions referred to in Article 104 and in this Article.

ARTICLE 104c

1. Member States shall avoid excessive government deficits.

2. The Commission shall monitor the development of the budgetary situation and of the stock of government debt in the Member States with a view to identifying gross errors. In particular it shall examine compliance with budgetary discipline on the basis of the following two criteria:

(a) whether the ratio of the planned or actual government deficit to gross domestic product exceeds a reference value, unless

— either the ratio has declined substantially and continuously and reached a level that comes close to the reference value;

— or, alternatively, the excess over the reference value is only exceptional and temporary and the ratio remains close to the reference value;

(b) whether the ratio of government debt to gross domestic product exceeds a reference value, unless the ratio is sufficiently diminishing and approaching the reference value at a satisfactory pace.

The reference values are specified in the Protocol on the excessive deficit procedure annexed to this Treaty.

3. If a Member State does not fulfil the requirements under one or both of these criteria, the Commission shall prepare a report. The report of the Commission shall also take into account whether the government deficit exceeds government investment expenditure and take into account all other relevant factors, including the medium term economic and budgetary position of the Member State.

The Commission may also prepare a report if, notwithstanding the fulfilment of the requirements under the criteria, it is of the opinion that there is a risk of an excessive deficit in a Member State.

4. The Committee provided for in Article 190c shall formulate an opinion on the report of the Commission.

5. If the Commission considers that an excessive deficit in a Member State exists or may occur, the Commission shall address an opinion to the Council.

6. The Council shall, acting by a qualified majority on a recommendation from the Commission, and having considered any observations which the Member State concerned may wish to make, decide after an overall assessment whether an excessive deficit exists.

7. Where the existence of an excessive deficit is decided according to paragraph 6, the Council shall make recommendations to the Member State concerned with a view to bringing that situation to an end within a given period. Subject to the provisions of paragraph 8, these recommendations shall not be made public.

8. Where it establishes that there has been no effective action in response to its recommendations within the period laid down, the Council may make its recommendations public.

9. If a Member State persists in failing to put into practice the recommendations of the Council, the Council may decide to give notice to the Member State to take, within a specified time limit, measures for the deficit reduction which is judged necessary by the Council in order to remedy the situation.

In such a case, the Council may request the Member State concerned to submit reports in accordance with a specific timetable in order to examine the adjustment efforts of that Member State.

10. The rights to bring actions provided for in Articles 169 and 170 may not be exercised within the framework of paragraphs 1 to 9 of this Article.

11. As long as a Member State fails to comply with a decision taken in accordance with paragraph 9, the Council may decide to apply or, as the case may be, intensify one or more of the following measures:

— to require that the Member State concerned shall publish additional information, to be specified by the Council, before issuing bonds and securities;

— to invite the European Investment Bank to reconsider its lending policy towards the Member State concerned;

— to require that the Member State concerned makes a non-interest-bearing deposit of an appropriate size with the Community until the excessive deficit has, in the view of the Council, been corrected;

— to impose fines of an appropriate size.

The President of the Council shall inform the European Parliament of the decisions taken.

12. The Council shall abrogate some or all of its decisions as referred to in paragraphs 6 to 9 and 11 to the extent that the excessive deficit in the Member State concerned has, in the view of the Council, been corrected.

If the Council previously had made public recommendations, it shall, as soon as the decision under paragraph 8 has been abrogated, make a public statement that an excessive deficit in the Member State concerned no longer exists.

13. When taking the decisions referred to in paragraphs 7 to 9, 11 and 12, the Council shall act on a recommendation from the Commission by a majority of two thirds of the votes of its members weighted in accordance with Article 148(2) and excluding the votes of the representative of the Member State concerned.

14. Further provisions relating to the implementation of the procedure described in this Article are set out in the Protocol on the excessive deficit procedure annexed to this Treaty.

The Council shall, acting unanimously on a proposal from the Commission and after consulting the European Parliament and the ECB, adopt the appropriate provisions which shall then replace the said Protocol.

Subject to the other provisions of this paragraph the Council shall, before 1 January 1994, acting by a qualified majority on a proposal from the Commission and after consulting the European Parliament, lay down detailed rules and definitions for the application of the provisions of the said Protocol.

CHAPTER 2

MONETARY POLICY

ARTICLE 105

1. The primary objective of the ESCB shall be to maintain price stability. Without prejudice to the objective of price stability, the ESCB shall support the general economic policies in the Community with a view to contributing to the achievement of the objectives of the Community as laid down in Article 2.

The ESCB shall act in accordance with the principle of an open market economy with free competition, favouring an efficient allocation of resources, and in compliance with the principles set out in Article 3a.

2. The basic tasks to be carried out through the ESCB shall be:

— to define and implement the monetary policy of the Community;

— to conduct foreign exchange operations consistent with the provisions of Article 109:

— to hold and manage the official foreign reserves of the Member States;

— to promote the smooth operation of payment systems.

3. The third indent of paragraph 2 shall be without prejudice to the holding and management by the governments of Member States of foreign exchange working balances.

4. The ECB shall be consulted:

— on any proposed Community act in its fields of competence;

— by national authorities regarding any draft legislative provision in its fields of competence, but within the limits and under the conditions set out by the Council in accordance with the procedure laid down in Article 106(6).

The ECB may submit opinions to the appropriate Community institutions or bodies or to national authorities on matters within its fields of competence.

5. The ESCB shall contribute to the smooth conduct of policies pursued by the competent authorities relating to the prudential supervision of credit institutions and the stability of the financial system.

6. The Council may, acting unanimously on a proposal from the Commission and after consulting the ECB and after receiving the assent of the European Parliament, confer upon the ECB specific tasks concerning policies relating to the prudential supervision of credit institutions and other financial institutions with the exception of insurance undertakings.

ARTICLE 105a

1. The ECB shall have the exclusive right to authorize the issue of bank notes within the Community. The ECB and the national central banks may issue such notes.

The bank notes issued by the ECB and the national central banks shall be the only such notes to have the status of legal tender within the Community.

2. Member States may issue coins subject to approval by the ECB of the volume of the issue. The Council may, acting in accordance with the procedure referred to in Article 189c and after consulting the ECB, adopt measures to harmonize the denominations and technical specifications of all coins intended for circulation to the extent necessary to permit their smooth circulation within the Community.

ARTICLE 106

1. The ESCB shall be composed of the ECB and of the national central banks.

2. The ECB shall have legal personality.

3. The ESCB shall be governed by the decision-making bodies of the ECB which shall be the Governing Council and the Executive Board.

4. The Statute of the ESCB is laid down in a Protocol annexed to this Treaty.
5. Articles 5.1, 5.2, 5.3, 17, 18, 19.1, 22, 23, 24, 26, 32.2, 32.3, 32.4, 32.6, 33.1(a) and 36 of the Statute of the ESCB may be amended by the Council, acting either by a qualified majority on a recommendation from the ECB and after consulting the Commission or unanimously on a proposal from the Commission and after consulting the ECB. In either case, the assent of the European Parliament shall be required.
6. The Council, acting by a qualified majority either on a proposal from the Commission and after consulting the European Parliament and the ECB, or on a recommendation from the ECB and after consulting the European Parliament and the Commission, shall adopt the provisions referred to in Articles 4, 5.4, 19.2, 20, 28.1, 29.2, 30.4 and 34.3 of the Statute of the ESCB.

ARTICLE 107
When exercising the powers and carrying out the tasks and duties conferred upon them by this Treaty and the Statute of the ESCB, neither the ECB, nor a national central bank, nor any member of their decision-making bodies shall seek or take instructions from Community institutions or bodies, from any government of a Member State or from any other body.
The Community institutions and bodies and the governments of the Member States undertake to respect this principle and not to seek to influence the members of the decision-making bodies of the ECB or of the national central banks in the performance of their tasks.

ARTICLE 108
Each Member State shall ensure, at the latest at the date of the establishment of the ESCB, that its national legislation including the statutes of its national central bank is compatible with this Treaty and the Statute of the ESCB.

ARTICLE 108a
1. In order to carry out the tasks entrusted to the ESCB, the ECB shall, in accordance with the provisions of this Treaty and under the conditions laid down in the Statute of the ESCB:
— make regulations to the extent necessary to implement the tasks defined in Article 3.1, first indent, Articles 19.1, 22 or 25.2 of the Statute of the ESCB and in cases which shall be laid down in the acts of the Council referred to in Article 106(6);
— take decisions necessary for carrying out the tasks entrusted to the ESCB under this Treaty and the Statute of the ESCB;
— make recommendations and deliver opinions.
2. A regulation shall have general application. It shall be binding in its entirety and directly applicable in all Member States.
Recommendations and opinions shall have no binding force.
A decision shall be binding in its entirety upon those to whom it is addressed.
Articles 190 to 192 shall apply to regulations and decisions adopted by the ECB.
The ECB may decide to publish its decisions, recommendations and opinions.
3. Within the limits and under the conditions adopted by the Council under the procedure laid down in Article 106(6), the ECB shall be entitled to impose fines or periodic penalty payments on undertakings for failure to comply with obligations under its regulations and decisions.

ARTICLE 109
1. By way of derogation from Article 228, the Council may, acting unanimously on a recommendation from the ECB or from the Commission, and after consulting the ECB in an endeavour to reach a consensus consistent with the objective of price stability, after consulting the European Parliament, in accordance with the procedure in paragraph 3 for determining the arrangements, conclude formal agreements on an exchange rate system for the ECU in relation to non-Community currencies.
The Council may, acting by a qualified majority on a recommendation from the ECB or from the Commission, and after consulting the ECB in an endeavour to reach a consensus consistent with the objective of price stability, adopt, adjust or abandon the central rates of the ECU within the exchange rate system.
The President of the Council shall inform the European Parliament of the adoption, adjustment or abandonment of the ECU central rates.
2. In the absence of an exchange rate system in relation to one or more non-Community currencies as referred to in paragraph 1, the Council, acting by a qualified majority either on a recommendation from the Commission and after consulting the ECB, or on a recommendation from the ECB, may formulate general orientations for exchange rate policy in relation to these currencies.
These general orientations shall be without prejudice to the primary objective of the ESCB to maintain price stability.
3. By way of derogation from Article 228, where agreements concerning monetary or foreign exchange regime matters need to be negotiated by the Community with one or more States or international organizations, the Council, acting by a qualified majority on a recommendation from the Commission and after consulting the ECB, shall decide the arrangements for the negotiation and for the conclusion of such agreements.
These arrangements shall ensure that the Community expresses a single position. The Commission shall be fully associated with the negotiations.
Agreements concluded in accordance with this paragraph shall be binding on the institutions of the Community, on the ECB and on Member States.
4. Subject to paragraph 1, the Council shall, on a proposal from the Commission and after consulting the ECB, acting by a qualified majority decide on the position of the Community at international level as regards issues of particular relevance to economic and monetary union and, acting unanimously, decide its representation in compliance with the allocation of powers laid down in Articles 103 and 105.
5. Without prejudice to Community competence and Community agreements as regards Economic and Monetary Union, Member States may negotiate in international bodies and conclude international agreements.

CHAPTER 3
INSTITUTIONAL PROVISIONS

ARTICLE 109a
1. The Governing Council of the ECB shall comprise the members of the Executive Board of the ECB and the Governors of the national central banks.
2. (a) The Executive Board shall compromise the President, the Vice-President and four other members.
(b) The President, the Vice-President and the other members of the Executive

Board shall be appointed from among persons of recognized standing and professional experience in monetary or banking matters by common accord of the Governments of the Member States at the level of Heads of State or of Government, on a recommendation from the Council, after it has consulted the European Parliament and the Governing Council of the ECB.
Their term of office shall be eight years and shall not be renewable. Only nationals of Member States may be members of the Executive Board.

ARTICLE 109b
1. The President of the Council and a member of the Commission may participate, without having the right to vote, in meetings of the Governing Council of the ECB.
The President of the Council may submit a motion for deliberation to the Governing Council of the ECB.
2. The President of the ECB shall be invited to participate in Council meetings when the Council is discussing matters relating to the objectives and tasks of the ESCB.
3. The ECB shall address an annual report on the activities of the ESCB and on the monetary policy of both the previous and current year to the European Parliament, the Council and the Commission, and also to the European Council.
The President of the ECB shall present this report to the Council and to the European Parliament, which may hold a general debate on that basis.
The President of the ECB and the other members of the Executive Board may, at the request of the European Parliament or on their own initiative, be heard by the competent Committees of the European Parliament.

ARTICLE 109c
1. In order to promote coordination of the policies of Member States to the full extent needed for the functioning of the internal market, a Monetary Committee with advisory status is hereby set up.

It shall have the following tasks:
— to keep under review the monetary and financial situation of the Member States and of the Community and the general payments system of the Member States and to report regularly thereon to the Council and to the Commission;
— to deliver opinions at the request of the Council or of the Commission, or on its own initiative for submission to those institutions;
— without prejudice to Article 151, to contribute to the preparation of the work of the Council referred to in Articles 73f, 73g, 103(2), (3), (4) and (5), 103a, 104a, 104b, 104c, 109e(2), 109f(6), 109h, 109i, 109j(2) and 109k(1);
— to examine, at least once a year, the situation regarding the movement of capital and the freedom of payments, as they result from the application of this Treaty and of measures adopted by the Council; the examination shall cover all measures relating to capital movements and payments; the Committee shall report to the Commission and to the Council on the outcome of this examination. The Member States and the Commission shall each appoint two members of the Monetary Committee.

2. At the start of the third stage, an Economic and Financial Committee shall be set up. The Monetary Committee provided for in paragraph 1 shall be dissolved.

The Economic and Financial Committee shall have the following tasks:
— to deliver opinions at the request of the Council or of the Commission, or on its own initiative for submission to those institutions;
— to keep under review the economic and financial situation of the Member States and of the Community and to report regularly thereon to the Council and to the Commission, in particular on financial relations with third countries and international institutions;
— without prejudice to Article 151, to contribute to the preparation of the work of the Council referred to in Articles 73f, 73g, 103(2), (3), (4) and (5), 103a, 104a, 104b, 104c, 105(6), 105a(2), 106(5) and (6), 109, 109h, 109i(2) and (3), 109k(2), 109l(4) and (5), and to carry out other advisory and preparatory tasks assigned to it by the Council;
— to examine, at least once a year, the situation regarding the movement of capital and the freedom of payments, as they result from the application of this Treaty and of measures adopted by the Council; the examination shall cover all measures relating to capital movements and payments: the Committee shall report to the Commission and to the Council on the outcome of this examination.
The Member States, the Commission and the ECB shall each appoint no more than two members of the Committee.

3. The Council shall, acting by a qualified majority on a proposal from the Commission and after consulting the ECB and the Committee referred to in this Article, lay down detailed provisions concerning the composition of the Economic and Financial Committee. The President of the Council shall inform the European Parliament of such a decision.

4. In addition to the tasks set out in paragraph 2, if and as long as there are Member States with a derogation as referred to in Articles 109k and 109l, the Committee shall keep under review the monetary and financial situation and the general payments system of those Member States and report regularly thereon to the Council and to the Commission.

ARTICLE 109d
For matters within the scope of Articles 103(4), 104c with the exception of paragraph 14, 109, 109j, 109k and 109l(4) and (5), the Council or a Member State may request the Commission to make a recommendation or a proposal, as appropriate. The Commission shall examine this request and submit its conclusions to the Council without delay.

CHAPTER 4

TRANSITIONAL PROVISIONS

ARTICLE 109e
1. The second stage for achieving economic and monetary union shall begin on 1 January 1994.
2. Before that date
(a) each Member State shall:
— adopt, where necessary, appropriate measures to comply with the prohibitions laid down in Article 73b, without prejudice to Article 73e, and in Articles 104 and 104a(1);

— adopt, if necessary, with a view to permitting the assessment provided for in subparagraph (b), multiannual programmes intended to ensure the lasting convergence necessary for the achievement of economic and monetary union, in particular with regard to price stability and sound public finances;

(b) the Council shall, on the basis of a report from the Commission, assess the progress made with regard to economic and monetary convergence, in particular with regard to price stability and sound public finances, and the progress made with the implementation of Community law concerning the internal market.

3. The provisions of Articles 104, 104a(1), 104b(1) and 104c with the exception of paragraphs 1, 9, 11 and 14 shall apply from the beginning of the second stage. The provisions of Articles 103a(2), 104c(1), (9) and (11), 105, 105a, 107, 109, 109a, 109b and 109c(2) and (4) shall apply from the beginning of the third stage.

4. In the second stage, Member States shall endeavour to avoid excessive government deficits.

5. During the second stage, each Member State shall, as appropriate, start the process leading to the independence of its central bank, in accordance with Article 108.

ARTICLE 109f

1. At the start of the second stage, a European Monetary Institute (hereinafter referred to as 'EMI') shall be established and take up its duties; it shall have legal personality and be directed and managed by a Council, consisting of a President and the Governors of the national central banks, one of whom shall be Vice-President.

The President shall be appointed by common accord of the Governments of the Member States at the level of Heads of State or of Government, on a recommendation from, as the case may be, the Committee of Governors of the central banks of the Member States (hereinafter referred to as 'Committee of Governors') or the Council of the EMI, and after consulting the European Parliament and the Council. The President shall be selected from among persons of recognized standing and professional experience in monetary or banking matters. Only nationals of Member States may be President of the EMI. The Council of the EMI shall appoint the Vice-President.

The Statute of the EMI is laid down in a Protocol annexed to this Treaty.

The Committee of Governors shall be dissolved at the start of the second stage.

2. The EMI shall:

— strengthen cooperation between the national central banks;

— strengthen the coordination of the monetary policies of the Member States, with the aim of ensuring price stability;

— monitor the functioning of the European Monetary System;

— hold consultations concerning issues falling within the competence of the national central banks and affecting the stability of financial institutions and markets;

— take over the tasks of the European Monetary Cooperation Fund, which shall be dissolved; the modalities of dissolution are laid down in the Statute of the EMI;

— facilitate the use of the ECU and oversee its development, including the smooth functioning of the ECU clearing system.

3. For the preparation of the third stage, the EMI shall:

— prepare the instruments and the procedures necessary for carrying out a single monetary policy in the third stage;

— promote the harmonization, where necessary, of the rules and practices governing the collection, compilation and distribution of statistics in the areas within its field of competence;
— prepare the rules for operations to be undertaken by the national central banks in the framework of the ESCB;
— promote the efficiency of cross-border payments;
— supervise the technical preparations of ECU bank notes.
At the latest by 31 December 1996, the EMI shall specify the regulatory, organizational and logistical framework necessary for the ESCB to perform its tasks in the third stage. This framework shall be submitted for decision to the ECB at the date of its establishment.
4. The EMI, acting by a majority of two thirds of the members of its Council may:
— formulate opinions or recommendations on the overall orientation of monetary policy and exchange rate policy as well as on related measures introduced in each Member State;
— submit opinions or recommendations to Governments and to the Council on policies which might affect the internal or external monetary situation in the Community and, in particular, the functioning of the European Monetary System;
— make recommendations to the monetary authorities of the Member States concerning the conduct of their monetary policy.
5. The EMI, acting unanimously, may decide to publish its opinions and its recommendations.
6. The EMI shall be consulted by the Council regarding any proposed Community act within its field of competence.
Within the limits and under the conditions set out by the Council, acting by a qualified majority on a proposal from the Commission and after consulting the European Parliament and the EMI, the EMI shall be consulted by the authorities of the Member States on any draft legislative provision within its field of competence.
7. The Council may, acting unanimously on a proposal from the Commission and after consulting the European Parliament and the EMI, confer upon the EMI other tasks for the preparation of the third stage.
8. Where this Treaty provides for a consultative role for the ECB, references to the ECB shall be read as referring to the EMI before the establishment of the ECB.
Where this Treaty provides for a consultative role for the EMI, references to the EMI shall be read, before 1 January 1994, as referring to the Committee of Governors.
9. During the second stage, the term 'ECB' used in Articles 173, 175, 176, 177, 180 and 215 shall be read as referring to the EMI.

ARTICLE 109g
The currency composition of the ECU basket shall not be changed. From the start of the third stage, the value of the ECU shall be irrevocably fixed in accordance with Article 109l(4).

ARTICLE 109h
1. Where a Member State is in difficulties or is seriously threatened with difficulties as regards its balance of payments either as a result of an overall disequilibrium in its balance of payments, or as a result of the type of currency at its disposal,

and where such difficulties are liable in particular to jeopardize the functioning of the common market or the progressive implementation of the common commercial policy, the Commission shall immediately investigate the position of the State in question and the action which, making use of all the means at its disposal, that State has taken or may take in accordance with the provisions of this Treaty.

The Commission shall state what measures it recommends the State concerned to take.

If the action taken by a Member State and the measures suggested by the Commission do not prove sufficient to overcome the difficulties which have arisen or which threaten, the Commission shall, after consulting the Committee referred to in Article 109c, recommend to the Council the granting of mutual assistance and appropriate methods therefor.

The Commission shall keep the Council regularly informed of the situation and of how it is developing.

2. The Council, acting by a qualified majority, shall grant such mutual assistance; it shall adopt directives or decisions laying down the conditions and details of such assistance, which may take such forms as:

(a) a concerted approach to or within any other international organizations to which Member States may have recourse;

(b) measures needed to avoid deflection of trade where the State which is in difficulties maintains or reintroduces quantitative restrictions against third countries;

(c) the granting of limited credits by other Member States, subject to their agreement.

3. If the mutual assistance recommended by the Commission is not granted by the Council or if the mutual assistance granted and the measures taken are insufficient, the Commission shall authorize the State which is in difficulties to take protective measures, the conditions and details of which the Commission shall determine.

Such authorization may be revoked and such conditions and details may be changed by the Council acting by a qualified majority.

4. Subject to Article 109k(6), this Article shall cease to apply from the beginning of the third stage.

ARTICLE 109i

1. Where a sudden crisis in the balance of payments occurs and a decision within the meaning of Article 109h(2) is not immediately taken, the Member State concerned may, as a precaution, take the necessary protective measures. Such measures must cause the least possible disturbance in the functioning of the common market and must not be wider in scope than is strictly necessary to remedy the sudden difficulties which have arisen.

2. The Commission and the other Member States shall be informed of such protective measures not later than when they enter into force. The Commission may recommend to the Council the granting of mutual assistance under Article 109h.

3. After the Commission has delivered an opinion and the Committee referred to in Article 109c has been consulted, the Council may, acting by a qualified majority, decide that the State concerned shall amend, suspend or abolish the protective measures referred to above.

4. Subject to Article 109k(6), this Article shall cease to apply from the beginning of the third stage.

ARTICLE 109j

1. The Commission and the EMI shall report to the Council on the progress made in the fulfilment by the Member States of their obligations regarding the achievement of economic and monetary union.

These reports shall include an examination of the compatibility between each Member State's national legislation, including the statutes of its national central bank, and Articles 107 and 108 of this Treaty and the Statute of the ESCB. The reports shall also examine the achievement of a high degree of sustainable convergence by reference to the fulfilment by each Member State of the folowing criteria:

— the achievement of a high degree of price stability; this will be apparent from a rate of inflation which is close to that of, at most, the three best performing Member States in terms of price stability;

— the sustainability of the government financial position; this will be apparent from having achieved a government budgetary position without a deficit that is excessive as determined in accordance with Article 104c(6);

— the observance of the normal fluctuation margins provided for by the Exchange Rate Mechanism of the European Monetary System, for at least two years, without devaluing against the currency of any other Member State;

— the durability of convergence achieved by the Member State and of its participation in the Exchange Rate Mechanism of the European Monetary System being reflected in the long-term interest rate levels.

The four criteria mentioned in this paragraph and the relevant periods over which they are to be respected are developed further in a Protocol annexed to this Treaty.

The reports of the Commission and the EMI shall also take account of the development of the ECU, the results of the integration of markets, the situation and development of the balances of payments on current account and an examination of the development of unit labour costs and other price indices.

2. On the basis of these reports, the Council, acting by a qualified majority on a recommendation from the Commission, shall assess:

— for each Member State, whether it fulfils the necessary conditions for the adoption of a single currency;

— whether a majority of the Member States fulfil the necessary conditions for the adoption of a single currency, and recommend its findings to the Council, meeting in the composition of the Heads of State or of Government. The European Parliament shall be consulted and forward its opinion to the Council, meeting in the composition of the Heads of State or of Government.

3. Taking due account of the reports referred to in paragraph 1 and the opinion of the European Parliament referred to in paragraph 2, the Council, meeting in the composition of Heads of State or of Government, shall, acting by a qualified majority, not later than 31 December 1996:

— decide, on the basis of the recommendations of the Council referred to in paragraph 2, whether a majority of the Member States fulfil the necessary conditions for the adoption of a single currency;

— decide whether it is appropriate for the Community to enter the third stage, and if so

— set the date for the beginning of the third stage.

4. If by the end of 1997 the date for the beginning of the third stage has not been set, the third stage shall start on 1 January 1999. Before 1 July 1998, the Council,

meeting in the composition of Heads of State or of Government, after a repetition of the procedure provided for in paragraphs 1 and 2, with the exception of the second indent of paragraph 2, taking into account the reports referred to in paragraph 1 and the opinion of the European Parliament, shall, acting by a qualified majority and on the basis of the recommendations of the Council referred to in paragraph 2, confirm which Member States fulfil the necessary conditions for the adoption of a single currency.

ARTICLE 109k

1. If the decision has been taken to set the date in accordance with Article 109j(3), the Council shall, on the basis of its recommendations as referred to in Article 109j(2), acting by a qualified majority on a recommendation from the Commission, decide whether any, and if so which, Member States shall have a derogation as defined in paragraph 3 of this Article. Such Member States shall in this Treaty be referred to as 'Member States with a derogation'. If the Council has confirmed which Member States fulfil the necessary conditions for the adoption of a single currency, in accordance with Article 109j(4) those Member States which do not fulfil the conditions shall have a derogation as defined in paragraph 3 of this Article. Such Member States shall in this Treaty be referred to as 'Member States with a derogation'.

2. At least once every two years, or at the request of a Member State with a derogation, the Commission and the ECB shall report to the Council in accordance with the procedure laid down in Article 109j(1). After consulting the European Parliament and after discussion in the Council, meeting in the composition of the Heads of State or of Government, the Council shall, acting by a qualified majority on a proposal from the Commission, decide which Member States with a derogation fulfil the necessary conditions on the basis of the criteria set out in Article 109j(1), and abrogate the derogations of the Member States concerned.

3. A derogation referred to in paragraph 1 shall entail that the following Articles do not apply to the Member State concerned: Articles 104c(9) and (11), 105(1), (2), (3) and (5), 105a, 108a, 109, and 109a(2)(b). The exclusion of such a Member State and its national central bank from rights and obligations within the ESCB is laid down in Chapter IX of the Statute of the ESCB.

4. In Articles 105(1), (2) and (3), 105a, 108a, 109 and 109a(2)(b), 'Member States' shall be read as 'Member States without a derogation'.

5. The voting rights of the Member States with a derogation shall be suspended for the Council decisions referred to in the Articles of this Treaty mentioned in paragraph 3. In that case, by way of derogation from Articles 148 and 189a(1), a qualified majority shall be defined as two thirds of the votes of the representatives of the Member States without a derogation weighted in accordance with Article 148(2), and unanimity of those Member States shall be required for an act requiring unanimity.

6. Articles 109h and 109i shall continue to apply to a Member State with a derogation.

ARTICLE 109l

1. Immediately after the decision on the date for the beginning of the third stage has been taken in accordance with Article 109j(3), or, as the case may be, immediately after 1 July 1998:

— the Council shall adopt the provisions referred to in Article 106(6);

— the governments of the Member States without a derogation shall appoint, in accordance with the procedure set out in Article 50 of the Statute of the ESCB, the President, the Vice-President and the other members of the Executive Board of the ECB.

If there are Member States with a derogation, the number of members of the Executive Board may be smaller than provided for in Article 11.1 of the Statute of the ESCB, but in no circumstances shall it be less than four.

As soon as the Executive Board is appointed, the ESCB and the ECB shall be established and shall prepare for their full operation as described in this Treaty and the Statute of the ESCB. The full exercise of their powers shall start from the first day of the third stage.

2. As soon as the ECB is established, it shall, if necessary, take over functions of the EMI. The EMI shall go into liquidation upon the establishment of the ECB; the modalities of liquidation are laid down in the Statute of the EMI.

3. If and as long as there are Member States with a derogation, and without prejudice to Article 106(3) of this Treaty, the General Council of the ECB referred to in Article 45 of the Statute of the ESCB shall be constituted as a third decision-making body of the ECB.

4. At the starting date of the third stage, the Council shall, acting with the unanimity of the Member States without a derogation, on a proposal from the Commission and after consulting the ECB, adopt the conversion rates at which their currencies shall be irrevocably fixed and at which irrevocably fixed rate the ECU shall be substituted for these currencies, and the ECU will become a currency in its own right. This measure shall by itself not modify the external value of the ECU. The Council shall, acting according to the same procedure, also take the other measures necessary for the rapid introduction of the ECU as the single currency of those Member States.

5. If it is decided, according to the procedure set out in Article 109k(2), to abrogate a derogation, the Council shall, acting with the unanimity of the Member States without a derogation and the Member State concerned, on a proposal from the Commission and after consulting the ECB, adopt the rate at which the ECU shall be substituted for the currency of the Member State concerned, and take the other measures necessary for the introduction of the ECU as the single currency in the Member State concerned.

ARTICLE 109m

1. Until the beginning of the third stage, each Member State shall treat its exchange rate policy as a matter of common interest. In so doing, Member States shall take account of the experience acquired in cooperation within the framework of the European Monetary System (EMS) and in developing the ECU, and shall respect existing powers in this field.

2. From the beginning of the third stage and for as long as a Member State has a derogation, paragraph 1 shall apply by analogy to the exchange rate policy of that Member State.'

26) In Title II of Part Three, the title of Chapter 4 shall be replaced by the following:
'TITLE VII
Commercial Commercial Policy'
27) Article 111 shall be repealed.

28) Article 113 shall be replaced by the following:

'ARTICLE 113
1. The common commercial policy shall be based on uniform principles, particularly in regard to changes in tariff rates, the conclusion of tariff and trade agreements, the achievement of uniformity in measures of liberalization, export policy and measures to protect trade such as those to be taken in the event of dumping or subsidies.
2. The Commission shall submit proposals to the Council for implementing the common commercial policy.
3. Where agreements with one or more States or international organizations need to be negotiated, the Commission shall make recommendations to the Council, which shall authorize the Commission to open the necessary negotiations.
The Commission shall conduct these negotiations in consultation with a special committee appointed by the Council to assist the Commission in this task and within the framework of such directives as the Council may issue to it.
The relevant provisions of Article 228 shall apply.
4. In exercising the powers conferred upon it by this Article, the Council shall act by a qualified majority.'

29) Article 114 shall be repealed.

30) Article 115 shall be replaced by the following:

'ARTICLE 115
In order to ensure that the execution of measures of commercial policy taken in accordance with this Treaty by any Member State is not obstructed by deflection of trade, or where differences between such measures lead to economic difficulties in one or more Member States, the Commission shall recommend the methods for the requisite cooperation between Member States. Failing this, the Commission may authorize Member States to take the necessary protective measures, the conditions and details of which it shall determine.
In case of urgency, Member States shall request authorization to take the necessary measures themselves from the Commission, which shall take a decision as soon as possible; the Member States concerned shall then notify the measures to the other Member States. The Commission may decide at any time that the Member States concerned shall amend or abolish the measures in question. In the selection of such measures, priority shall be given to those which cause the least disturbance to the functioning of the common market.'

31) Article 116 shall be repealed.

32) In Part Three, the title of Title III shall be replaced by the following:
'TITLE VIII
Social Policy, Education,
Vocational Training and Youth'
33) The first subparagraph of Article 118a(2) shall be replaced by the following:
'2. In order to help achieve the objective laid down in the first paragraph, the Council, acting in accordance with the procedure referred to in Article 189c and

after consulting the Economic and Social Committee, shall adopt by means of directives, minimum requirements for gradual implementation, having regard to the conditions and technical rules obtaining in each of the Member States.'

34) Article 123 shall be replaced by the following:

'ARTICLE 123
In order to improve employment opportunities for workers in the internal market and to contribute thereby to raising the standard of living, a European Social Fund is hereby established in accordance with the provisions set out below; it shall aim to render the employment of workers easier and to increase their geographical and occupational mobility within the Community, and to facilitate their adaptation to industrial changes and to changes in production systems, in particular through vocational training and retraining.'

35) Article 125 shall be replaced by the following:

'ARTICLE 125
The Council, acting in accordance with the procedure referred to in Article 189c and after consulting the Economic and Social Committee, shall adopt implementing decisions relating to the European Social Fund.'

36) Articles 126, 127 and 128 shall be replaced by the following:

'CHAPTER 3
EDUCATION, VOCATIONAL TRAINING AND YOUTH

ARTICLE 126
1. The Community shall contribute to the development of quality education by encouraging cooperation between Member States and, if necessary, by supporting and supplementing their action, while fully respecting the responsibility of the Member States for the content of teaching and the organization of education systems and their cultural and linguistic diversity.
2. Community action shall be aimed at:
— developing the European dimension in education, particularly through the teaching and dissemination of the languages of the Member States;
— encouraging mobility of students and teachers, inter alia by encouraging the academic recognition of diplomas and periods of study;
— promoting cooperation between educational establishments;
— developing exchanges of information and experience on issues common to the education systems of the Member States;
— encouraging the developments of youth exchanges and of exchanges of socio-educational instructors;
— encouraging the development of distance education.
3. The Community and the Member States shall foster co-operation with third countries and the competent international organizations in the sphere of education, in particular the Council of Europe.

4. In order to contribute to the achievement of the objectives referred to in this Article, the Council:
— acting in accordance with the procedure referred to in Article 189b, after consulting the Economic and Social Committee and the Committee of the Regions, shall adopt incentive measures, excluding any harmonization of the laws and regulations of the Member States;
— acting by qualified majority on a proposal from the Commission, shall adopt recommendations.

ARTICLE 127
1. The Community shall implement a vocational training policy which shall support and supplement the action of the Member States, while fully respecting the responsibility of the Member States for the content and organization of vocational training.
2. Community action shall aim to:
— facilitate adaptation to industrial changes, in particular through vocational training and retraining;
— improve initial and continuing vocational training in order to facilitate vocational integration and reintegration into the labour market;
— facilitate access to vocational training and encourage mobility of instructors and trainees and particularly young people;
— stimulate cooperation on training between educational or training establishments and firms;
— develop exchanges of information and experience on issues common to the training systems of the Member States.
3. The Community and the Member States shall foster cooperation with third countries and the competent international organizations in the sphere of vocational training.
4. The Council, acting in accordance with the procedure referred to in Article 189c and after consulting the Economic and Social Committee, shall adopt measures to contribute to the achievement of the objectives referred to in this Article, excluding any harmonization of the laws and regulations of the Member States.'

37) The following shall be inserted:
'TITLE IX
Culture

ARTICLE 128
1. The Community shall contribute to the flowering of the cultures of the Member States, while respecting their national and regional diversity and at the same time bringing the common cultural heritage to the fore.
2. Action by the Community shall be aimed at encouraging cooperation between Member States and, if necessary, supporting and supplementing their action in the following areas:
— improvement of the knowledge and dissemination of the culture and history of the European peoples;
— conservation and safeguarding of cultural heritage of European significance;
— non-commercial cultural exchanges;
— artistic and literary creation, including in the audiovisual sector.
3. The Community and the Member States shall foster cooperation with third

countries and the competent international organizations in the sphere of culture, in particular the Council of Europe.

4. The Community shall take cultural aspects into account in its action under other provisions of this Treaty.

5. In order to contribute to the achievement of the objectives referred to in this Article, the Council:

— acting in accordance with the procedure referred to in Article 189b and after consulting the Committee of the Regions, shall adopt incentive measures, excluding any harmonization of the laws and regulations of the Member States.

The Council shall act unanimously throughout the procedures referred to in Article 189b;

— acting unanimously on a proposal from the Commission, shall adopt recommendations.'

38) Titles IV, V, VI and VII shall be replaced by the following:
'TITLE X
Public Health

ARTICLE 129

1. The Community shall contribute towards ensuring a high level of human health protection by encouraging cooperation between the Member States and, if necessary, lending support to their action.

Community action shall be directed towards the prevention of diseases, in particular the major health scourges, including drug dependence, by promoting research into their causes and their transmission, as well as health information and education.

Health protection requirements shall form a constituent part of the Community's other policies.

2. Member States shall, in liaison with the Commission, coordinate among themselves their policies and programmes in the areas referred to in paragraph 1. The Commission may, in close contact with the Member States, take any useful initiative to promote such coordination.

3. The Community and the Member States shall foster cooperation with third countries and the competent international organizations in the sphere of public health.

4. In order to contribute to the achievement of the objectives referred to in this Article, the Council:

— acting in accordance with the procedure referred to in Article 189b, after consulting the Economic and Social Committee and the Committee of the Regions, shall adopt incentive measures, excluding any harmonization of the laws and regulations of the Member States;

— acting by a qualified majority on a proposal from the Commission, shall adopt recommendations.

TITLE XI
Consumer protection

ARTICLE 129a

1. The Community shall contribute to the attainment of a high level of consumer protection through:

(a) measures adopted pursuant to Article 100a in the context of the completion of the internal market;

(b) specific action which supports and supplements the policy pursued by the Member States to protect the health, safety and economic interests of consumers and to provide adequate information to consumers.

2. The Council, acting in accordance with the procedure referred to in Article 189b and after consulting the Economic and Social Committee, shall adopt the specific action referred to in paragraph 1(b).

3. Action adopted pursuant to paragraphs 2 shall not prevent any Member State from maintaining or introducing more stringent protective measures. Such measures must be compatible with this Treaty. The Commission shall be notified of them.

TITLE XII
Trans-European networks

ARTICLE 129b

1. To help achieve the objectives referred to in Articles 7a and 130a and to enable citizens of the Union, economic operators and regional and local communities to derive full benefit from the setting up of an area without internal frontiers, the Community shall contribute to the establishment and development of trans-European networks in the areas of transport, telecommunications and energy infrastructures.

2. Within the framework of a system of open and competitive markets, action by the Community shall aim at promoting the interconnection and inter-operability of national networks as well as access to such networks. It shall take account in particular of the need to link island, landlocked and peripheral regions with the central regions of the Community.

ARTICLE 129c

1. In order to achieve the objectives referred to in Article 129b, the Community:
— shall establish a series of guidelines covering the objectives, priorities and broad lines of measures envisaged in the sphere of trans-European networks; these guidelines shall identify projects of common interest;
— shall implement any measures that may prove necessary to ensure the inter-operability of the networks, in particular in the field of technical standardization;
— may support the financial efforts made by the Member States for projects of common interest financed by Member States, which are identified in the framework of the guidelines referred to in the first indent, particularly through feasibility studies, loan guarantees or interest rate subsidies; the Community may also contribute, through the Cohesion Fund to be set up no later than 31 December 1993 pursuant to Article 130d, to the financing of specific projects in Member States in the area of transport infrastructure.

The Community's activities shall take into account the potential economic viability of the projects.

2. Member States shall, in liaison with the Commission, coordinate among themselves the policies pursued at national level which may have a significant impact on the achievement of the objectives referred to in Article 129b.

The Commission may, in close cooperation with the Member States, take any useful initiative to promote such coordination.

3. The Community may decide to cooperate with third countries to promote projects of mutual interest and to ensure the interoperability of networks.

ARTICLE 129d
The guidelines referred to in Article 129c(1) shall be adopted by the Council, acting in accordance with the procedure referred to in Article 189b and after consulting the Economic and Social Committee and the Committee of the Regions. Guidelines and projects of common interest which relate to the territory of a Member State shall require the approval of the Member State concerned.
The Council, acting in accordance with the procedure referred to in Article 189c and after consulting the Economic and Social Committee and the Committee of the Regions, shall adopt the other measures provided for in Article 129c(1).

TITLE XIII
Industry
ARTICLE 130
1. The Community and the Member States shall ensure that the conditions necessary for the competitiveness of the Community's industry exist.
For that purpose, in accordance with a system of open and competitive markets, their action shall be aimed at:
— speeding up the adjustments of industry to structural changes;
— encouraging an environment favourable to initiative and to the development of undertakings throughout the Community, particularly small and medium-sized undertakings;
— encouraging an environment favourable to cooperation between undertakings;
— fostering better exploitation of the industrial potential of policies of innovation, research and technological development.
2. The Member States shall consult each other in liaison with the Commission and, where necessary, shall coordinate their action. The Commission may take any useful initiative to promote such coordination.
3. The Community shall contribute to the achievement of the objectives set out in paragraph 1 through the policies and activities it pursues under other provisions of this Treaty. The Council, acting unanimously on a proposal from the Commission, after consulting the European Parliament and the Economic and Social Committee, may decide on specific measures in support of action taken in the Member States to achieve the objectives set out in paragraph 1.
This Title shall not provide a basis for the introduction by the Community of any measure which could lead to a distortion of competition.

TITLE XIV
Economic and Social Cohesion
ARTICLE 130a
In order to promote its overall harmonious development, the Community shall develop and pursue its actions leading to the strengthening of its economic and social cohesion.
In particular, the Community shall aim at reducing disparities between the levels of development of the various regions and the backwardness of the least-favoured regions, including rural areas.

ARTICLE 130b

Member States shall conduct their economic policies and shall coordinate them in such a way as, in addition, to attain the objectives set out in Article 130a. The formulation and implementation of the Community's policies and actions and the implementation of the internal market shall take into account the objectives set out in Article 130a and shall contribute to their achievement.

The Community shall also support the achievement of these objectives by the action it takes through the Structural Funds (European Agricultural Guidance and Guarantee Fund, Guidance Section; European Social Fund; European Regional Development Fund), the European Investment Bank and the other existing financial instruments.

The Commission shall submit a report to the European Parliament, the Council, the Economic and Social Committee and the Committee of the Regions every three years on the progress made towards achieving economic and social cohesion and on the manner in which the various means provided for in this Article have contributed to it. This report shall, if necessary, be accompanied by appropriate proposals.

If specific actions prove necessary outside the Funds and without prejudice to the measures decided upon within the framework of the other Community policies, such actions may be adopted by the Council acting unanimously on a proposal from the Commission and after consulting the European Parliament, the Economic and Social Committee and the Committee of the Regions.

ARTICLE 130c

The European Regional Development Fund is intended to help to redress the main regional imbalances in the Community through participation in the development and structural adjustment of regions whose development is lagging behind and in the conversion of declining industrial regions.

ARTICLE 130d

Without prejudice to Article 130e, the Council, acting unanimously on a proposal from the Commission and after obtaining the assent of the European Parliament and consulting the Economic and Social Committee and the Committee of the Regions, shall define the tasks, priority objectives and the organization of the Structural Funds, which may involve grouping the Funds. The Council, acting by the same procedure, shall also define the general rules applicable to them and the provisions necessary to ensure their effectiveness and the coordination of the Funds with one another and with the other existing financial instruments.

The Council, acting in accordance with the same procedure, shall before 31 December 1993 set up a Cohesion Fund to provide a financial contribution to projects in the fields of environment and trans-European networks in the area of transport infrastructure.

ARTICLE 130e

Implementing decisions relating to the European Regional Development Fund shall be taken by the Council, acting in accordance with the procedure referred to in Article 189c and after consulting the Economic and Social Committee and the Committee of the Regions.

With regard to the European Agricultural Guidance and Guarantee Fund, Guidance Section, and the European Social Fund, Articles 43 and 125 respectively shall continue to apply.

TITLE XV
Research and Technological Development

ARTICLE 130f

1. The Community shall have the objective of strengthening the scientific and technological bases of Community industry and encouraging it to become more competitive at international level, while promoting all the research activities deemed necessary by virtue of other Chapters of this Treaty.

2. For this purpose the Community shall, throughout the Community, encourage undertakings, including small and medium-sized undertakings, research centres and universities in their research and technological development activities of high quality; it shall support their efforts to cooperate with one another, aiming, notably, at enabling undertakings to exploit the internal market potential to the full, in particular through the opening up of national public contracts, the definition of common standards and the removal of legal and fiscal obstacles to that cooperation.

3. All Community activities under this Treaty in the area of research and technological development, including demonstration projects, shall be decided on and implemented in accordance with the provisions of this Title.

ARTICLE 130g

In pursuing these objectives, the Community shall carry out the following activities, complementing the activities carried out in the Member States:

(a) implementation of research, technological development and demonstration programmes, by promoting cooperation with and between undertakings, research centres and universities;

(b) promotion of cooperation in the field of Community research, technological development and demonstration with third countries and international organizations;

(c) dissemination and optimization of the results of activities in Community research, technological development and demonstration;

(d) stimulation of the training and mobility of researchers in the Community.

ARTICLE 130h

1. The Community and the Member States shall coordinate their research and technological development activities so as to ensure that national policies and Community policy are mutually consistent.

2. In close cooperation with the Member States, the Commission may take any useful initiative to promote the coordination referred to in paragraph 1.

ARTICLE 130i

1. A multiannual framework programme, setting out all the activities of the Community, shall be adopted by the Council, acting in accordance with the procedure referred to in Article 189b after consulting the Economic and Social Committee. The Council shall act unanimously throughout the procedures referred to in Article 189b.

The framework programme shall:
— establish the scientific and technological objectives to be achieved by the activities provided for in Article 130g and fix the relevant priorities:
— indicate the broad lines of such activities;
— fix the maximum overall amount and the detailed rules for Community financial participation in the framework programme and the respective shares in each of the activities provided for.
2. The framework programme shall be adapted or supplemented as the situation changes.
3. The framework programme shall be implemented through specific programmes developed within each activity. Each specific programme shall define the detailed rules for implementing it, fix its duration and provide for the means deemed necessary. The sum of the amounts deemed necessary, fixed in the specific programmes, may not exceed the overall maximum amount fixed for the framework programme and each activity.
4. The Council, acting by a qualified majority on a proposal from the Commission and after consulting the European Parliament and the Economic and Social Committee, shall adopt the specific programmes.

ARTICLE 130j
For the implementation of the multiannual framework programme the Council shall:
— determine the rules for the participation of undertakings, research centres and universities;
— lay down the rules governing the dissemination of research results.

ARTICLE 130k
In implementing the multiannual framework programme, supplementary programmes may be decided on involving the participation of certain Member States only, which shall finance them subject to possible Community participation.
The Council shall adopt the rules applicable to supplementary programmes, particularly as regards the dissemination of knowledge and access by other Member States.

ARTICLE 130l
In implementing the multiannual framework programme the Community may make provision, and agreement with the Member States concerned, for participation in research and development programmes undertaken by several Member States, including participation in the structures created for the execution of those programmes.

ARTICLE 130m
In implementing the multiannual framework programme the Community may make provision for cooperation in Community research, technological development and demonstration with third countries or international organizations.
The detailed arrangements for such cooperation may be the subject of agreements between the Community and the third parties concerned, which shall be negotiated and concluded in accordance with Article 228.

ARTICLE 130n
The Community may set up joint undertakings or any other structure necessary for the efficient execution of Community research, technological development and demonstration programmes.

ARTICLE 130o
The Council, acting unanimously on a proposal from the Commission and after consulting the European Parliament and the Economic and Social Committee, shall adopt the provisions referred to in Article 130n.
The Council, acting in accordance with the procedure referred to in Article 189c and after consulting the Economic and Social Committee, shall adopt the provisions referred to in Articles 130j to l. Adoption of the supplementary programmes shall require the agreement of the Member States concerned.

ARTICLE 130p
At the beginning of each year the Commission shall send a report to the European Parliament and the Council. The report shall include information on research and technological development activities and the dissemination of results during the previous year, and the work programme for the current year.

TITLE XVI
Environment

ARTICLE 130r
1. Community policy on the environment shall contribute to pursuit of the following objectives:
— preserving, protecting and improving the quality of the environment;
— protecting human health;
— prudent and rational utilization of natural resources;
— promoting measures at international level to deal with regional or worldwide environmental problems.
2. Community policy on the environment shall aim at a high level of protection taking into account the diversity of situations in the various regions of the Community. It shall be based on the precautionary principle and on the principles that preventive action should be taken, that environmental damage should as a priority be rectified at source and that the polluter should pay. Environmental protection requirements must be integrated into the definition and implementation of other Community policies.
In this context, harmonization measures answering these requirements shall include, where appropriate, a safeguard clause allowing Member States to take provisional measures, for non-economic environmental reasons, subject to a Community inspection procedure.
3. In preparing its policy on the environment, the Community shall take account of:
— available scientific and technical data;
— environmental conditions in the various regions of the Community;
— the potential benefits and costs of action or lack of action;
— the economic and social development of the Community as a whole and the balanced development of its regions.

4. Within their respective spheres of competence, the Community and the Member States shall cooperate with third countries and with the competent international organizations.

The arrangements for Community cooperation may be the subject of agreements between the Community and the third parties concerned, which shall be negotiated and concluded in accordance with Article 228.

The previous subparagraph shall be without prejudice to Member States' competence to negotiate in international bodies and to conclude international agreements.

ARTICLE 130s

1. The Council, acting in accordance with the procedure referred to in Article 189c and after consulting the Economic and Social Committee, shall decide what action is to be taken by the Community in order to achieve the objectives referred to in Article 130r.

2. By way of derogation from the decision-making procedure provided for in paragraph 1 and without prejudice to Article 100a, the Council, acting unanimously on a proposal from the Commission and after consulting the European Parliament and the Economic and Social Committee, shall adopt:
— provisions primarily of a fiscal nature;
— measures concerning town and country planning, land use with the exception of waste management and measures of a general nature, and management of water resources;
— measures significantly affecting a Member State's choice between different energy sources and the general structure of its energy supply.

The Council may, under the conditions laid down in the preceding subparagraph, define those matters referred to in this paragraph on which decisions are to be taken by a qualified majority.

3. In other areas, general action programmes setting out priority objectives to be attained shall be adopted by the Council, acting in accordance with the procedure referred to in Article 189b and after consulting the Economic and Social Committee.

The Council, acting under the terms of paragraph 1 or paragraph 2 according to the case, shall adopt the measures necessary for the implementation of these programmes.

4. Without prejudice to certain measures of a Community nature, the Member States shall finance and implement the environment policy.

5. Without prejudice to the principle that the polluter should pay, if a measure based on the provisions of paragraph 1 involves costs deemed disproportionate for the public authorities of a Member State, the Council shall, in the act adopting that measure, lay down appropriate provisions in the form of:
— temporary derogations and/or
— financial support from the Cohesion Fund to be set up no later than 31 December 1993 pursuant to Article 130d.

ARTICLE 130t

The protective measures adopted pursuant to Article 130s shall not prevent any Member State from maintaining or introducing more stringent protective measures.

Such measures must be compatible with this Treaty. They shall be notified to the Commission.

TITLE XVII
Development cooperaton

ARTICLE 130u

1. Community policy in the sphere of development cooperation, which shall be complementary to the policies pursued by the Member States, shall foster:
— the sustainable economic and social development of the developing countries, and more particularly the most disadvantaged among them;
— the smooth and gradual integration of the developing countries into the world economy;
— the campaign against poverty in the developing countries.
2. Community policy in this area shall contribute to the general objective of developing and consolidating democracy and the rule of law, and to that of respecting human rights and fundamental freedoms.
3. The Community and the Member States shall comply with the commitments and take account of the objectives they have approved in the context of the United Nations and other competent international organizations.

ARTICLE 130v

The Community shall take account of the objectives referred to in Article 130u in the policies that it implements which are likely to affect developing countries.

ARTICLE 130w

1. Without prejudice to the other provisions of this Treaty the Council, acting in accordance with the procedure referred to in Article 189c, shall adopt the measures necessary to further the objectives referred to in Article 130u. Such measures may take the form of multiannual programmes.
2. The European Investment Bank shall contribute, under the terms laid down in its Statute, to the implementation of the measures referred to in paragraph 1.
3. The provisions of this Article shall not affect cooperation with the African, Caribbean and Pacific countries in the framework of the ACP-EEC Convention.

ARTICLE 130x

1. The Community and the Member States shall coordinate their policies on development cooperation and shall consult each other on their aid programmes, including the international organizations and during international conferences. They may undertake joint action. Member States shall contribute if necessary to the implementation of Community aid programmes.
2. The Commission may take any useful initiative to promote the coordination referred to in paragraph 1.

ARTICLE 130y

Within their respective spheres of competence, the Community and the Member States shall cooperate with third countries and with the competent international organizations. The arrangements for Community cooperation may be the subject of agreements between the Community and the third parties concerned, which shall be negotiated and concluded in accordance with Article 228.

The previous paragraph shall be without prejudice to Member States' competence to negotiate in international bodies and to conclude international agreements.'

E. In Part Five 'Institutions of the Community'
39) Article 137 shall be replaced by the following:

'ARTICLE 137
The European Parliament, which shall consist of representatives of the peoples of the States brought together in the Community, shall exercise the powers conferred upon it by this Treaty.'

40) Paragraph 3 of Article 138 shall be replaced by the following:
'3. The European Parliament shall draw up proposals for elections by direct universal suffrage in accordance with a uniform procedure in all Member States. The Council shall, acting unanimously after obtaining the assent of the European Parliament, which shall act by a majority of its component members, lay down the appropriate provisions, which it shall recommend to Member States for adoption in accordance with their respective constitutional requirements.'

41) The following Articles shall be inserted:

'ARTICLE 138a
Political parties at European level are important as a factor for integration within the Union. They contribute to forming a European awareness and to expressing the political will of the citizens of the Union.

ARTICLE 138b
In so far as provided in this Treaty, the European Parliament shall participate in the process leading up to the adoption of Community acts by exercising its powers under the procedures laid down in Articles 189b and 189c and by giving its assent to delivering advisory opinions. The European Parliament may, acting by a majority of its members, request the Commission to submit any appropriate proposals on matters on which it considers that a Community act is required for the purpose of implementing this Treaty.

ARTICLE 138c
In the course of its duties, the European Parliament may, at the request of a quarter of its members, set up a temporary Committee of Inquiry to investigate, without prejudice to the powers conferred by this Treaty on other institutions or bodies, alleged contraventions or maladministration in the implementation of Community law, except where the alleged facts are being examined before a court and while the case is still subject to legal proceedings.
The temporary Committee of Inquiry shall cease to exist on the submission of its report.
The detailed provisions governing the exercise of the right of inquiry shall be determined by common accord of the European Parliament, the Council and the Commission.

ARTICLE 138d

Any citizen of the Union, and any natural or legal person residing or having its registered office in a Member State, shall have the right to address, individually or in association with other citizens or persons, a petition to the European Parliament on a matter which comes within the Community's fields of activity and which affects him, her or it directly.

ARTICLE 138e

1. The European Parliament shall appoint an Ombudsman empowered to receive complaints from any citizen of the Union or any natural or legal person residing or having its registered office in a Member State concerning instances of maladministration in the activities of the Community institutions or bodies, with the exception of the Court of Justice and the Court of First Instance acting in their judicial role.

In accordance with his duties, the Ombudsman shall conduct inquiries for which he finds grounds, either on his own initiative or on the basis of complaints submitted to him direct or through a member of the European Parliament, except where the alleged facts are or have been the subject of legal proceedings. Where the Ombudsman establishes an instance of maladministration, he shall refer the matter to the institution concerned, which shall have a period of three months in which to inform him of its views.

The Ombudsman shall then forward a report to the European Parliament and the institution concerned. The person lodging the complaint shall be informed of the outcome of such inquiries.

The Ombudsman shall submit an annual report to the European Parliament on the outcome of his inquiries.

2. The Ombudsman shall be appointed after each election of the European Parliament for the duration of its term of office. The Ombudsman shall be eligible for reappointment.

The Ombudsman may be dismissed by the Court of Justice at the request of the European Parliament if he no longer fulfils the conditions required for the performance of his duties or if he is guilty of serious misconduct.

3. The Ombudsman shall be completely independent in the performance of his duties. In the performance of those duties he shall neither seek nor take instructions from any body.

The Ombudsman may not, during his term of office, engage in any other occupation, whether gainful or not.

4. The European Parliament shall, after seeking an opinion from the Commission and with the approval of the Council acting by a qualified majority, lay down the regulations and general conditions governing the performance of the Ombudsman's duties.'

42) The second subparagraph of Article 144 shall be supplemented by the following sentence:

'In this case, the term of office of the members of the Commission appointed to replace them shall expire on the date on which the term of office of the members of the Commission obliged to resign as a body would have expired.'

43) The following Article shall be inserted:

'ARTICLE 146
The Council shall consist of a representative of each Member State at ministerial level, authorized to commit the government of that Member State.
The office of President shall be held in turn by each Member State in the Council for a term of six months, in the following order of Member States:
— for a first cycle of six years: Belgium, Denmark, Germany, Greece, Spain, France, Ireland, Italy, Luxembourg, Netherlands, Portugal, United Kingdom:
— for the following cycle of six years: Denmark, Belgium, Greece, Germany, France, Spain, Italy, Ireland, Netherlands, Luxembourg, United Kingdom, Portugal.'

44) The following Article shall be inserted:

'ARTICLE 147
The Council shall meet when convened by its President on his own initiative or at the request of one of its members or of the Commission.'

45) Article 149 shall be repealed.

46) The following Article shall be inserted:

'ARTICLE 151
1. A committee consisting of the Permanent Representatives of the Member States shall be responsible for preparing the work of the Council and for carrying out the tasks assigned to it by the Council.
2. The Council shall be assisted by a General Secretariat, under the direction of a Secretary-General. The Secretary-General shall be appointed by the Council acting unanimously.
The Council shall decide on the organization of the General Secretariat.
3. The Council shall adopt its rules of procedure.'

47) The following Article shall be inserted:

'ARTICLE 154
The Council, shall, acting by a qualified majority, determine the salaries, allowances and pensions of the President and members of the Commission, and of the President, Judges, Advocates-General and Registrar of the Court of Justice. It shall also, again by a qualified majority, determine any payment to be made instead of remuneration.'

48) The following Articles shall be inserted:

'ARTICLE 156
The Commission shall publish annually, not later than one month before the opening of the session of the European Parliament, a general report on the activities of the Community.

ARTICLE 157
1. The Commission shall consist of seventeen members, who shall be chosen on the grounds of their general competence and whose independence is beyond doubt.

The number of members of the Commission may be altered by the Council acting unanimously.

Only nationals of Member States may be members of the Commission.

The Commission must include at least one national of each of the Member States, but may not include more than two members having the nationality of the same State.

2. The members of the Commission shall, in the general interest of the Community, be completely independent in the performance of their duties. In the performance of these duties, they shall neither seek nor take instructions from any government or from any other body. They shall refrain from any action incompatible with their duties. Each Member State undertakes to respect this principle and not to seek to influence the members of the Commission in the performance of their tasks.

The members of the Commission may not, during their term of office, engage in any other occupation, whether gainful or not. When entering upon their duties they shall give a solemn undertaking that, both during and after their term of office, they will respect the obligations arising therefrom and in particular their duty to behave with integrity and discretion as regards the acceptance, after they have ceased to hold office, of certain appointments or benefits. In the event of any breach of these obligations, the Court of Justice may, on application by the Council or the Commission, rule that the member concerned be, according to the circumstances, either compulsorily retired in accordance with Article 160 or deprived of his right to a pension or other benefits in its stead.

ARTICLE 158

1. The members of the Commission shall be appointed, in accordance with the procedure referred to in paragraph 2, for a period of five years, subject, if need be, to Article 144.

Their term of office shall be renewable.

2. The governments of the Member States shall nominate by common accord, after consulting the European Parliament, the person they intend to appoint as President of the Commission.

The governments of the Member States shall, in consultation with the nominee for President, nominate the other persons whom they intend to appoint as members of the Commission.

The President and the other members of the Commission thus nominated shall be subject as a body to a vote of approval by the European Parliament. After approval by the European Parliament, the President and the other members of the Commission shall be appointed by common accord of the governments of the Member States.

3. Paragraphs 1 and 2 shall be applied for the first time to the President and the other members of the Commission whose term of office begins on 7 January 1995. The President and the other members of the Commission whose term of office begins on 7 January 1993 shall be appointed by common accord of the governments of the Member States. Their term of office shall expire on 6 January 1995.

ARTICLE 159

Apart from normal replacement, or death, the duties of a member of the Commission shall end when he resigns or is compulsorily retired.

The vacancy thus caused shall be filled for the remainder of the member's term of office by a new member appointed by common accord of the governments of the Member States. The Council may, acting unanimously, decide that such a vacancy need not be filled. In the event of resignation, compulsory retirement or death, the President shall be replaced for the remainder of his term of office. The procedure laid down in Article 158(2) shall be applicable for the replacement of the President.

Save in the case of compulsory retirement under Article 160, members of the Commission shall remain in office until they have been replaced.

ARTICLE 160
If any member of the Commission no longer fulfils the conditions required for the performance of his duties or if he has been guilty of serious misconduct, the Court of Justice may, on application by the Council or the Commission, compulsorily retire him.

ARTICLE 161
The Commission may appoint a Vice-President or two Vice-Presidents from among its members.

ARTICLE 162
1. The Council and the Commission shall consult each other and shall settle by common accord their methods of cooperation.
2. The Commission shall adopt its rules of procedure so as to ensure that both it and its department operate in accordance with the provisions of this Treaty.
It shall ensure that these rules are published.

ARTICLE 163
The Commission shall act by a majority of the number of members provided for in Article 157.
A meeting of the Commission shall be valid only if the number of members laid down in the rules of procedure is present.'

49) Article 165 shall be replaced by the following:

'ARTICLE 165
The Court of Justice shall consist of thirteen judges.
The Court of Justice shall sit in plenary session. It may, however, form chambers, each consisting of three or five judges, either to undertake certain preparatory inquiries or to adjudicate on particular categories of cases in accordance with rules laid down for these purposes. The Court of Justice shall sit in plenary session when a Member State or a Community institution that is a party to the proceedings so requests. Should the Court of Justice so request, the Council may, acting unanimously, increase the number of judges and make the necessary adjustments to the second and third paragraphs of this Article and to the second paragraph of Article 167.'

50) Article 168a shall be replaced by the following:

'ARTICLE 168a

1. A Court of First Instance shall be attached to the Court of Justice with jurisdiction to hear and determine at first instance, subject to a right of appeal to the Court of Justice on points of law only and in accordance with the conditions laid down by the Statute, certain classes of action or proceeding defined in accordance with the conditions laid down in paragraph 2. The Court of First Instance shall not be competent to hear and determine questions referred for a preliminary ruling under Article 177.

2. At the request of the Court of Justice and after consulting the European Parliament and the Commission, the Council, acting unanimously, shall determine the classes of action or proceeding referred to in paragraph 1 and the composition of the Court of First Instance and shall adopt the necessary adjustments and additional provisions to the Statute of the Court of Justice. Unless the Council decides otherwise, the provisions of this Treaty relating to the Court of Justice, in particular the provisions of the Protocol on the Statute of the Court of Justice, shall apply to the Court of First Instance.

3. The members of the Court of First Instance shall be chosen from persons whose independence is beyond doubt and who possess the ability required for appointment to judicial office; they shall be appointed by common accord of the governments of the Member States for a term of six years. The membership shall be partially renewed every three years. Retiring members shall be eligible for re-appointment.

4. The Court of First Instance shall establish its rules of procedure in agreement with the Court of Justice. Those rules shall require the unanimous approval of the Council.'

51) Article 171 shall be replaced by the following:

'ARTICLE 171

1. If the Court of Justice finds that a Member State has failed to fulfil an obligation under this Treaty, the State shall be required to take the necessary measures to comply with the judgment of the Court of Justice.

2. If the Commission considers that the Member State concerned has not taken such measures it shall, after giving that State the opportunity to submit its observations, issue a reasoned opinion specifying the points on which the Member State concerned has not complied with the judgment of the Court of Justice. If the Member State concerned fails to take the necessary measures to comply with the Court's judgment within the time-limit laid down by the Commission, the latter may bring the case before the Court of Justice. In so doing it shall specify the amount of the lump sum or penalty payment to be paid by the Member State concerned which it considers appropriate in the circumstances. If the Court of Justice finds that the Member State concerned has not complied with its judgment it may impose a lump sum or penalty payment on it.

This procedure shall be without prejudice to Article 170.'

52) Article 172 shall be replaced by the following:

'ARTICLE 172

Regulations adopted jointly by the European Parliament and the Council, and by the Council, pursuant to the provisions of this Treaty, may give the Court of

Justice unlimited jurisdiction with regard to the penalties provided for in such regulations.'

53) Article 173 shall be replaced by the following:

'ARTICLE 173
The Court of Justice shall review the legality of acts adopted jointly by the European Parliament and the Council, of acts of the Council, of the Commission and of the ECB, other than recommendations and opinions, and of acts of the European Parliament intended to produce legal effects vis-à-vis third parties.
It shall for this purpose have jurisdiction in actions brought by a Member State, the Council or the Commission on grounds of lack of infringement of this Treaty or of any rule relating to its application, or misuse of powers.
The Court shall have jurisdiction under the same conditions in actions brought by the European Parliament and by the ECB for the purpose of protecting their prerogatives. Any natural or legal person may, under the same conditions, institute proceedings against a decision addressed to that person or against a decision which, although in the form of a regulation or a decision addressed to another person, is of direct and individual concern to the former. The proceedings provided for in this Article shall be instituted within two months of the publication of the measure, or of its notification to the plaintiff, or, in the absence thereof, of the day on which it came to the knowledge of the latter, as the case may be.'

54) Article 175 shall be replaced by the following:

'ARTICLE 175
Should the European Parliament, the Council or the Commission, in infringement of this Treaty, fail to act, the Member States and the other institutions of the Community may bring an action before the Court of Justice to have the infringement established.
The action shall be admissible only if the institution concerned has first been called upon to act. If, within two months of being so called upon, the institution concerned has not defined its position, the action may be brought within a further period of two months.
Any natural or legal person may, under the conditions laid down in the preceding paragraphs, complain to the Court of Justice that an institution of the Community has failed to address to that person any act other than a recommendation or an opinion.
The Court of Justice shall have jurisdiction, under the same conditions, in actions or proceedings brought by the ECB in the areas falling within the latter's field of competence and in actions or proceedings brought against the latter.'

55) Article 176 shall be replaced by the following:

'ARTICLE 176
The institution or institutions whose act has been declared void or whose failure to act has been declared contrary to this Treaty shall be required to take the necessary measures to comply with the judgment of the Court of Justice.
This obligation shall not affect any obligation which may result from the application of the second paragraph of Article 215.

This Article shall also apply to the ECB.'

56) Article 177 shall be replaced by the following:

'ARTICLE 177
The Court of Justice shall have jurisdiction to give preliminary rulings concerning:
(a) the interpretation of this Treaty;
(b) the validity and interpretation of acts of the institutions of the Community and of the ECB;
(c) the interpretation of the statutes of bodies established by an act of the Council, where those statutes so provide.
Where such a question is raised before any court or tribunal of a Member State, that court or tribunal may, if it considers that a decision on the question is necessary to enable it to give judgment, request the Court of Justice to give a ruling thereon.
Where any such question is raised in a case pending before a court or tribunal of a Member State against whose decision there is no judicial remedy under national law, that court or tribunal shall bring the matter before the Court of Justice.'

57) Article 180 shall be replaced by the following:

'ARTICLE 180
The Court of Justice shall, within the limits hereinafter laid down, have jurisdiction in disputes concerning:
(a) the fulfilment by Member States of obligations under the Statute of the European Investment Bank. In this connection, the Board of Directors of the Bank shall enjoy the powers conferred upon the Commission by Article 169;
(b) measures adopted by the Board of Governors of the European Investment Bank. In this connection, any Member State, the Commission or the Board of Directors of the Bank may institute proceedings under the conditions laid down in Article 173;
(c) measures adopted by the Board of Directors of the European Investment Bank. Proceedings against such measures may be instituted only by Member States or by the Commission, under the conditions laid down in Article 173, and solely on the grounds of non-compliance with the procedure provided for in Article 21(2), (5), (6) and (7) of the Statute of the Bank;
(d) the fulfilment by national central banks of obligations under this Treaty and the Statute of the ESCB. In this connection the powers of the Council of the ECB in respect of national central banks shall be the same as those conferred upon the Commission in respect of Member States by Article 169. If the Court of Justice finds that a national central bank has failed to fulfil an obligation under this Treaty, that bank shall be required to take the necessary measures to comply with the judgment of the Court of Justice.'

58) Article 184 shall be replaced by the following:

'ARTICLE 184
Notwithstanding the expiry of the period laid down in the fifth paragraph of Article 173, any party may, in proceedings in which a regulation adopted jointly by the European Parliament and the Council, or a regulation of the Council, of the

Commission, or of the ECB is at issue, plead the grounds specified in the second paragraph of Article 173 in order to invoke before the Court of Justice the inapplicability of that regulation.'

59) The following section shall be inserted:
'SECTION 5
THE COURT OF AUDITORS

ARTICLE 188a
The Court of Auditors shall carry out the audit.

ARTICLE 188b
1. The Court of Auditors shall consist of twelve members.
2. The members of the Court of Auditors shall be chosen from among persons who belong or have belonged in their respective countries to external audit bodies or who are especially qualified for this office. Their independence must be beyond doubt.
3. The members of the Court of Auditors shall be appointed for a term of six years by the Council, acting unanimously after consulting the European Parliament. However, when the first appointments are made, four members of the Court of Auditors, chosen by lot, shall be appointed for a term of office of four years only.
The members of the Court of Auditors shall be eligible for reappointment.
They shall elect the President of the Court of Auditors from among their number for a term of three years.
The President may be re-elected.
4. The members of the Court of Auditors shall, in the general interest of the Community, be completely independent in the performance of their duties.
In the performance of these duties, they shall neither seek nor take instructions from any government or from any other body. They shall refrain from any action incompatible with their duties.
5. The members of the Court of Auditors may not, during their term of office, engage in any other occupation, whether gainful or not. When entering upon their duties they shall give a solemn undertaking that, both during and after their term of office, they will respect the obligations arising therefrom and in particular their duty to behave with integrity and discretion as regards the acceptance, after they have ceased to hold office, of certain appointments or benefits.
6. Apart from normal replacement, or death, the duties of a member of the Court of Auditors shall end when he resigns, or is compulsorily retired by a ruling of the Court of Justice pursuant to paragraph 7. The vacancy thus caused shall be filled for the remainder of the member's term of office.
Save in the case of compulsory retirement, members of the Court of Auditors shall remain in office until they have been replaced.
7. A member of the Court of Auditors may be deprived of his office or of his right to a pension or other benefits in its stead only if the Court of Justice, at the request of the Court of Auditors, finds that he no longer fulfils the requisite conditions or meets the obligations arising from his office.
8. The Council, acting by a qualified majority, shall determine the conditions of employment of the President and the members of the Court of Auditors and in particular their salaries, allowances and pensions. It shall also, by the same majority, determine any payment to be made instead of remuneration.

9. The provisions of the Protocol on the Privileges and Immunities of the European Communities applicable to the Judges of the Court of Justice shall also apply to the members of the Court of Auditors.

ARTICLE 188c
1. The Court of Auditors shall examine the accounts of all revenue and expenditure of the Community. It shall also examine the accounts of all revenue and expenditure of all bodies set up by the Community in so far as the relevant constituent instrument does not preclude such examination.
The Court of Auditors shall provide the European Parliament and the Council with a statement of assurance as to the reliability of the accounts and the legality and regularity of the underlying transactions.
2. The Court of Auditors shall examine whether all revenue has been received and all expenditure incurred in a lawful and regular manner and whether the financial management has been sound.
The audit of revenue shall be carried out on the basis both of the amounts established as due and the amounts actually paid to the Community.
The audit of expenditure shall be carried out on the basis both of commitments undertaken and payments made.
These audits may be carried out before the closure of accounts for the financial year in question.
3. The audit shall be based on records and, if necessary, performed on the spot in the other institutions of the Community and in the Member States. In the Member States the audit shall be carried out in liaison with the national audit bodies or, if these do not have the necessary powers, with the competent national departments. These bodies or departments shall inform the Court of Auditors whether they intend to take part in the audit.
The other institutions of the Community and the national audit bodies or, if these do not have the necessary powers, the competent national department, shall forward to the Court of Auditors, at its request, any document or information necessary to carry out its task.
4. The Court of Auditors shall draw up an annual report after the close of each financial year. It shall be forwarded to the other institutions of the Community and shall be published, together with the replies of these institutions to the observations of the Court of Auditors, in the Office Journal of the European Communities.
The Court of Auditors may also, at any time, submit observations, particularly in the form of special reports, on specific questions and deliver opinions at the request of one of the other institutions of the Community.
It shall adopt its annual report, special reports or opinions by a majority of its members.
It shall assist the European Parliament and the Council in exercising their powers of control over the implementation of the budget.'

60) Article 189 shall be replaced by the following:

'ARTICLE 189
In order to carry out their task and in accordance with the provisions of this Treaty, the European Parliament acting jointly with the Council, the Council and

the Commissions shall make regulations and issue directives, take decisions, make recommendations or deliver opinions.

A regulation shall have general application. It shall be binding in its entirety and directly applicable in all Member States.

A directive shall be binding, as to the result to be achieved, upon each Member State to which it is addressed, but shall leave to the national authorities the choice of form and methods.

A decision shall be binding in its entirety upon those to whom it is addressed.

Recommendations and opinions shall have no binding force.'

61) The following Articles shall be inserted:

'ARTICLE 189a

1. Where, in pursuance of this Treaty, the Council acts on a proposal from the Commission, unanimity shall be required for an act constituting an amendment to that proposal, subject to Article 189b(4) and (5).

2. As long as the Council has not acted, the Commission may alter its proposal at any time during the procedures leading to the adoption of a Community act.

ARTICLE 189b

1. Where reference is made in this Treaty to this Article for the adoption of an act, the following procedure shall apply.

2. The Commission shall submit a proposal to the European Parliament and the Council.

The Council, acting by a qualified majority after obtaining the Opinion of the European Parliament, shall adopt a common position. The common position shall be communicated to the European Parliament. The Council shall inform the European Parliament fully of its position.

If, within three months of such communication, the European Parliament:

(a) approves the common position, the Council shall definitively adopt the act in question in accordance with that common position;

(b) has not taken a decision, the Council shall adopt the act in question in accordance with its common position;

(c) indicates, by an absolute majority of its component members, that it intends to reject the common position, it shall immediately inform the Council. The Council may convene a meeting of the Conciliation Committee referred to in paragraph 3 to explain further its position. The European Parliament shall thereafter either confirm, by an absolute majority of its component members, its rejection of the common position, in which event the proposed act shall be deemed not to have been adopted, or propose amendments in accordance with subparagraph (d) of this paragraph;

(d) proposes amendments to the common position by an absolute majority of its component members, the amended text shall be forwarded to the Council and to the Commission, which shall deliver an opinion on those amendments.

3. If, within three months of the matter being referred to it, the Council, acting by a qualified majority, approves all the amendments of the European Parliament, it shall amend its common position accordingly and adopt the act in question; however, the Council shall act unanimously on the amendments on which the Commission has delivered a negative opinion. If the Council does not approve the act in question, the President of the Council, in agreement with the President

of the European Parliament, shall forthwith convene a meeting of the Conciliation Committee.

4. The Conciliation Committee, which shall be composed of the members of the Council or their representatives and an equal number of representatives of the European Parliament, shall have the task of reaching agreement on a joint text, by a qualified majority of the members of the Council or their representatives and by a majority of the representatives of the European Parliament. The Commission shall take part in the Conciliation Committee's proceedings and shall take all the necessary initiatives with a view to reconciling the positions of the European Parliament and the Council.

5. If, within six weeks of its being convened, the Conciliation Committee approves a joint text, the European Parliament, acting by an absolute majority of the votes cast, and the Council, acting by a qualified majority, shall have a period of six weeks from that approval in which to adopt the act in question in accordance with the joint text. If one of the two institutions fails to approve the proposed act, it shall be deemed not to have been adopted.

6. Where the Conciliation Committee does not approve a joint text, the proposed act shall be deemed not to have been adopted unless the Council, acting by a qualified majority within six weeks of expiry of the period granted to the Conciliation Committee, confirms the common position to which it agreed before the conciliation procedure was initiated, possibly with amendments proposed by the European Parliament. In this case, the act in question shall be finally adopted unless the European Parliament, within six weeks of the date of confirmation by the Council, rejects the text by an absolute majority of its component members, in which case the proposed act shall be deemed not to have been adopted.

7. The periods of three months and six weeks referred to in this Article may be extended by a maximum of one month and two weeks respectively by common accord of the European Parliament and the Council. The period of three months referred to in paragraph 2 shall be automatically extended by two months where paragraph 2(c) applies.

8. The scope of the procedure under this Article may be widened, in accordance with the procedure provided for in Article N(2) of the Treaty on European Union, on the basis of a report to be submitted to the Council by the Commission by 1996 at the latest.

ARTICLE 189c
Where reference is made in this Treaty to this Article for the adoption of an act, the following procedure shall apply:

(a) The Council, acting by a qualified majority on a proposal from the Commission and after obtaining the Opinion of the European Parliament, shall adopt a common position.

(b) The Council's common position shall be communicated to the European Parliament. The Council and the Commission shall inform the European Parliament fully of the reasons which led the Council to adopt its common position and also of the Commission's position.

If, within three months of such communication, the European Parliament approves this common position or has not taken a decision within that period, the Council shall definitively adopt the act in question in accordance with the common position.

(c) The European Parliament may, within the period of three months referred to in point (b), by an absolute majority of its component members, propose amendments to the Council's common position.

The European Parliament may also, by the same majority, reject the Council's common position. The result of the proceedings shall be transmitted to the Council and the Commission.

If the European Parliament has rejected the Council's common position, unanimity shall be required for the Council to act on a second reading.

(d) The Commission shall, within a period of one month, re-examine the proposal on the basis of which the Council adopted its common position, by taking into account the amendments proposed by the European Parliament.

The Commission shall forward to the Council, at the same time as its re-examined proposal, the amendments of the European Parliament which it has not accepted, and shall express its opinion on them. The Council may adopt these amendments unanimously.

(e) The Council, acting by a qualified majority, shall adopt the proposal as re-examined by the Commission.

Unanimity shall be required for the Council to amend the proposal as re-examined by the Commission.

(f) In the cases referred to in points (c), (d) and (e), the Council shall be required to act within a period of three months. If no decision is taken within this period, the Commission proposal shall be deemed not to have been adopted.

(g) The periods referred to in points (b) and (f) may be extended by a maximum of one month by common accord between the Council and the European Parliament.'

62) Article 190 shall be replaced by the following:

'ARTICLE 190
Regulations, directives and decisions adopted jointly by the European Parliament and the Council, and such acts adopted by the Council or the Commission, shall state the reasons on which they are based and shall refer to any proposals or opinions which were required to be obtained pursuant to this Treaty.'

63) Article 191 shall be replaced by the following:

'ARTICLE 191
1. Regulations, directives and decisions adopted in accordance with the procedure referred to in Article 189b shall be signed by the President of the European Parliament and by the President of the Council and published in the Official Journal of the Community. They shall enter into force on the date specified in them or, in the absence thereof, on the twentieth day following that of their publication.
2. Regulations of the Council and of the Commission, as well as directives of those institutions which are addressed to all Member States, shall be published in the Official Journal of the Community. They shall enter into force on the date specified in them or, in the absence thereof, on the twentieth day following that of their publication.
3. Other directives, and decisions, shall be notified to those to whom they are addressed and shall take effect upon such notification.'

64) Article 194 shall be replaced by the following:

'**ARTICLE 194**

The number of members of the Economic and Social Committee shall be as follows:

Belgium 12; Denmark 9; Germany 24; Greece 12; Spain 21; France 24; Ireland 9; Italy 24; Luxembourg 6; Netherlands 12; Portugal 12; United Kingdom 24.

The members of the Committee shall be appointed by the Council, acting unanimously, for four years. Their appointments shall be renewable. The members of the Committee may not be bound by any mandatory instructions. They shall be completely independent in the performance of their duties, in the general interest of the Community. The Council, acting by a qualified majority, shall determine the allowances of members of the Committee.'

65) Article 196 shall be replaced by the following:

'**ARTICLE 196**

The Committee shall elect its chairman and officers from among its members for a term of two years. It shall adopt its rules of procedure. The Committee shall be convened by its chairman at the request of the Council or of the Commission. It may also meet on its own initiative.'

66) Article 198 shall be replaced by the following:

'**ARTICLE 198**

The Committee must be consulted by the Council or by the Commission where this Treaty so provides. The Committee may be consulted by these institutions in all cases in which they consider it appropriate. It may take the initiative of issuing an opinion in cases in which it considers such action appropriate.

The Council or the Commission shall, if it considers it necessary, set the Committee, for the submission of its opinion, a time limit which may not be less than one month from the date on which the chairman receives notification to this effect. Upon expiry of the time limit, the absence of an opinion shall not prevent further action.

The opinion of the Committee and that of the specialized section, together with a record of the proceedings, shall be forwarded to the Council and to the Commission.'

67) The following Chapter shall be inserted:

'*CHAPTER 4*
THE COMMITTEE OF THE REGIONS

ARTICLE 198a

A Committee consisting of representatives of regional and local bodies, hereinafter referred to as the 'Committee of the Regions', is hereby established with advisory status.

The number of members of the Committee of the Regions shall be as follows: Belgium 12; Denmark 9; Germany 24; Greece 12; Spain 21; France 24; Ireland 9; Italy 24; Luxembourg 6; Netherlands 12; Portugal 12; United Kingdom 24.

The members of the Committee and an equal number of alternate members shall be appointed for four years by the Council acting unanimously on proposals from the respective Member States. Their term of office shall be renewable.

The members of the Committee may not be bound by any mandatory instructions. They shall be completely independent in the performance of their duties, in the general interest of the Community.

ARTICLE 198b

The Committee of the Regions shall elect its chairman and officers from among its members for a term of two years.

It shall adopt its rules of procedure and shall submit them for approval to the Council, acting unanimously.

The Committee shall be convened by its chairman at the request of the Council or of the Commission. It may also meet on its own initiative.

ARTICLE 198c

The Committee of the Regions shall be consulted by the Council or by the Commission where this Treaty so provides and in all other cases in which one of these two institutions considers it appropriate. The Council or the Commission shall, if it considers it necessary, set the Committee, for the submission of its opinion, a time-limit which may not be less than one month from the date on which the chairman receives notification to this effect. Upon expiry of the time-limit, the absence of an opinion shall not prevent further action.

Where the Economic and Social Committee is consulted pursuant to Article 198, the Committee of the Regions shall be informed by the Council or the Commission of the request for an opinion. Where it considers that specific regional interests are involved, the Committee of the Regions may issue an opinion on the matter.

It may take the initiative of issuing an opinion in cases in which it considers such action appropriate. The opinion of the Committee, together with the record of the proceedings, shall be forwarded to the Council and to the Commission.'

68) The following chapter shall be inserted:

'*CHAPTER 5*
EUROPEAN INVESTMENT BANK

ARTICLE 198d

The European Investment Bank shall have legal personality.

The members of the European Investment Bank shall be the Member States.

The Statute of the European Investment Bank is laid down in a Protocol annexed to this Treaty.

ARTICLE 198e

The task of the European Investment Bank shall be to contribute, by having recourse to the capital market and utilizing its own resources, to the balanced and steady development of the common market in the interest of the Community. For this purpose the Bank shall, operating on a non-profit-making basis, grant loans and give guarantees which facilitate the financing of the following projects in all sectors of the economy:

(a) projects for developing less-developed regions;

(b) projects for modernizing or converting undertakings or for developing fresh activities called for by the progressive establishment of the common market, where these projects are of such a size or nature that they cannot be entirely financed by the various means available in the individual Member States;

(c) projects of common interest to several Member States which are of such a size or nature that they cannot be entirely financed by the various means available in the individual Member States.

In carrying out its task, the Bank shall facilitate the financing of investment programmes in conjunction with assistance from the structural Funds and other Community financial instruments.'

69) Article 199 shall be replaced by the following:

'ARTICLE 199

All items of revenue and expenditure of the Community, including those relating to the European Social Fund, shall be included in estimates to be drawn up for each financial year and shall be shown in the budget.

The administrative expenditure occasioned for the institutions by the provisions of the Treaty on European Union relating to common foreign and security policy and to co-operation in the spheres of justice and home affairs shall be charged to the budget. The operational expenditure occasioned by the implementation of the said provisions may, under the conditions referred to therein, be charged to the budget.

The revenue and expenditure shown in the budget shall be in balance.'

70) Article 200 shall be repealed.

71) Article 201 shall be replaced by the following:

'ARTICLE 201

Without prejudice to other revenue, the budget shall be financed wholly from own resources. The Council, acting unanimously on a proposal from the Commission and after consulting the European Parliament, shall lay down provisions relating to the system of own resources of the Community, which it shall recommend to the Member States for adoption in accordance with their respective constitutional requirements.'

72) The following Article shall be inserted:

'ARTICLE 201a

With a view to maintaining budgetary discipline, the Commission shall not make any proposal for a Community act, or alter its proposals, or adopt any implementing measure which is likely to have appreciable implications for the budget without providing the assurance that that proposal or that measure is capable of being financed within the limits of the Community's own resources arising under provision laid down by the Council pursuant to Article 201.'

73) Article 205 shall be replaced by the following:

'ARTICLE 205

The Commission shall implement the budget, in accordance with the provisions of the regulations made pursuant to Article 209, on its own responsibility and within the limits of the appropriations, having regard to the principles of sound financial management.

The regulations shall lay down detailed rules for each institution concerning its part in effecting its own expenditure.

Within the budget, the Commission may, subject to the limits and conditions laid down in the regulations made pursuant to Article 209, transfer appropriations from one chapter to another or from one subdivision to another.'

74) Article 206 shall be replaced by the following:

'ARTICLE 206

1. The European Parliament, acting on a recommendation from the Council which shall act by a qualified majority, shall give a discharge to the Commission in respect of the implementation of the budget.

To this end, the Council and the European Parliament in turn shall examine the accounts and the financial statement referred to in Article 205a, the annual report by the Court of Auditors together with the replies of the institutions under audit to the observations of the Court of Auditors and any relevant special reports by the Court of Auditors.

2. Before giving a discharge to the Commission, or for any other purpose in connection with the exercise of its powers over the implementation of the budget, the European Parliament may ask to hear the Commission give evidence with regard to the execution of expenditure or the operation of financial control systems. The Commission shall submit any necessary information to the European Parliament at the latter's request.

3. The Commission shall take all appropriate steps to act on the observations in the decisions giving discharge and on other observations by the European Parliament relating to the execution of expenditure, as well as on comments accompanying the recommendations on discharge adopted by the Council.

At the request of the European Parliament or the Council, the Commission shall report on the measures taken in the light of these observations and comments and in particular on the instructions given to the departments which are responsible for the implementation of the budget. These reports shall also be forwarded to the Court of Auditors.'

75) Articles 206a and 206b shall be repealed.

76) Article 209 shall be replaced by the following:

'ARTICLE 209

The Council, acting unanimously on a proposal from the Commission and after consulting the European Parliament and obtaining the opinion of the Court of Auditors, shall:

(a) make Financial Regulations specifying in particular the procedure to be adopted for establishing and implementing the budget and for presenting and auditing accounts;

(b) determine the methods and procedure whereby the budget revenue provided under the arrangements relating to the Communities' own resources shall be made available to the Commissions, and determine the measures to be applied, if need be, to meet cash requirements;

(c) lay down rules concerning the responsibility of financial controllers, authorizing officers and accounting officers, and concerning appropriate arrangements for inspection.'

77) The following Article shall be inserted:

'ARTICLE 209a

Member States shall take the same measures to counter fraud affecting the financial interests of the Community as they take to counter fraud affecting their own financial interests.

Without prejudice to other provisions of this Treaty, Member States shall co-ordinate their action aimed at protecting the financial interests of the Community against fraud. To this end they shall organize, with the help of the Commission, close and regular co-operation between the competent departments of their administrations.'

78) Article 215 shall be replaced by the following:

'ARTICLE 215

The contractual liability of the Community shall be governed by the law applicable to the contract in question.

In the case of non-contractual liability, the Community shall, in accordance with the general principles common to the laws of the Member States, make good any damage caused by its institutions or by its servants in performing of their duties.

The preceding paragraph shall apply under the same conditions to damage caused by the ECB or by its servants in the performance of their duties.

The personal liability of its servants towards the Community shall be governed by the provisions laid down in their Staff Regulations or in the Conditions of Employment applicable to them.'

79) Article 227 shall be amended as follows:

(a) paragraph 2 shall be replaced by the following:

'2. With regard to the French overseas departments, the general and particular provisions of this Treaty relating to:

— the free movement of goods;
— agriculture, save for Article 40 (4);
— the liberalization of services;
— the rules on competition;
— the protective measures provided for in Articles 109h, 109i and 226;
— the institutions,

shall apply as soon as this Treaty enters into force.

The conditions under which the other provisions of this Treaty are to apply shall be determined, within two years of the entry into force of this Treaty, by decisions of the Council, acting unanimously on a proposal from the Commission.

The institutions of the Community will, within the framework of the procedures provided for in this Treaty, in particular Article 226, take care that the economic and social development of these areas is made possible';

(b) in paragraph 5, subparagraph (a) shall be replaced by the following:
'(a) this Treaty shall not apply to the Faroe Islands.'

80) Article 228 shall be replaced by the following:

'ARTICLE 228
1. Where this Treaty provides for the conclusion of agreements between the Community and one or more States or international organizations, the Commission shall make recommendations to the Council, which shall authorize the Commission to open the necessary negotiations. The Commission shall conduct these negotiations in consultation with special committees appointed by the Council to assist it in this task and within the framework of such directives as the Council may issue to it.
In exercising the powers conferred upon it by this paragraph, the Council shall act by a qualified majority, except in the cases provided for in the second sentence of paragraph 2, for which it shall act unanimously.
2. Subject to the powers vested in the Commission in this field, the agreements shall be concluded by the Council, acting by a qualified majority on a proposal from the Commission. The Council shall act unanimously when the agreement covers a field for which unanimity is required for the adoption of internal rules, and for the agreements referred to in Article 238.
3. The Council shall conclude agreements after consulting the European Parliament, except for the agreements referred to in Article 113(3), including cases where the agreement covers a field for which the procedure referred to in Article 189b or that referred to in Article 189c is required for the adoption of internal rules. The European Parliament shall deliver its Opinion within a time limit which the Council may lay down according to the urgency of the matter. In the absence of an Opinion within that time limit, the Council may act. By way of derogation from the previous subparagraph, agreements referred to in Article 238, other agreements establishing a specific institutional framework by organizing cooperation procedures, agreements having important budgetary implications for the Community and agreements entailing amendment of an act adopted under the procedure referred to in Article 189b shall be concluded after the assent of the European Parliament has been obtained.
The Council and the European Parliament may, in an urgent situation, agree upon a time limit for the assent.
4. When concluding an agreement, the Council may, by way of derogation from paragraph 2, empower the Commission to approve modifications on behalf of the Community where the agreement provides for them to be adopted by a simplified procedure or by a body set up by the agreement; it may attach specific conditions to such empowerment.
5. When the Council envisages concluding an agreement which calls for amendments to this Treaty, the amendments must first be adopted in accordance with the procedure laid down in Article N of the Treaty on European Union.
6. The Council, the Commission or a Member State may obtain the opinion of the Court of Justice as to whether an agreement envisaged is compatible with the provisions of this Treaty. Where the opinion of the Court of Justice is adverse, the agreement may enter into force only in accordance with Article N of the Treaty on European Union.

7. Agreements concluded under the conditions set out in this Article shall be binding on the institutions of the Community and on Member States.'

81) The following Article shall be inserted:

'ARTICLE 228a
Where it is provided, in a common position or in a joint action adopted according to the provisions of the Treaty on European Union relating to the common foreign and security policy, for an action by the Community to interrupt or to reduce, in part or completely, economic relations with one or more third countries, the Council shall take the necessary urgent measures.
The Council shall act by a qualified majority on a proposal from the Commission.'

82) Article 231 shall be replaced by the following:

'ARTICLE 231
The Community shall establish close cooperation with the Organization for Economic Cooperation and Development, the details of which shall be determined by common accord.'

83) Articles 236 and 237 shall be repealed.
84) Article 238 shall be replaced by the following:

'ARTICLE 238
The Community may conclude with one or more States or international organizations agreements establishing an association involving reciprocal rights and obligations, common action and special procedures.'

F. In Annex III:
85) The title shall be replaced by the following:
'List of invisible transactions referred to in Article 73h of this Treaty.'
G. In the Protocol on the Statute off the European Investment Bank:
86) The reference to Articles 129 and 130 shall be replaced by a reference to Articles 198d and 198e.

TITLE III
PROVISIONS AMENDING THE TREATY ESTABLISHING THE EUROPEAN COAL AND STEEL COMMUNITY

ARTICLE H
The Treaty establishing the European Coal and Steel Community shall be amended in accordance with the provisions of this Article.

1) Article 7 shall be replaced by the following:

'ARTICLE 7
The institutions of the Community shall be:
— a HIGH AUTHORITY (hereinafter referred to as 'the Commission');

— a COMMON ASSEMBLY (hereinafter referred to as 'the European Parliament');
— a SPECIAL COUNCIL OF MINISTERS (hereinafter referred to as 'the Council');
— a COURT OF JUSTICE;
— a COURT OF AUDITORS.
The Commission shall be assisted by a Consultative Committee.'

2) The following Articles shall be inserted:

'ARTICLE 9
1. The Commission shall consist of seventeen members, who shall be chosen on the grounds of their general competence and whose independence is beyond doubt. The number of members of the Commission may be altered by the Council, acting unanimously.
Only nationals of the Member States may be members of the Commission.
The Commission must include at least one national of each of the Member States, but may not include more than two members having the nationality of the same State.
2. The members of the Commission shall, in the general interest of the Community, be completely independent in the performance of their duties. In the performance of these duties, they shall neither seek nor take instructions from any government or from any other body. They shall refrain from any action incompatible with their duties. Each Member State undertakes to respect this principle and not to seek to influence the members of the Commission in the performance of their tasks. The members of the Commission may not, during their term of office, engage in any other occupation, whether gainful or not. When entering upon their duties they shall give a solemn undertaking that, both during and after their term of office, they will respect the obligations arising therefrom and in particular their duty to behave with integrity and discretion as regards the acceptance, after they have ceased to hold office, of certain appointments or benefits. In the event of any breach of these obligations, the Court of Justice may, on application by the Council or the Commission, rule that the member concerned be, according to the circumstances, either compulsorily retired in accordance with Article 12a or deprived of his right to a pension or other benefits in its stead.

ARTICLE 10
1. The members of the Commission shall be appointed, in accordance with the procedure referred to in paragraph 2, for a period of five years, subject, if need be, to Article 24.
Their term of office shall be renewable.
2. The governments of the Member States shall nominate by common accord, after consulting the European Parliament, the person they intend to appoint as President of the Commission.
The governments of the Member States shall, in consultation with the nominee for President, nominate the other persons whom they intend to appoint as members of the Commission.
The President and the other members of the Commission thus nominated shall be subject as a body to a vote of approval by the European Parliament. After approval by the European Parliament, the President and the other members of the

Commission shall be appointed by common accord of the governments of the Member States.

3. Paragraphs 1 and 2 shall be applied for the first time to the President and the other members of the Commission whose term of office begins on 7 January 1995. The President and the other members of the Commission whose term of office begins on 7 January 1993 shall be appointed by common accord of the governments of the Member States. Their term of office shall expire on 6 January 1995.

ARTICLE 11
The Commission may appoint a Vice-President or two Vice-Presidents from among its members.

ARTICLE 12
Apart from normal replacement, or death, the duties of a member of the Commission shall end when he resigns or is compulsorily retired. The vacancy thus caused shall be filled for the remainder of the member's term of office by a new member appointed by common accord of the governments of the Member States. The Council may, acting unanimously, decide that such a vacancy need not be filled. In the event of resignation, compulsory retirement or death, the President shall be replaced for the remainder of his term of office. The procedure laid down in Article 10(2) shall be applicable for the replacement of the President. Save in the case of compulsory retirement under Article 12a, members of the Commission shall remain in office until they have been replaced.

ARTICLE 12a
If any member of the Commission no longer fulfils the conditions required for the performance of his duties or if he has been guilty of serious misconduct, the Court of Justice may, on application by the Council or the Commission, compulsorily retire him.

ARTICLE 13
The Commission shall act by a majority of the number of members provided for in Article 9.

A meeting of the Commission shall be valid only if the number of members laid down in its rules of procedure is present.'

3) Article 16 shall be replaced by the following:

'ARTICLE 16
The Commission shall make all appropriate administrative arrangements for the operation of its departments.

It may set up study committees, including an economic study committee. The Council and the Commission shall consult each other and shall settle by common accord their methods of cooperation. The Commission shall adopt its rules of procedure so as to ensure that both it and its departments operate in accordance with the provisions of this Treaty. It shall ensure that these rules are published.'

4) The following Article shall be inserted:

'ARTICLE 17

The Commission shall publish annually, not later than one month before the opening of the session of the European Parliament, a general report on the activities of the Community.'

5) The following subparagraph shall be added to Article 18:

'The Council shall, acting by a qualified majority, determine any payment to be made instead of remuneration.'

6) The following Articles shall be inserted:

'ARTICLE 20a

The European Parliament may, acting by a majority of its members, request the Commission to submit any appropriate proposal on matters on which it considers that a Community act is required for the purpose of implementing this Treaty.

ARTICLE 20b

In the course of its duties, the European Parliament may, at the request of a quarter of its members, set up a temporary Committee of Inquiry to investigate, without prejudice to the powers conferred by this Treaty on other institutions or bodies, alleged contraventions or maladministration in the implementation of Community law, except where the alleged facts are being examined before a court and while the case is still subject to legal proceedings. The temporary Committee of Inquiry shall cease to exist on the submission of its report. The detailed provisions governing the exercise of the right of inquiry shall be determined by common accord of the European Parliament, the Council and the Commission.

ARTICLE 20c

Any citizen of the Union, and any natural or legal person residing or having its registered office in a Member State, shall have the right to address, individually or in association with other citizens or persons, a petition to the European Parliament on a matter which comes within the Community's fields of activity and which affects him, her or it directly.

ARTICLE 20d

1. The European Parliament shall appoint an Ombudsman empowered to receive complaints from any citizen of the Union or any natural or legal person residing or having its registered office in a Member State concerning instances of maladministration in the activities of the Community institutions or bodies, with the exception of the Court of Justice and the Court of First Instance acting in their judicial role. In accordance with his duties, the Ombudsman shall conduct inquiries for which he finds grounds, either on his own initiative or on the basis of complaints submitted to him direct or through a member of the European Parliament, except where the alleged facts are or have been the subject of legal proceedings. Where the Ombudsman establishes an instance of maladministration, he shall refer the matter to the institution concerned, which shall have a period of three months in which to inform him of its views. The Ombudsman shall then forward a report to the European Parliament and the institution concerned. The person lodging the complaint shall be informed of the outcome of such inquiries. The Ombudsman shall submit an annual report to the European Parliament on the outcome of his inquiries.

2. The Ombudsman shall be appointed after each election of the European Parliament for the duration of its term of office. The Ombudsman shall be eligible for reappointment.
The Ombudsman may be dismissed by the Court of Justice at the request of the European Parliament if he no longer fulfils the conditions required for the performance of his duties or if he is guilty of serious misconduct.
3. The Ombudsman shall be completely independent in the performance of his duties. In the performance of those duties he shall neither seek nor take instructions from any body. The Ombudsman may not, during his term of office, engage in any other occupation, whether gainful or not.
4. The European Parliament shall, after seeking an opinion from the Commission and with the approval of the Council acting by a qualified majority, lay down the regulations and general conditions governing the performance of the Ombudsman's duties.'

7) Paragraph 3 of Article 21 shall be replaced by the following:
'3. The European Parliament shall draw up proposals for elections by direct universal suffrage in accordance with a uniform procedure in all Member States. The Council shall, acting unanimously after obtaining the assent of the European Parliament, which shall act by a majority of its component members, lay down the appropriate provisions, which it shall recommend to Member States for adoption in accordance with their respective constitutional requirements.'

8) Article 24 shall be replaced by the following:

'ARTICLE 24
The European Parliament shall discuss in open session the general report submitted to it by the Commission. If a motion of censure on the activities of the Commission is tabled before it, the European Parliament shall not vote thereon until at least three days after the motion has been tabled and only by open vote. If a motion of censure is carried by a two-thirds majority of the votes cast, representing a majority of the members of the European Parliament, the members of the Commission shall resign as a body. They shall continue to deal with current business until they are replaced in accordance with Article 10. In this case, the term of office of the members of the Commission appointed to replace them shall expire on the date on which the term of office of the members of the Commission obliged to resign as a body would have expired.'

9) The following Articles shall be inserted:

'ARTICLE 27
The Council shall consist of a representative of each Member State at ministerial level, authorized to commit the government of that Member State.
The office of President shall be held in turn by each Member State in the Council for a term of six months, in the following order of Member States:
— for a first cycle of six years: Belgium, Denmark, Germany, Greece, Spain, France, Ireland, Italy, Luxembourg, Netherlands, Portugal, United Kingdom.
— for the following cycle of six years: Denmark, Belgium, Greece, Germany, France, Spain, Italy, Ireland, Netherlands, Luxembourg, United Kingdom, Portugal.

ARTICLE 27a
The Council shall meet when convened by its President on his own initiative or at the request of one of its members or of the Commission.'

10) The following Articles shall be inserted:

'ARTICLE 29
The Council shall, acting by a qualified majority, determine the salaries, allowances and pensions of the President and members of the Commission, and of the President. Judges, Advocates-General and Registrar of the Court of Justice. It shall also, again by a qualified majority, determine any payment to be made instead of remuneration.

ARTICLE 30
1. A committee consisting of the Permanent Representatives of the Member States shall be responsible for preparing the work of the Council and for carrying out the tasks assigned to it by the Council.
2. The Council shall be assisted by a General Secretariat, under the direction of a Secretary-General. The Secretary-General shall be appointed by the Council acting unanimously. The Council shall decide on the organization of the General Secretariat.
3. The Council shall adopt its rules of procedure.'

11) Article 32 shall be replaced by the following:

'ARTICLE 32
The Court of Justice shall consist of thirteen judges.
The Court of Justice shall sit in plenary session. It may, however, form chambers, each consisting of three or five judges, either to undertake certain preparation inquiries or to adjudicate on particular categories of cases in accordance with the rules laid down for these purposes.
The Court of Justice shall sit in plenary session when a Member State or a Community institution that is a party to the proceedings so requests. Should the Court of Justice so request, the Council may, acting unanimously, increase the number of judges and make the necessary adjustments to the second and third paragraphs of this Article and to the second paragraph of Article 32b.'

12) Article 32d shall be replaced by the following:

'ARTICLE 32d
1. A Court of First Instance shall be attached to the Court of Justice with jurisdiction to hear and determine at first instance, subject to a right of appeal to the Court of Justice on points of law only and in accordance with the conditions laid down by the Statute, certain classes of action or proceeding defined in accordance with the conditions laid down in paragraph 2. The Court of First Instance shall not be competent to hear and determine questions referred for a preliminary ruling under Article 41.
2. At the request of the Court of Justice and after consulting the European Parliament and the Commission, the Council, acting unanimously, shall determine the classes of action or proceeding referred to in paragraph 1, and the composition

to the Court of First Instance and shall adopt the necessary adjustments and additional provisions to the Statute of the Court of Justice. Unless the Council decides otherwise, the provisions of this Treaty relating to the Court of Justice, in particular the provisions of the Protocol on the Statute of the Court of Justice, shall apply to the Court of First Instance.

3. The members of the Court of First Instance shall be chosen from persons whose independence is beyond doubt and who possess the ability required for appointment to judicial office; they shall be appointed by common accord of the governments of the Member States for a term of six years. The membership shall be partially renewed every three years. Retiring members shall be eligible for re-appointment.

4. The Court of First Instance shall establish its rules of procedure in agreement with the Court of Justice. Those rules shall require the unanimous approval of the Council.'

13) Article 33 shall be replaced by the following:

'ARTICLE 33

The Court of Justice shall have jurisdiction in actions brought by a Member State or by the Council to have decisions or recommendations of the Commission declared void on grounds of lack of competence, infringement of an essential procedural requirement, infringement of this Treaty or of any rule of law relating to its application, or misuse of powers. The Court of Justice may not, however, examine the evaluation of the situation, resulting from economic facts or circumstances, in the light of which the Commission took its decisions or made its recommendations, save where the Commission is alleged to have misused its powers or to have manifestly failed to observe the provisions of this Treaty or any rule of law relating to its application.

Undertakings or associations referred to in Article 48 may, under the same conditions, institute proceedings against decisions or recommendations concerning them which are individual in character or against general decisions or recommendations which they consider to involve a misuse of powers affecting them.

The proceedings provided for in the first two paragraphs of this Article shall be instituted within one month of the notification or publication, as the case may be, of the decision or recommendation.

The Court of Justice shall have jurisdiction under the same conditions in actions brought by the European Parliament for the purpose of protecting its prerogatives.'

14) The following chapter shall be inserted:

'CHAPTER V

THE COURT OF AUDITORS

ARTICLE 45a

The Court of Auditors shall carry out the audit.

ARTICLE 45b

1. The Court of Auditors shall consist of twelve members.

2. The members of the Court of Auditors shall be chosen from among persons who belong or have belonged in their respective countries to external audit bodies

or who are especially qualified for this office. Their independence must be beyond doubt.

3. The members of the Court of Auditors shall be appointed for a term of six years by the Council, acting unanimously after consulting the European Parliament. However, when the first appointments are made, four members of the Court of Auditors, chosen by lot, shall be appointed for a term of office of four years only. The members of the Court of Auditors shall be eligible for reappointment. They shall elect the President of the Court of Auditors from among their number for a term of three years. The President may be re-elected.

4. The members of the Court of Auditors shall, in the general interest of the Community, be completely independent in the performance of their duties.

In the performance of these duties, they shall neither seek nor take instructions from any government or from any other body. They shall refrain from any action incompatible with their duties.

5. The members of the Court of Auditors may not, during their term of office, engage in any other occupation, whether gainful or not. When entering upon their duties they shall give a solemn undertaking that, both during and after their term of office, they will respect the obligations arising therefrom and in particular their duty to behave with integrity and discretion as regards the acceptance, after they have ceased to hold office, of certain appointments or benefits.

6. Apart from normal replacement, or death, the duties of a member of the Court of Auditors shall end when he resigns, or is compulsorily retired by a ruling of the Court of Justice pursuant to paragraph 7. The vacancy thus caused shall be filled for the remainder of the member's term of office.

Save in the case of compulsory retirement, members of the Court of Auditors shall remain in office until they have been replaced.

7. A member of the Court of Auditors may be deprived of his office or of his right to a pension or other benefits in its stead only if the Court of Justice, at the request of the Court of Auditors, finds that he no longer fulfils the requisite conditions or meets the obligations arising from his office.

8. The Council, acting by a qualified majority, shall determine the conditions of employment of the President and the members of the Court of Auditors and in particular their salaries, allowances and pensions. It shall also, by the same majority, determine any payment to be made instead of remuneration.

9. The provisions of the Protocol on the Privileges and Immunities of the European Communities applicable to the Judges of the Court of Justice shall also apply to the members of the Court of Auditors.

ARTICLE 45c

1. The Court of Auditors shall examine the accounts of all revenue and expenditure of the Community. It shall also examine the accounts of all revenue and expenditure of all bodies set up by the Community in so far as the relevant constituent instrument does not preclude such examination. The Court of Auditors shall provide the European Parliament and the Council with a statement of assurance as to the reliability of the accounts and the legality and regularity of the underlying transactions.

2. The Court of Auditors shall examine whether all revenue referred to in paragraph 1 has been received and all expenditure referred to in that paragraph has been incurred in a lawful and regular manner and whether the financial management has been sound.

The audit of revenue shall be carried out on the basis of the amounts established as due and the amounts actually paid to the Community.

The audit of expenditure shall be carried out on the basis both of commitments undertaken and payments made.

These audits may carried out before the closure of accounts for the financial year in question.

3. The audit shall be based on records and, if necessary, performed on the spot in the other institutions of the Community and in the Member States. In the Member States the audit shall be carried out in liaison with the national audit bodies or, if these do not have the necessary powers, with the competent national departments. These bodies or departments shall inform the Court of Auditors whether they intend to take part in the audit.

The other institutions of the Community and the national audit bodies or, if these do not have the necessary powers, the competent national department, shall forward to the Court of Auditors, as its request, any document or information necessary to carry out its task.

4. The Court of Auditors shall draw up an annual report after the close of each financial year. It shall be forwarded to the other institutions of the Community and shall be published, together with the replies of these institutions to the observations of the Court of Auditors in the Official Journal of the European Communities.

The Court of Auditors may also, at any time, submit observations, particularly in the form of special reports, on specific questions and deliver opinions at the request of one of the other institutions of the Community. It shall adopt its annual reports, special reports or opinions by a majority of its members.

It shall assist the European Parliament and the Council in exercising their powers of control over the implementation of the budget.

5. The Court of Auditors shall also draw up a separate annual report stating whether the accounting other than that for the expenditure and revenue referred to in paragraph 1 and the financial management by the Commission relating thereto have been effected in a regular manner. It shall draw up this report within six months of the end of the financial year to which the accounts refer and shall submit it to the Commission and the Council. The Commission shall foward it to the European Parliament.'

15) Article 78c shall be replaced by the following:

'ARTICLE 78c
The Commission shall implement the administrative budget, in accordance with the provisions of the regulations made pursuant to Article 78h, on its own responsibility and within the limits of the appropriations, having regard to the principles of sound financial management.

The regulations shall lay down detailed rules for each institution concerning its part in effecting its own expenditure.

Within the administrative budget, the Commission may, subject to the limits and conditions laid down in the regulations made pursuant to Article 78h, transfer appropriations from one chapter to another or from one subdivision to another.'

16) Articles 78e and 78f shall be repealed.

17) Article 78g shall be replaced by the following:

'ARTICLE 78g
1. The European Parliament, acting on a recommendation from the Council, which shall act by a qualified majority, shall give a discharge to the Commission in respect of the implementation of the administrative budget. To this end, the Council and the European Parliament in turn shall examine the accounts and the financial statement referred to in Article 78d, the annual report by the Court of Auditors together with the replies of the institutions under audit to the observations of the Court of Auditors, and any relevant special reports by the Court of Auditors.
2. Before giving a discharge to the Commission, or for any other purpose in connection with the exercise of its powers over the implementation of the administrative budget, the European Parliament may ask to hear the Commission give evidence with regard to the execution of expenditure or the operation of financial control systems. The Commission shall submit any necessary information to the European Parliament at the latter's request.
3. The Commission shall take all appropriate steps to act on the observations in the decisions giving discharge and on other observations by the European Parliament relating to the execution of expenditure, as well as on comments accompanying the recommendations on discharge adopted by the Council.
At the request of the European Parliament or the Council, the Commission shall report on the measures taken in the light of these observations and comments and in particular on the instructions given to the departments which are responsible for the implementation of the administrative budget. These reports shall also be forwarded to the Court of Auditors.'

18) Article 78h shall be replaced by the following:

'ARTICLE 78h
The Council, acting unanimously on a proposal from the Commission and after consulting the European Parliament and obtaining the opinion of the Court of Auditors, shall:
(a) make Financial Regulations specifying in particular the procedure to be adopted for establishing and implementing the administrative budget and for presenting and auditing accounts;
(b) determine the methods and procedure whereby the budget revenue provided for under the arrangements relating to the Communities' own resources shall be made available to the Commission, and determine the measures to be applied, if need be, to meet cash requirements;
(c) lay down rules concerning the responsibility of financial controllers, authorizing officers and accounting officers, and concerning appropriate arrangements for inspection.'

19) The following Article shall be inserted:

'ARTICLE 78i
Member States shall take the same measures to counter fraud affecting the financial interests of the Community as they take to counter fraud affecting their own financial interests.

Without prejudice to other provisions of this Treaty, Member States shall co-ordinate their action aimed at protecting the financial interests of the Community against fraud. To this end they shall organize, with the help of the Commission, close and regular co-operation between the competent departments of their administrations.'

20) Article 79(a) shall be replaced by the following:
'(a) This Treaty shall not apply to the Faroe Islands.'

21) Articles 96 and 98 shall be repealed.

TITLE IV
PROVISIONS AMENDING THE TREATY
ESTABLISHING
THE EUROPEAN ATOMIC ENERGY COMMUNITY

ARTICLE I
The Treaty establishing the European Atomic Energy Community shall be amended in accordance with the provisions of this Article.
1) Article 3 shall be replaced by the following:

'ARTICLE 3
1. The tasks entrusted to the Community shall be carried out by the following institutions:
— a EUROPEAN PARLIAMENT,
— a COUNCIL,
— a COMMISSION,
— a COURT OF JUSTICE,
— a COURT OF AUDITORS.
Each institution shall act within the limits of the powers conferred upon it by this Treaty.
2. The Council and the Commission shall be assisted by an Economic and Social Committee acting in an advisory capacity.'

2) The following Articles shall be inserted:

'ARTICLE 107a
The European Parliament may, acting by a majority of its members, request the Commission to submit any appropriate proposal on matters on which it considers that a Community act is required for the purpose of implementing this Treaty.

ARTICLE 107b
In the course of its duties, the European Parliament may, at the request of a quarter of its members, set up a temporary Committee of Inquiry to investigate, without prejudice to the powers conferred by this Treaty on other institutions or bodies, alleged contraventions or maladministration in the implementation of Community law, except where the alleged facts are being examined before a court and while the case is still subject to legal proceedings.

The temporary Committee of Inquiry shall cease to exist on the submission of its report.

The detailed provisions governing the exercise of the right of inquiry shall be determined by common accord of the European Parliament, the Council and the Commission.

ARTICLE 107c

Any citizen of the Union, and any natural or legal person residing or having its registered office in a Member State, shall have the right to address, individually or in association with other citizens or persons, a petition to the European Parliament on a matter which comes within the Community's fields of activity and which affects him, her or it directly.

ARTICLE 107d

1. The European Parliament shall appoint an Ombudsman empowered to receive complaints from any citizen of the Union or any natural or legal person residing or having its registered office in a Member State concerning instances of maladministration in the activities of the Community institutions or bodies, with the exception of the Court of Justice and the Court of First Instance acting in their judicial role. In accordance with his duties, the Ombudsman shall conduct inquiries for which he finds grounds, either on his own initiative or on the basis of complaints submitted to him direct or through a member of the European Parliament, except where the alleged facts are or have been the subject of legal proceedings. Where the Ombudsman establishes an instance of maladministration, he shall refer the matter to the institution concerned, which shall have a period of three months in which to inform him of its views. The Ombudsman shall then forward a report to the European Parliament and the institution concerned. The person lodging the complaint shall be informed of the outcome of such inquiries.

The Ombudsman shall submit an annual report to the European Parliament on the outcome of his inquiries.

2. The Ombudsman shall be appointed after each election of the European Parliament for the duration of its term of office. The Ombudsman shall be eligible for reappointment.

The Ombudsman may be dismissed by the Court of Justice at the request of the European Parliament if he no longer fulfils the conditions required for the performance of his duties or if he is guilty of serious misconduct.

3. The Ombudsman shall be completely independent in the performance of his duties. In the performance of those duties he shall neither seek nor take instructions from any body. The Ombudsman may not, during his term of office, engage in any other occupation, whether gainful or not.

4. The European Parliament shall, after seeking an opinion from the Commission and with the approval of the Council acting by a qualified majority, lay down the regulations and general conditions governing the performance of the Ombudsman's duties.'

3) Paragraph 3 of Article 108 shall be replaced by following:

'3. The European Parliament shall draw up proposals for elections by direct universal suffrage in accordance with a uniform procedure in all Member States. The Council shall, acting unanimously after obtaining the assent of the European Parliament, which shall act by a majority of its component members, lay down the appropriate provisions, which it shall recommend to Member States for adoption in accordance with their respective constitutional requirements.'

4) The second subparagraph of Article 114 shall be supplemented by the following sentence:
'In this case, the term of office of the members of the Commission appointed to replace them shall expire on the date on which the term of office of the members of the Commission obliged to resign as a body would have expired.'

5) The following Articles shall be inserted:

'ARTICLE 116
The Council shall consist of a representative of each Member State at ministerial level, authorized to commit the government of that Member State. The office of President shall be held in turn by each Member State in the Council for a term of six months, in the following order of Member States:
— for a first cycle of six years: Belgium, Denmark, Germany, Greece, Spain, France, Ireland, Italy, Luxembourg, Netherlands, Portugal, United Kingdom;
— for the following cycle of six years: Denmark, Belgium, Greece, Germany, France, Spain, Italy, Ireland, Netherlands, Luxembourg, United Kingdom, Portugal.

ARTICLE 117
The Council shall meet when convened by its President on his own initiative or at the request of one of its members or of the Commission.'

6) The following Article shall be inserted:

'ARTICLE 121
1. A committee consisting of the Permanent Representatives of the Member States shall be responsible for preparing the work of the Council and for carrying out the tasks assigned to it by the Council.
2. The Council shall be assisted by a General Secretariat, under the direction of a Secretary-General. The Secretary-General shall be appointed by the Council acting unanimously.
The Council shall decide on the organization of the General Secretariat.
3. The Council shall adopt its rules of procedure.'

7) The following Article shall be inserted:

'ARTICLE 123
The Council shall, acting by qualified majority, determine the salaries, allowances and pensions of the President and members of the Commission, and the President, Judges, Advocates-General and Registrar of the Court of Justice. It shall also, again by a qualified majority, determine any payment to be made instead of remuneration.'

8) The following Articles shall be inserted:

'ARTICLE 125
The Commission shall publish annually, not later than one month before the opening of the session of the European Parliament, a general report on the activities of the Community.

ARTICLE 126
1. The Commission shall consist of seventeen members, who shall be chosen on the grounds of their general competence and whose independence is beyond doubt. The number of members of the Commission may be altered by the Council, acting unanimously.
Only nationals of the Member States may be members of the Commission.
The Commission must include at least one national of each of the Member States, but may not include more than two members having the nationality of the same State.
2. The members of the Commission shall, in the general interest of the Community, be completely independent in the performance of their duties. In the performance of these duties, they shall neither seek nor take instructions from any government or from any other body. They shall refrain from any action incompatible with their duties. Each Member State undertakes to respect this principle and not to seek to influence the members of the Commission in the performance of their tasks.
The members of the Commission may not, during their term of office, engage in any other occupation, whether gainful or not. When entering upon their duties they shall give a solemn undertaking that, both during and after their term of office, they will respect the obligations arising therefrom and in particular their duty to behave with integrity and discretion as regards the acceptance, after they have ceased to hold office, of certain appointments or benefits. In the event of any breach of these obligations, the Court of Justice may, on application by the Council or the Commission, rule that the member concerned be, according to the circumstances, either compulsorily retired in accordance with Article 129 or deprived of his right to a pension or other benefits in its stead.

ARTICLE 127
1. The members of the Commission shall be appointed, in accordance with the procedure referred to in paragraph 2, for a period of five years, subject, if need be, to Article 114.
Their term of office shall be renewable.
2. The governments of the Member States shall nominate by common accord, after consulting the European Parliament, the person they intend to appoint as President of the Commission.
The governments of the Member States shall, in consultation with the nominee for President, nominate the other persons whom they intend to appoint as members of the Commission.
The President and the other members of the Commission thus nominated shall be subject as a body to a vote of approval by the European Parlimaent. After approval by the European Parliament. After approval by the European Parliament, the President and the other members of the Commission shall be appointed by common accord of the governments of the Member States.
3. Paragraphs 1 and 2 shall be applied for the first time to the President and the other members of the Commission whose term of office begins on 7 January 1995.

The President and the other members of the Commission whose term of office begins on 7 January 1993 shall be appointed by common accord of the governments of the Member States. Their term of office shall expire on 6 January 1995.

ARTICLE 128
Apart from normal replacement, or death, the duties of a member of the Commission shall end when he resigns or is compulsorily retired.
The vacancy thus caused shall be filled for the remainder of the member's term of office by a new member appointed by common accord of the governments of the Member States. The Council may, acting unanimously, decide that such a vacancy need not be filled. In the event of resignation, compulsory retirement or death, the President shall be replaced for the remainder of his term of office. The procedure laid down in Article 127(2) shall be applicable for the replacement of the President.
Save in the case of compulsory retirement under Article 129, members of the Commission shall remain in office until they have been replaced.

ARTICLE 129
If any member of the Commission no longer fulfils the conditions required for the performance of his duties or if he has been guilty of serious misconduct, the Court of Justice may, on application by the Council or the Commission, compulsorily retire him.

ARTICLE 130
The Commission may appoint a Vice-President or two Vice-Presidents from among its members.

ARTICLE 131
The Council and the Commission shall consult each other and shall settle by common accord their methods of cooperation.
The Commission shall adopt its rules of procedure so as to ensure that both it and its departments operate in accordance with the provisions of this Treaty. It shall ensure that these rules are published.

ARTICLE 132
The Commission shall act by a majority of the number of members provided for in Article 126.
A meeting of the Commission shall be valid only if the number of members laid down in its rules of procedure is present'.

9) Article 133 shall be repealed.

10) Article 137 shall be replaced by the following:

'ARTICLE 137
'The Court of Justice shall consist of thirteen judges.
The Court of Justice shall sit in plenary session. It may, however, form chambers, each consisting of three or five judges, either to undertake certain preparatory inquiries or to adjudicate on particular categories of cases in accordance with the rules laid down for these purposes.

The Court of Justice shall sit in plenary session when a Member State or a Community institution that is a party to the proceedings so requests.

Should the Court of Justice so request, the Council may, acting unanimously, increase the number of judges and make the necessary adjustments to the second and third paragraphs of this Article and to the second paragraph of Article 139.'

11) Article 140a shall be replaced by the following:

'ARTICLE 140a

1. A Court of First Instance shall be attached to the Court of Justice with jurisdiction to hear and determine at first instance, subject to a right of appeal to the Court of Justice on points of law only and in accordance with the conditions laid down by the Statute, certain classes of action or proceeding defined in accordance with the conditions laid down in paragraph 2. The Court of First Instance shall not be competent to hear and determine questions referred for a preliminary ruling under Article 150.

2. At the request of the Court of Justice and after consulting the European Parliament and the Commission, the Council, acting unanimously, shall determine the classes of action or proceeding referred to in paragraph 1 and the composition of the Court of First Instance and shall adopt the necessary adjustments and additional provisions to the Statute of the Court of Justice. Unless the Council decides otherwise, the provisions of this Treaty relating to the Court of Justice, in particular the provisions of the Protocol on the Statute of the Court of Justice, shall apply to the Court of First Instance.

3. The members of the Court of First Instance shall be chosen from persons whose independence is beyond doubt and who possess the ability required for appointment to judicial office; they shall be appointed by common accord of the governments of the Member States for a term of six years. The membership shall be partially renewed every three years. Retiring members shall be eligible for re-appointment.

4. The Court of First Instance shall establish its rules of procedure in agreement with the Court of Justice. Those rules shall require the unanimous approval of the Council.'

12) Article 143 shall be replaced by the following:

'ARTICLE 143

1. If the Court of Justice finds that a Member State has failed to fulfil an obligation under this Treaty, the State shall be required to take the necessary measures to comply with the judgment of the Court of Justice.

2. If the Commission considers that the Member State concerned has not taken such measures it shall, after giving that State the opportunity to submit its observations, issue a reasoned opinion specifying the points on which the Member State concerned has not complied with the judgment of the Court of Justice.

If the Member State concerned fails to take the necessary measures to comply with the Court's judgment within the time-limit laid down by the Commission, the latter may bring the case before the Court of Justice. In so doing it shall specify the amount of the lump sum or penalty payment to be paid by the Member State concerned which it considers appropriate in the circumstances.

If the Court of Justice finds that the Member State concerned has not complied with its judgment it may impose a lump sum or penalty payment on it.
This procedure shall be without prejudice to Article 142.'

13) Article 146 shall be replaced by the following:

'ARTICLE 146
The Court of Justice shall review the legality of acts of the Council and of the Commission, other than recommendations and opinions, and of acts of the European Parliament intended to produce legal effects vis-à-vis third parties.
It shall for this purpose have jurisdiction in actions brought by a Member State, the Council or the Commission on grounds of lack of competence, infringement of an essential procedural requirement, infringement of this Treaty or of any rule of law relating to its application, or misuse of powers.
The Court shall have jurisdiction under the same conditions in actions brought by the European Parliament for the purpose of protecting its prerogatives.
Any natural or legal person may, under the same conditions, institute proceedings against a decision addressed to that person or against a decision which, although in the form of a regulation or a decision addressed to another person, is of direct and individual concern to the former.
The proceedings provided for in this Article shall be instituted within two months of the publication of the measure, or of its notification to the plaintiff, or, in the absence thereof, of the day on which it came to the knowledge of the latter, as the case may be.'

14) The following Section shall be inserted:
'SECTION V
THE COURT OF AUDITORS

ARTICLE 160a
The audit shall be carried out by the Court of Auditors.

ARTICLE 160b
1. The Court of Auditors shall consist of twelve members.
2. The members of the Court of Auditors shall be chosen from among persons who belong or have belonged in their respective countries to external audit bodies or who are especially qualified for this office. Their independence must be beyond doubt.
3. The members of the Court of Auditors shall be appointed for a term of six years by the Council, acting unanimously after consulting the European Parliament. However, when the first appointments are made, four members of the Court of Auditors, chosen by lot, shall be appointed for a term of office of four years only. The members of the Court of Auditors shall be eligible for reappointment.
They shall elect the President of the Court of Auditors from among their number for a term of three years. The President may be re-elected.
4. The members of the Court of Auditors shall, in the general interest of the Community, be completely independent in the performance of their duties.
In the performance of these duties, they shall neither seek nor take instructions from any government or from any other body. They shall refrain from any action incompatible with their duties.

5. The members of the Court of Auditors may not, during their term of office, engage in any other occupation, whether gainful or not. When entering upon their duties they shall give a solemn undertaking that, both during and after their term of office, they will respect the obligations arising therefrom and in particular their duty to behave with integrity and discretion as regards the acceptance, after they have ceased to hold office, of certain appointments or benefits.

6. Apart from normal replacement, or death, the duties of a member of the Court of Auditors shall end when he resigns, or is compulsorily retired by a ruling of the Court of Justice pursuant to paragraph 7. The vacancy thus caused shall be filled for the remainder of the member's term of office.

Save in the case of compulsory retirement, members of the Court of Auditors shall remain in office until they have been replaced.

7. A member of the Court of Auditors may be deprived of his office or of his right to a pension or other benefits in its stead only if the Court of Justice, at the request of the Court of Auditors, finds that he no longer fulfils the requisite conditions or meets the obligations arising from his office.

8. The Council, acting by a qualified majority, shall determine the conditions of employment of the President and the members of the Court of Auditors and in particular their salaries, allowances and pensions. It shall also, by the same majority, determine any payment to be made instead of remuneration.

9. The provisions of the Protocol on the Privileges and Immunities of the European Communities applicable to the judges of the Court of Justice shall also apply to the members of the Court of Auditors.

ARTICLE 160c

1. The Court of Auditors shall examine the accounts of all revenue and expenditure of the Community. It shall also examine the accounts of all revenue and expenditure of all bodies set up by the Community insofar as the relevant constituent instrument does not preclude such examination. The Court of Auditors shall provide the European Parliament and the Council with a statement of assurance as to the reliability of the accounts and the legality and regularity of the underlying transactions.

2. The Court of Auditors shall examine whether all revenue has been received and all expenditure incurred in a lawful and regular manner and whether the financial management has been sound.

The audit of revenue shall be carried out on the basis of the amounts established as due and the amounts actually paid to the Community. The audit of expenditure shall be carried out on the basis both of commitments undertaken and payments made.

These audits may be carried out before the closure of accounts for the financial year in question.

3. The audit shall be based on records and, if necessary, performed on the spot in the other institutions of the Community and in the Member States. In the Member States the audit shall be carried out in liaison with the national audit bodies or, if these do not have the necessary powers, with the competent national departments. These bodies or departments shall inform the Court of Auditors whether they intend to take part in the audit.

The other institutions of the Community and the national audit bodies or, if these do not have the necessary powers, the competent national department, shall forward to the Court of Auditors, at its request, any document or information necessary to carry out its task.

4. The Court of Auditors shall draw up an annual report after the close of each financial year. It shall be forwarded to the other institutions of the Community and shall be published, together with the replies of these institutions to the observations of the Court of Auditors, in the Official Journal of the European Communities.

The Court of Auditors may also, at any time, submit observations, particularly in the form of special reports, on specific questions and deliver opinions at the request of one of the other institutions of the Community.

It shall adopt its annual reports, special reports or opinions by a majority of its members.

It shall assist the European Parliament and the Council in exercising their powers of control over the implementation of the budget.'

15) Article 166 shall be replaced by the following:

'ARTICLE 166
The number of members of the Economic and Social Committee shall be as follows: Belgium 12; Denmark 9; Germany 24; Greece 12; Spain 21; France 24; Ireland 9; Italy 24; Luxembourg 6; Netherlands 12; Portugal 12; United Kingdom 24.

The members of the Committee shall be appointed by the Council, acting unanimously, for four years. Their appointments shall be renewable.

The members of the Committee may not be bound by any mandatory instructions. They shall be completely independent in the performance of their duties, in the general interest of the Community.

The Council, acting by a qualified majority, shall determine the allowances of members of the Committee.'

16) Article 168 shall be replaced by the following:

'ARTICLE 168
The Committee shall elect its chairman and officers from among its members for a term of two years. It shall adopt its rules of procedure.

The Committee shall be convened by its chairman at the request of the Council or of the Commission. It may also meet on its own initiative.'

17) Article 170 shall be replaced by the following:

'ARTICLE 170
The Committee must be consulted by the Council or by the Commission where this Treaty so provides. The Committee may be consulted by these institutions in all cases in which they consider it appropriate. It may take the initiative of issuing an opinion in cases in which it considers such action appropriate.

The Council or the Commission shall, if it considers it necessary, set the Committee, for the submission of its opinion, a time limit which may not be less than one month from the date on which the chairman receives notification to this effect.

Upon expiry of the time limit, the absence of an opinion shall not prevent further action.

The opinion of the Committee and that of the specialized section, together with a record of the proceedings, shall be forwarded to the Council and to the Commission.'

18) Paragraphs 1 to 3 of Article 172 shall be repealed.

19) Article 173 shall be replaced by the following:

'ARTICLE 173

Without prejudice to other revenue, the budgets shall be financed wholly from own resources.

The Council, acting unanimously on a proposal from the Commission and after consulting the European Parliament, shall lay down provisions relating to the system of own resources of the Community, which it shall recommend to the Member States for adoption in accordance with their respective constitutional requirements.'

20) The following Article shall be inserted:

'ARTICLE 173a

With a view to maintaining budgetary discipline, the Commission shall not make any proposal for a Community act, or alter its proposals, or adopt any implementing measure which is likely to have appreciable implications for the budget without providing the assurance that that proposal or that measure is capable of being financed within the limit of the Community's own resources arising under provisions laid down by the Council pursuant to Article 173.'

21) Article 179 shall be replaced by the following:

'ARTICLE 179

The Commission shall implement the budgets, in accordance with the provisions of the regulations made pursuant to Article 183, on its own responsibility and within the limits of the appropriations, having regard to the principles of sound financial management.

The regulations shall lay down detailed rules for each institution concerning its part in effecting its own expenditure.

Within the budgets, the Commission may, subject to the limits and conditions laid down in the regulations made pursuant to Article 183, transfer appropriations from one chapter to another or from one subdivision to another.'

22) Articles 180 and 180a shall be repealed.

23) Article 180b shall be replaced by the following:

'ARTICLE 180b

1. The European Parliament, acting on a recommendation from the Council which shall act by a qualified majority, shall give a discharge to the Commission in

respect of the implementation of the budgets. To this end, the Council and the European Parliament in turn shall examine the accounts and the financial statement referred to in Article 179a, the annual report by the Court of Auditors together with the replies of the institutions under audit to the observations of the Court of Auditors, and any relevant special reports by the Court of Auditors.

2. Before giving a discharge to the Commission, or for any other purpose in connection with the exercise of its powers over the implementation of the budgets, the European Parliament may ask to hear the Commission give evidence with regard to the execution of expenditure or the maintenance of financial control systems. The Commission shall submit any necessary information to the European Parliament at the latter's request.

3. The Commission shall take all appropriate steps to act on the observations in the decisions giving discharge and on other observations by the European Parliament relating to the execution of expenditure, as well as on comments accompanying the recommendations on discharge adopted by the Council.

At the request of the European Parliament or the Council, the Commission shall report on the measures taken in the light of these observations and comments and in particular on the instructions given to the departments which are responsible for the implementation of the budgets. These reports shall also be forwarded to the Court of Auditors.'

24) Article 183 shall be replaced by the following:

'ARTICLE 183
The Council, acting unanimously on a proposal from the Commission and after consulting the European Parliament and obtaining the opinion of the Court of Auditors, shall:

(a) make Financial Regulations specifying in particular the procedure to be adopted for establishing and implementing the budgets and for presenting and auditing accounts;

(b) determine the methods and procedure whereby the budget revenue provided for under the arrangements relating to the Communities' own resources shall be made available to the Commission, and determine the measures to be applied, if need be, to meet cash requirements;

(c) lay down rules concerning the responsibility of financial controllers, authorizing officers and accounting officers, and concerning appropriate arrangements for inspection.'

25) The following Article shall be inserted:

'ARTICLE 183a
Member States shall take the same measures to counter fraud affecting the financial interests of the Community as they take to counter fraud affecting their own financial interests.

Without prejudice to other provisions of this Treaty, Member States shall co-ordinate their actions aimed at protecting the financial interests of the Community against fraud. To this end they shall organize, with the help of the Commission, close and regular co-operation between the component services of their administrations.'

26) Article 198(a) shall be replaced by the following:

'(a) This Treaty shall not apply to the Faroe Islands.'

27) Article 201 shall be replaced by the following:

'ARTICLE 201
The Community shall establish close cooperation with the Organization for Economic Cooperation and Development, the details of which shall be determined by common accord.'

28) Articles 204 and 205 shall be repealed.

29) Article 206 shall be replaced by the following:

'ARTICLE 206
The Community may conclude with one or more States or international organizations agreements establishing an association involving reciprocal rights and obligations, common action and special procedures.
These agreements shall be concluded by the Council, acting unanimously after consulting the European Parliament.
Where such agreements call for amendments to this Treaty, these amendments shall first be adopted in accordance with the procedure laid down in Article N of the Treaty on European Union.'

TITLE V

PROVISIONS
ON A COMMON FOREIGN AND SECURITY POLICY

ARTICLE J
A common foreign and security policy is hereby established which shall be governed by the following provisions.

ARTICLE J.1
1. The Union and its Member States shall define and implement a common foreign and security policy, governed by the provisions of this Title and covering all areas of foreign and security policy.
2. The objectives of the common foreign and security policy shall be:
— to safeguard the common values, fundamental interests and independence of the Union;
— to strengthen the security of the Union and its Member States in all ways;
— to preserve peace and strengthen international security, in accordance with the principles of the United Nations Charter as well as the principles of the Helsinki Final Act and the objectives of the Paris Charter;
— to promote international co-operation;
— to develop and consolidate democracy and the rule of law, and respect for human rights and fundamental freedoms.
3. The Union shall pursue these objectives:
— by establishing systematic cooperation between Member States in the conduct of policy, in accordance with Article J.2;

— by gradually implementing, in accordance with Article J.3, joint action in the areas in which the Member States have important interests in common.

4. The Member States shall support the Union's external and security policy actively and unreservedly in a spirit of loyalty and mutual solidarity.

They shall refrain from any action which is contrary to the interests of the Union or likely to impair its effectiveness as a cohesive force in international relations. The Council shall ensure that these principles are complied with.

ARTICLE J.2

1. Member States shall inform and consult one another within the Council on any matter of foreign and security policy of general interest in order to ensure that their combined influence is exerted as effectively as possible by means of concerted and convergent action.

2. Whenever it deems it necessary, the Council shall define a common position.

Member States shall ensure that their national policies conform to the common positions.

3. Member States shall coordinate their action in international organizations and at international conferences. They shall uphold the common positions in such fora. In international organizations and at international conferences where not all the Member States participate, those which do take part shall uphold the common positions.

ARTICLE J.3

The procedure for adopting joint action in matters covered by the foreign and security policy shall be the following:

1. The Council shall decide, on the basis of general guidelines from the European Council, that a matter should be the subject of joint action.

Whenever the Council decides on the principle of joint action, it shall lay down the specific scope, the Union's general and specific objectives in carrying out such action, if necessary its duration, and the means, procedures and conditions for its implementation.

2. The Council shall, when adopting the joint action and at any stage during its development, define those matters on which decisions are to be taken by a qualified majority.

Where the Council is required to act by a qualified majority pursuant to the preceding subparagraph, the votes of its members shall be weighted in accordance with Article 148(2) of the Treaty establishing the European Community, and for their adoption, acts of the Council shall require at least fifty-four votes in favour, cast by at least eight members.

3. If there is a change in circumstances having a substantial effect on a question subject to joint action, the Council shall review the principles and objectives of that action and take the necessary decisions. As long as the Council has not acted, the joint action shall stand.

4. Joint actions shall commit the Member States in the positions they adopt and in the conduct of their activity.

5. Whenever there is any plan to adopt a national position or take national action pursuant to a joint action, information shall be provided in time to allow, if necessary, for prior consultations within the Council. The obligation to provide prior information shall not apply to measures which are merely a national transposition of Council decisions.

6. In cases of imperative need arising from changes in the situation and failing a Council decision, Member States may take the necessary measures as a matter of urgency having regard to the general objectives of the joint action. The Member State concerned shall inform the Council immediately of any such measures.

7. Should there by any major difficulties in implementing a joint action, a Member State shall refer them to the Council which shall discuss them and seek appropriate solutions. Such solutions shall not run counter to the objectives of the joint action or impair its effectiveness.

ARTICLE J.4

1. The common foreign and security policy shall include all questions related to the security of the Union, including the eventual framing of a common defence policy, which might in time lead to a common defence.

2. The Union requests the Western European Union (WEU), which is an integral part of the development of the Union, to elaborate and implement decisions and actions of the Union which have defence implications. The Council shall, in agreement with the institutions of the WEU, adopt the necessary practical arrangements.

3. Issues having defence implications dealt with under this Article shall not be subject to the procedures set out in Article J.3.

4. The policy of the Union in accordance with this Article shall not prejudice the specific character of the security and defence policy of certain Member States and shall respect the obligations of certain Member States under the North Atlantic Treaty and be compatible with the common security and defence policy established within that framework.

5. The provisions of this Article shall not prevent the development of closer cooperation between two or more Member States on a bilateral level, in the framework of the WEU and the Atlantic Alliance, provided such cooperation does not run counter to or impede that provided for in this Title.

6. With a view to furthering the objective of this Treaty, and having in view the date of 1998 in the context of Article XII of the Brussels Treaty, the provisions of this Article may be revised as provided for in Article N (2) on the basis of a report to be presented in 1996 by the Council to the European Council, which shall include an evaluation of the progress made and the experience gained until then.

ARTICLE J.5

1. The Presidency shall represent the Union in matters coming within the common foreign and security policy.

2. The Presidency shall be responsible for the implementation of common measures; in that capacity it shall in principle express the position of the Union in international organizations and international conferences.

3. In the tasks referred to in paragraphs 1 and 2, the Presidency shall be assisted if need be by the previous and next Member States to hold the Presidency. The Commission shall be fully associated in these tasks.

4. Without prejudice to Article J.2(3) and Article J.3(4). Member States represented in international organizations or international conferences where not all the Member States participate shall keep the latter informed of any matter of common interest.

Member States which are also members of the United Nations Security Council will concert and keep the other Member States fully informed. Member States which are permanent members of the Security Council will, in the execution of their functions, ensure the defence of the positions and the interests of the Union, without prejudice to their responsibilities under the provisions of the United Nations Charter.

ARTICLE J.6

The diplomatic and consular missions of the Member States and the Commission Delegations in third countries and international conferences, and their representatives to international organizations, shall co-operate in ensuring that the common positions and common measures adopted by the Council are complied with and implemented. They shall step up cooperation by exchanging information, carrying out joint assessments and contributing to the implementation of the provisions referred to in Article 8c of the Treaty establishing the European Community.

ARTICLE J.7

The Presidency shall consult the European Parliament on the main aspects and the basic choices of the common foreign and security policy and shall ensure that the views of the European Parliament are duly taken into consideration. The European Parliament shall be kept regularly informed by the Presidency and the Commission of the development of the Union's foreign and security policy.

The European Parliament may ask questions of the Council or make recommendations to it. It shall hold an annual debate on progress in implementing the common foreign and security policy.

ARTICLE J.8

1. The European Council shall define the principles of and general guidelines for the common foreign and security policy.

2. The Council shall take the decisions necessary for defining and implementing the common foreign and security policy on the basis of the general guidelines adopted by the European Council. It shall ensure the unity, consistency and effectiveness of action by the Union.

The Council shall act unanimously, except for procedural questions and in the case referred to in Article J.3(2).

3. Any Member State or the Commission may refer to the Council any question relating to the common foreign and security policy and may submit proposals to the Council.

4. In cases requiring a rapid decision, the Presidency, of its own motion, or at the request of the Commission or a Member State, shall convene an extraordinary Council meeting within forty-eight hours or, in an emergency, within a shorter period.

5. Without prejudice to Article 151 of the Treaty establishing the European Community, a Political Committee consisting of Political Directors shall monitor the international situation in the areas covered by common foreign and security policy and contribute to the definition of policies by delivering opinions to the Council at the request of the Council or on its own initiative. It shall also monitor the implementation of agreed policies, without prejudice to the responsibility of the Presidency and the Commission.

ARTICLE J.9
The Commission shall be fully associated with the work carried out in the common foreign and security policy field.

ARTICLE J.10
On the occasion of any review of the security provisions under Article J.4, the Conference which is convened to that effect shall also examine whether any other amendments need to be made to provisions relating to the common foreign and security policy.

ARTICLE J.11
1. The provisions referred to in Articles 137, 138 to 142, 146, 147, 150 to 153, 157 to 163 and 217 of the Treaty establishing the European Community shall apply to the provisions relating to the areas referred to in this Title.
2. Administrative expenditure which the provisions relating to the areas referred to in this Title entail for the institutions shall be charged to the budget of the European Communities.
The Council may also:
— either decide unanimously that operating expenditure to which the implementation of those provisions gives rise is to be charged to the budget of the European Communities; in that event, the budgetary procedure laid down in the Treaty establishing the European Community shall be applicable;
— or determine that such expenditure shall be charged to the Member States, where appropriate in accordance with a scale to be decided.

TITLE VI

PROVISIONS ON COOPERATION
IN THE FIELDS OF JUSTICE AND HOME AFFAIRS

ARTICLE K
Cooperation in the fields of justice and home affairs shall be governed by the following provisions.

ARTICLE K.1
For the purposes of achieving the objectives of the Union, in particular the free movement of persons, and without prejudice to the powers of the European Community, Member States shall regard the following areas as matters of common interest:
1. asylum policy;
2. rules governing the crossing by persons of the external borders of the Member States and the exercise of controls thereon;
3. immigration policy and policy regarding nationals of third countries:
(a) conditions of entry and movement by nationals of third countries on the territory of Member States;
(b) conditions of residence by nationals of third countries on the territory of Member States, including family reunion and access to employment;
(c) combatting unauthorized immigration, residence and work by nationals of third countries on the territory of Member States;
4. combatting drug addiction in so far as this is not covered by 7 to 9;

5. combatting fraud on an international scale in so far as this is not covered by 7 to 9;
6. judicial cooperation in civil matters;
7. judicial cooperation in criminal matters;
8. customs cooperation;
9. police cooperation for the purposes of preventing and combatting terrorism, unlawful drug trafficking and other serious forms of international crime, including if necessary certain aspects of customs cooperation, in connection with the organization of a Union-wide system for exchanging information within a European Police Office (Europol).

ARTICLE K.2
1. The matters referred to in Article K.1 shall be dealt with in compliance with the European Convention for the Protection of Human Rights and Fundamental Freedoms of 4 November 1950 and the Convention relating to the Status of Refugees of 28 July 1951 and having regard to the protection afforded by Member States to persons persecuted on political grounds.
2. This Title shall not affect the exercise of the responsibilities incumbent upon Member States with regard to the maintenance of law and order and the safeguarding of internal security.

ARTICLE K.3
1. In the areas referred to in Article K.1, Member States shall inform and consult one another within the Council with a view to co-ordinating their action. To that end, they shall establish collaboration between the relevant departments of their administrations.
2. The Council may:
— on the initiative of any Member State or of the Commission, in the areas referred to in Article K.1(1) to (6);
— on the initiative of any Member State, in the areas referred to in Article K1(7) to (9):
(a) adopt joint positions and promote, using the appropriate form and procedures, any cooperation contributing to the pursuit of the objectives of the Union;
(b) adopt joint action in so far as the objectives of the Union can be attained better by joint action than by the Member States acting individually on account of the scale or effects of the action envisaged; it may decide that measures implementing joint action are to be adopted by a qualified majority;
(c) without prejudice to Article 220 of the Treaty establishing the European Community, draw up conventions which it shall recommend to the Member States for adoption in accordance with their respective constitutional requirements.
Unless otherwise provided by such conventions, measures implementing them shall be adopted within the Council by a majority of two-thirds of the High Contracting Parties.
Such conventions may stipulate that the Court of Justice shall have jurisdiction to interpret their provisions and to rule on any disputes regarding their application, in accordance with such arrangements as they may lay down.

ARTICLE K.4
1. A Coordinating Committee shall be set up consisting of senior officials. In addition to its coordinating role, it shall be the task of the Committee to:

— give opinions for the attention of the Council, either at the Council's request or on its own initiative;
— contribute, without prejudice to Article 151 of the Treaty establishing the European Community, to the preparation of the Council's discussions in the areas referred to in Article K.1 and, in accordance with the conditions laid down in Article 100d of the Treaty establishing the European Community, in the areas referred to in Article 100c of that Treaty.
2. The Commission shall be fully associated with the work in the areas referred to in this Title.
3. The Council shall act unanimously, except on matters of procedure and in cases where Article K.3 expressly provides for other voting rules.
Where the Council is required to act by a qualified majority, the votes of its members shall be weighted as laid down in Article 148(2) of the Treaty establishing the European Community, and for their adoption, acts of the Council shall require at least fifty-four votes in favour, cast by at least eight members.

ARTICLE K.5
Within international organizations and at international conferences in which they take part, Member States shall defend the common positions adopted under the provisions of this Title.

ARTICLE K.6
The Presidency and the Commission shall regularly inform the European Parliament of discussions in the areas covered by this Title. The Presidency shall consult the European Parliament on the principal aspects of activities in the areas referred to in this Title and shall ensure that the views of the European Parliament are duly taken into consideration. The European Parliament may ask questions of the Council or make recommendations to it. Each year, it shall hold a debate on the progress made in implementation of the areas referred to in this Title.

ARTICLE K.7
The provisions of this Title shall not prevent the establishment or development of closer cooperation between two or more Member States in so far as such cooperation does not conflict with, or impede, that provided for in this Title.

ARTICLE K.8
1. The provisions referred to in Articles 137, 138 to 142, 146, 147, 150 to 153, 157 to 163 and 217 of the Treaty establishing the European Community shall apply to the provisions relating to the areas referred to in this Title.
2. Administrative expenditure which the provisions relating to the areas referred to in this Title entail for the institutions shall be charged to the budget of the European Communities.
The Council may also:
— either decide unanimously that operating expenditure to which the implementation of those provisions gives rise is to be charged to the budget of the European Communities; in that event, the budgetary procedure laid down in the Treaty establishing the European Community shall be applicable;
— or determine that such expenditure shall be charged to the Member States, where appropriate in accordance with a scale to be decided.

ARTICLE K.9

The Council, acting unanimously on the initiative of the Commission or a Member State, may decide to apply Article 100c to the Treaty establishing the European Community to action in areas referred to in Article K.1(1) to (6), and at the same time determine the relevant voting conditions relating to it. It shall recommend the Member States to adopt that decision in accordance with their respective constitutional requirements.

TITLE VII

FINAL PROVISIONS

ARTICLE L

The provisions of the Treaty establishing the European Community, the Treaty establishing the European Coal and Steel Community and the Treaty establishing the European Atomic Energy Community concerning the powers of the Court of Justice of the European Communities and the exercise of those powers shall apply only to the following provisions of this Treaty:

(a) provisions amending the Treaty establishing the European Economic Community with a view to establishing the European Community, the Treaty establishing the European Coal and Steel Community and the Treaty establishing the European Atomic Energy Community;

(b) the third subparagraph of Article K.3(2c);

(c) Articles L to S.

ARTICLE M

Subject to the provisions amending the Treaty establishing the European Economic Community with a view to establishing the European Community, the Treaty establishing the European Coal and Steel Community and the Treaty establishing the European Atomic Energy Community, and to these final provisions, nothing in this Treaty shall affect the Treaties establishing the European Communities or the subsequent Treaties and Acts modifying or supplementing them.

ARTICLE N

1. The government of any Member State or the Commission may submit to the Council proposals for the amendment of the Treaties on which the Union is founded.

If the Council, after consulting the European Parliament and, where appropriate, the Commission, delivers an opinion in favour of calling a conference of representatives of the governments of the Member States, the conference shall be convened by the President of the Council for the purpose of determining by common accord the amendments to be made to those Treaties. The European Central Bank shall also be consulted in the case of institutional changes in the monetary area.

The amendments shall enter into force after being ratified by all the Member States in accordance with their respective constitutional requirements.

2. A conference of representatives of the governments of the Member States shall be convened in 1996 to examine those provisions of this Treaty for which revision is provided, in accordance with the objectives set out in Articles A and B.

ARTICLE O

Any European State may apply to become a Member of the Union. It shall address its application to the Council, which shall act unanimously after consulting the Commission and after receiving the assent of the European Parliament, which shall act by an absolute majority of its component members.

The conditions of admission and the adjustments to the Treaties on which the Union is founded which such admission entails shall be the subject of an agreement between the Member States and the applicant State. This agreement shall be submitted for ratification by all the Contracting States in accordance with their respective constitutional requirements.

ARTICLE P

1. Articles 2 to 7 and 10 to 19 of the Treaty establishing a single Council and a single Commission of the European Communities, signed in Brussels on 8 April 1965, are hereby repealed.

2. Article 2, Article 3(2) and Title III of the Single European Act signed in Luxembourg on 17 February 1986 and in The Hague on 28 February 1986 are hereby repealed.

ARTICLE Q

This Treaty is concluded for an unlimited period.

ARTICLE R

1. This Treaty shall be ratified by the High Contracting Parties in accordance with their respective constitutional requirements. The instruments of ratification shall be deposited with the government of the Italian Republic.

2. This Treaty shall enter into force on 1 January 1993, provided that all the instruments of ratification have been deposited, or, failing that, on the first day of the month following the deposit of the instrument of ratification by the last signatory State to take this step.

ARTICLE S

This Treaty, drawn up in a single original in the Danish, Dutch, English, French, German, Greek, Irish, Italian, Portuguese and Spanish languages, the texts in each of these languages being equally authentic, shall be deposited in the archives of the government of the Italian Republic, which will transmit a certified copy to each of the governments of the other signatory States.

IN WITNESS WHEREOF, the undersigned Plenipotentiaries have signed this Treaty.

Done at   , on

PROTOCOLS
PROTOCOL
ON THE ACQUISITION OF PROPERTY IN DENMARK

THE HIGH CONTRACTING PARTIES,

DESIRING to settle certain particular problems relating to Denmark,

HAVE AGREED UPON the following provision, which shall be annexed to the Treaty establishing the European Community: Notwithstanding the provisions of this Treaty, Denmark may maintain the existing legislation on the acquisition of second homes.

PROTOCOL CONCERNING ARTICLE 119
OF THE TREATY ESTABLISHING THE EUROPEAN COMMUNITY
THE HIGH CONTRACTING PARTIES,

HAVE AGREED UPON the following provision, which shall be annexed to the Treaty establishing the European Community:

For the purposes of Article 119 of this Treaty, benefits under occupational social security schemes shall not be considered as remuneration if and in so far as they are attributable to periods of employment prior to 17 May 1990, except in the case of workers or those claiming under them who have before that date initiated legal proceedings or introduced an equivalent claim under the applicable national law.

PROTOCOL ON THE STATUTE
OF THE EUROPEAN SYSTEM OF CENTRAL BANKS AND OF THE
EUROPEAN CENTRAL BANK
THE HIGH CONTRACTING PARTIES,

DESIRING to lay down the Statute of the European System of Central Banks and of the European Central Bank provided for in Article 4a of the Treaty establishing the European Community,

HAVE AGREED upon the following provisions, which shall be annexed to the Treaty establishing the European Community:

CHAPTER 1
CONSTITUTION OF THE ESCB

ARTICLE 1
The European System of Central Banks
1.1. The European System of Central Banks (ESCB) and the European Central Bank (ECB) shall be established in accordance with Article 4a of this Treaty; they shall perform their tasks and carry on their activities in accordance with the provisions of this Treaty and of this Statute.
1.2. In accordance with Article 106(1) of this Treaty, the ESCB shall be composed of the ECB and of the central banks of the Member States ('national central banks'). The Institut monétaire luxembourgeois will be the central bank of Luxembourg.

CHAPTER II

OBJECTIVES AND TASKS OF THE ESCB

ARTICLE 2
Objectives
In accordance with Article 105(1) of this Treaty, the primary objective of the ESCB shall be to maintain price stability.
Without prejudice to the objective of price stability, it shall support the general economic policies in the Community with a view to contributing to the achievement of the objectives of the Community as laid down in Article 2 of this Treaty.
The ESCB shall act in accordance with the principle of an open market economy with free competition, favouring an efficient allocation of resources, and in compliance with the principles set out in Article 3a of this Treaty.

ARTICLE 3
Tasks
3.1. In accordance with Article 105(2) of this Treaty, the basic tasks to be carried out through the ESCB shall be:
— to define and implement the monetary policy of the Community;
— to conduct foreign exchange operations consistent with the provisions of Article 109 of this Treaty;
— to hold and manage the official foreign reserves of the Member States;
— to promote the smooth operation of payment systems.

3.2. In accordance with Article 105(3) of this Treaty, the third indent of Article 3.1 shall be without prejudice to the holding and management by the governments of Member States of foreign exchange working balances.
3.3. In accordance with Article 105(5) of this Treaty, the ESCB shall contribute to the smooth conduct of policies pursued by the competent authorities relating to the prudential supervision of credit institutions and the stability of the financial system.

ARTICLE 4
Advisory functions
In accordance with Article 105(4) of this Treaty:

(a) the ECB shall be consulted:
— on any proposed Community act in its fields of competence;
— by national authorities regarding any draft legislative provision in its fields of competence, but within the limits and under the conditions set out by the Council in accordance with the procedure laid down in Article 42;
(b) the ECB may submit opinions to the appropriate Community institutions or bodies or to national authorities on matters in its fields of competence.

ARTICLE 5
Collection of statistical information
5.1. In order to undertake the tasks of the ESCB, the ECB, assisted by the national central banks, shall collect the necessary statistical information either from the competent national authorities or directly from economic agents. For these purposes it shall cooperate with the Community institutions or bodies and

with the competent authorities of the Member States or third countries and with international organizations.

5.2. The national central banks shall carry out, to the extent possible, the tasks described in Article 5.1.

5.3. The ECB shall contribute to the harmonization, where necessary, of the rules and practices governing the collection, compilation and distribution of statistics in the areas within its fields of competence.

5.4. The Council, in accordance with the procedure laid down in Article 42, shall define the natural and legal persons subject to reporting requirements, the confidentiality regime and the appropriate provisions for enforcement.

ARTICLE 6
International cooperation

6.1. In the field of international cooperation involving the tasks entrusted to the ESCB, the ECB shall decide how the ESCB shall be represented.

6.2. The ECB and, subject to its approval, the national central banks may participate in international monetary institutions.

6.3. Articles 6.1 and 6.2 shall be without prejudice to Article 109(4) of this Treaty.

CHAPTER III
ORGANIZATION OF THE ESCB

ARTICLE 7
Independence

In accordance with Article 107 of this Treaty, when exercising the powers and carrying out the tasks and duties conferred upon them by this Treaty and this Statute, neither the ECB, nor a national central bank, nor any member of their decision-making bodies shall seek or take instructions from Community institutions or bodies, from any government of a Member State or from any other body. The Community institutions and bodies and the governments of the Member States undertake to respect this principle and not to seek to influence the members of the decision-making bodies of the ECB or of the national central banks in the performance of their tasks.

ARTICLE 8
General principle

The ESCB shall be governed by the decision-making bodies of the ECB.

ARTICLE 9
The European Central Bank

9.1. The ECB which, in accordance with Article 106(2) of this Treaty, shall have legal personality, shall enjoy in each of the Member States the most extensive legal capacity accorded to legal persons under its law; it may, in particular, acquire or dispose of movable and immovable property and may be a party to legal proceedings.

9.2. The ECB shall ensure that the tasks conferred upon the ESCB under Article 105(2), (3) and (5) of this Treaty are implemented either by its own activities pursuant to this Statute or through the national central banks pursuant to Articles 12.1 and 14.

9.3. In accordance with Article 106(3) of this Treaty, the decision-making bodies of the ECB shall be the Governing Council and the Executive Board.

ARTICLE 10
The Governing Council
10.1. In accordance with Article 109a(1) of this Treaty, the Governing Council shall comprise the members of the Executive Board of the ECB and the Governors of the national central banks.

10.2. Subject to Article 10.3, only members of the Governing Council present in person shall have the right to vote. By way of derogation from this rule, The Rules of Procedure referred to in Article 12.3 may lay down that members of the Governing Council may cast their vote by means of teleconferencing. These rules shall also provide that a member of the Governing Council who is prevented from voting for a prolonged period may appoint an alternate as a member of the Governing Council.

Subject to Articles 10.3 and 11.3, each member of the Governing Council shall have one vote. Save as otherwise provided for in this Statute, the Governing Council shall act by a simple majority. In the event of a tie, the President shall have the casting vote.

In order for the Governing Council to vote, there shall be a quorum of two-thirds of the members. If the quorum is not met, the President may convene an extraordinary meeting at which decisions may be taken without regard to the quorum.

10.3. For any decisions to be taken under Articles 28, 29, 30, 32, 33 and 51, the votes in the Governing Council shall be weighted according to the national central banks' shares in the subscribed capital of the ECB. The weights of the votes of the members of the Executive Board shall be zero. A decision requiring a qualified majority shall be adopted if the votes cast in favour represent at least two thirds of the subscribed capital of the ECB and represent at least half of the shareholders. If a Governor is unable to be present, he may nominate an alternate to cast his weighted vote.

10.4. The proceedings of the meetings shall be confidential. The Governing Council may decide to make the outcome of its deliberations public.

10.5. The Governing Council shall meet at least ten times a year.

ARTICLE 11
The Executive Board
11.1. In accordance with Article 109a(2)(a) of this Treaty, the Executive Board shall comprise the President, the Vice-President and four other members.

The members shall perform their duties on a full-time basis. No member shall engage in any occupation, whether gainful or not, unless exemption is exceptionally granted by the Governing Council.

11.2. In accordance with Article 109a(2)(b) of this Treaty, the President, the Vice-President and the other Members of the Executive Board shall be appointed from among persons of recognized standing and professional experience in monetary or banking matters by common accord by the governments of the Member States at the level of the Heads of State or of Government, on a recommendation from the Council after it has consulted the European Parliament and the Governing Council.

Their term of office shall be 8 years and shall not be renewable. Only nationals of Member States may be members of the Executive Board.

11.3. The terms and conditions of employment of the members of the Executive Board, in particular their salaries, pensions and other social security benefits shall be the subject of contracts with the ECB and shall be fixed by the Governing Council on a proposal from a Committee comprising three members appointed by the Governing Council and three members appointed by the Council. The members of the Executive Board shall not have the right to vote on matters referred to in this paragraph.

11.4. If a member of the Executive Board no longer fulfils the conditions required for the performance of his duties or if he has been guilty of serious misconduct, the Court of Justice may, on application by the Governing Council or the Executive Board, compulsorily retire him.

11.5. Each member of the Executive Board present in person shall have the right to vote and shall have, for that purpose, one vote. Save as otherwise provided, the Executive Board shall act by simple majority of the votes cast. In the event of a tie, the President shall have the casting vote. The voting arrangements shall be specified in the Rules of Procedure referred to in Article 12.3.

11.6. The Executive Board shall be responsible for the current business of the ECB.

11.7. Any vacancy on the Executive Board shall be filled by the appointment of a new member in accordance with Article 11.2.

ARTICLE 12
Responsibilities of the decision-making bodies

12.1. The Governing Council shall adopt the guidelines and take the decisions necessary to ensure the performance of the tasks entrusted to the ESCB under this Treaty and this Statute. The Governing Council shall formulate the monetary policy of the Community including, as appropriate, decisions relating to intermediate monetary objectives, key interest rates and the supply of reserves in the ESCB, and shall establish the necessary guidelines for their implementation.

The Executive Board shall implement monetary policy in accordance with the guidelines and decisions laid down by the Governing Council. In doing so the Executive Board shall give the necessary instructions to national central banks. In addition the Executive Board may have certain powers delegated to it where the Governing Council so decides.

To the extent deemed possible and appropriate and without prejudice to the provisions of this Article, the ECB shall have recourse to the national central banks to carry out operations which form part of the tasks of the ESCB.

12.2. The Executive Board shall have responsibility for the preparation of meetings of the Governing Council.

12.3. The Governing Council shall adopt Rules of Procedure which determine the internal organization of the ECB and its decision-making bodies.

12.4. The Governing Council shall exercise the advisory functions referred to in Article 4.

12.5. The Governing Council shall take the decisions referred to in Article 6.

ARTICLE 13
The President
13.1. The President or, in his absence, the Vice-President shall chair the Governing Council and the Executive Board of the ECB.
13.2. Without prejudice to Article 39, the President or his nominee shall represent the ECB externally.

ARTICLE 14
National central banks
14.1. In accordance with Article 108 of this Treaty, each Member State shall ensure, at the latest at the date of the establishment of the ESCB, that its national legislation, including the statutes of its national central bank, is compatible with this Treaty and this Statute.
14.2. The statutes of the national central banks shall, in particular, provide that the term of office of a Governor of a national central bank shall be no less than 5 years.
A Governor may be relieved from office only if he no longer fulfils the conditions required for the performance of his duties or if he has been guilty of serious misconduct.
A decision to this effect may be referred to the Court of Justice by the Governor concerned or the Governing Council on grounds of infringement of this Treaty or of any rule of law relating to its application. Such proceedings shall be instituted within two months of the publication of the decision or of its notification to the plaintiff or, in the absence thereof, of the day on which it came to the knowledge of the latter, as the case may be.
14.3. The national central banks are an integral part of the ESCB and shall act in accordance with the guidelines and instructions of the ECB. The Governing Council shall take the necessary steps to ensure compliance with the guidelines and instructions of the ECB, and shall require that any necessary information be given to it.
14.4. National central banks may perform functions other than those specified in this Statute unless the Governing Council finds, by a majority of two thirds of the votes cast, that these interfere with the objectives and tasks of the ESCB. Such functions shall be performed on the responsibility and liability of national central banks and shall not be regarded as being part of the functions of the ESCB.

ARTICLE 15
Reporting commitments
15.1. The ECB shall draw up and publish reports on the activities of the ESCB at least quarterly.
15.2. A consolidated financial statement of the ESCB shall be published each week.
15.3. In accordance with Article 109b(3) of this Treaty, the ECB shall address an annual report on the activities of the ESCB and on the monetary policy of both the previous and the current year to the European Parliament, the Council and the Commission, and also to the European Council.
15.4. The reports and statements referred to in this Article shall be made available to interested parties free of charge.

ARTICLE 16
Bank notes
In accordance with Article 105a(1) of this Treaty, the Governing Council shall have the exclusive right to authorize the issue of bank notes within the Community. The ECB and the national central banks may issue such notes. The bank notes issued by the ECB and the national central banks shall be the only such notes to have the status of legal tender within the Community.
The ECB shall respect as far as possible existing practices regarding the issue and design of bank notes.

CHAPTER IV
MONETARY FUNCTIONS
AND OPERATIONS OF THE ESCB

ARTICLE 17
Accounts with the ECB and the national central banks
In order to conduct their operations, the ECB and the national central banks may open accounts for credit institutions, public entities and other market participants and accept assets, including book-entry securities, as collateral.

ARTICLE 18
Open market and credit operations
18.1. In order to achieve the objectives of the ESCB and to carry out its tasks, the ECB and the national central banks may:
— operate in the financial markets by buying and selling outright (spot and forward) or under repurchase agreement and by lending or borrowing claims and marketable instruments, whether in Community or in non-Community currencies, as well as precious metals;
— conduct credit operations with credit institutions and other market participants, with lending being based on adequate collateral.
18.2. The ECB shall establish general principles for open markets and credit operations carried out by itself or the national central banks, including for the announcement of conditions under which they stand ready to enter into such transactions.

ARTICLE 19
Minimum reserves
19.1. Subject to Article 2, the ECB may require credit institutions established in Member States to hold minimum reserves on accounts with the ECB and national central banks in pursuance of monetary policy objectives. Regulations concerning the calculation and determination of the required minimum reserves may be established by the Governing Council. In cases of non-compliance the ECB shall be entitled to levy penalty interest and to impose other sanctions with comparable effect.
19.2. For the application of this Article, the Council shall, in accordance with the procedure laid down in Article 42, define the basis for minimum reserves and the maximum permissible ratios between those reserves and their basis, as well as the appropriate sanctions in cases on non-compliance.

ARTICLE 20
Other instruments of monetary control
The Governing Council may, by a majority of two thirds of the votes cast, decide upon the use of such other operational methods of monetary control as it sees fit, respecting Article 2.
The Council shall, in accordance with the procedure laid down in Article 42, define the scope of such methods if they impose obligations on third parties.

ARTICLE 21
Operations with public entities
21.1. In accordance with Article 104 of this Treaty, overdrafts or any other type of credit facility with the ECB or with the national central banks in favour of Community institutions or bodies, central governments, regional, local or other public authorities, other bodies governed by public law or public undertakings of Member States shall be prohibited, as shall the purchase directly from them by the ECB or national central banks of debt instruments.
21.2. The ECB and national central banks may act as fiscal agents for the entities referred to in Article 21.1.
21.3. The provisions of this Article shall not apply to publicly-owned credit institutions which, in the context of the supply of reserves by central banks, shall be given the same treatment by national central banks and the ECB as private credit institutions.

ARTICLE 22
Clearing and payment systems
The ECB and national central banks may provide facilities, and the ECB may make regulations, to ensure efficient and sound clearing and payment systems within the Community and with other countries.

ARTICLE 23
External operations
The ECB and national central banks may:
— establish relations with central banks and financial institutions in other countries and, where appropriate, with international organizations;
— acquire and sell spot and forward all types of foreign exchange assets and precious metals; the term 'foreign exchange asset' shall include securities and all other assets in the currency of any country or units of account and in whatever form held;
— hold and manage the assets referred to in this Article;
— conduct all types of banking transactions in relations with third countries and international organizations, including borrowing and lending operations.

ARTICLE 24
Other operations
In addition to operations arising from their tasks, the ECB and national central banks may enter into operations for their administrative purposes or for their staff.

CHAPTER V
PRUDENTIAL SUPERVISION

ARTICLE 25
Prudential supervision
25.1. The ECB may offer advice to and be consulted by the Council, the Commission and the competent authorities of the Member States on the scope and implementation of Community legislation relating to the prudential supervision of credit institutions and to the stability of the financial system.
25.2. In accordance with any decision of the Council under Article 105(6) of this Treaty, the ECB may perform specific tasks concerning policies relating to the prudential supervision of credit institutions and other financial institutions with the exception of insurance undertakings.

CHAPTER VI
FINANCIAL PROVISIONS OF THE ESCB

ARTICLE 26
Financial accounts
26.1. The financial year of the ECB and national central banks shall begin on the first day of January and end on the last day of December.
26.2. The annual accounts of the ECB shall be drawn up by the Executive Board, in accordance with the principles established by the Governing Council.
The accounts shall be approved by the Governing Council and shall thereafter be published.
26.3. For analytical and operational purposes, the Executive Board shall draw up a consolidated balance sheet of the ESCB, comprising those assets and liabilities of the national central banks that fall within the ESCB.
26.4. For the application of this Article, the Governing Council shall establish the necessary rules for standardizing the accounting and reporting of operations undertaken by the national central banks.

ARTICLE 27
Auditing
27.1. The accounts of the ECB and national central banks shall be audited by independent external auditors recommended by the Governing Council and approved by the Council.
The auditors shall have full power to examine all books and accounts of the ECB and national central banks and obtain full information about their transactions.
27.2. The provisions of Article 188b of this Treaty shall only apply to an examination of the operational efficiency of the management of the ECB.

ARTICLE 28
Capital of the ECB
28.1. The capital of the ECB, which shall become operational upon its establishment, shall be ECU 5 000 million.
The capital may be increased by such amounts as may be decided by the Governing Council acting by the qualified majority provided for in Article 10.3, within the limits and under the conditions set by the Council under the procedure laid down in Article 42.
28.2. The national central banks shall be the sole subscribers to and holders of the capital of the ECB. The subscription of capital shall be according to the key established in accordance with Article 29.

28.3. The Governing Council, acting by the qualified majority provided for in Article 10.3, shall determine the extent to which and the form in which the capital shall be paid up.

28.4. Subject to Article 28.5, the shares of the national central banks in the subscribed capital of the ECB may not be transferred, pledged or attached.

28.5. If the key referred to in Article 29 is adjusted, the national central banks shall transfer among themselves capital shares to the extent necessary to ensure that the distribution of capital shares corresponds to the adjusted key.

The Governing Council shall determine the terms and conditions of such transfers.

ARTICLE 29
Key for capital subscription

29.1. When in accordance with the procedure referred to in Article 109(1) of this Treaty the ESCB and the ECB have been established, the key for subscription of the ECB's capital shall be established. Each national central bank shall be assigned a weighting in this key which shall be equal to the sum of:

— 50% of the share of its respective Member State in the population of the Community in the penultimate year preceding the establishment of the ESCB;

— 50% of the share of its respective Member State in the gross domestic product at market prices of the Community as recorded in the last five years preceding the penultimate year before the establishment of the ESCB;

The percentages shall be rounded up to the nearest multiple of 0,05% points.

29.2. The statistical data to be used for the application of this Article shall be provided by the Commission in accordance with the rules adopted by the Council under the procedure provided for in Article 42.

29.3. The weightings assigned to the national central banks shall be adjusted every five years after the establishment of the ESCB by analogy with the provisions laid down in Article 29.1.

The adjusted key shall apply with effect from the first day of the following year.

29.4. The Governing Council shall take all other measures necessary for the application of this Article.

ARTICLE 30
Transfer of foreign reserve assets to the ECB

30.1. Without prejudice to Article 28, the ECB shall be provided by the national central banks with foreign reserve assets, other than Member States' currencies, ECUs, IMF reserve positions and SDRs, up to an amount equivalent to ECU 50 000 million. The Governing Council shall decide upon the proportion to be called up by the ECB following its establishment and the amounts called up at later dates.

The ECB shall have the full right to hold and manage the foreign reserves that are transferred to it and to use them for the purposes set out in this Statute.

30.2. The contributions of each national central bank shall be fixed in proportion to its share in the subscribed capital of the ECB.

30.3. Each national central bank shall be credited by the ECB with a claim equivalent to its contribution.

The Governing Council shall determine the denomination and remuneration of such claims.

30.4. Further calls of foreign reserve assets beyond the limit set in Article 30.1 may be effected by the ECB, in accordance with Article 30.2, within the limits and under the conditions set by the Council in accordance with the procedure laid down in Article 42.

30.5. The ECB may hold and manage IMF reserve positions and SDRs and provide for the pooling of such assets.

30.6. The Governing Council shall take all other measures necessary for the application of this Article.

ARTICLE 31
Foreign reserve assets held by national central banks

31.1. The national central banks shall be allowed to perform transactions in fulfilment of their obligations towards international organizations in accordance with Article 23.

31.2. All other operations in foreign reserve assets remaining with the national central banks after the transfers referred to in Article 30, and Member States' transactions with their foreign exchange working balances shall, above a certain limit to be established within the framework of Article 31.3, be subject to approval by the ECB in order to ensure consistency with the exchange rate and monetary policies of the Community.

31.3. The Governing Council shall issue guidelines with a view to facilitating such operations.

ARTICLE 32
Allocation of monetary income of national central banks

32.1. The income accruing to the national central banks in the performance of the ESCB's monetary policy function (hereinafter referred to as 'monetary income') shall be allocated at the end of each financial year in accordance with the provisions of this Article.

32.2. Subject to Article 32.3, the amount of each national central bank's monetary income shall be equal to its annual income derived from its assets held against notes in circulation and deposit liabilities to credit institutions. These assets shall be earmarked by national central banks in accordance with guidelines to be established by the Governing Council.

32.3. If, after the start of the third stage, the balance sheet structures of the national central banks do not, in the judgment of the Governing Council, permit the application of Article 32.2, the Governing Council, acting by a qualified majority, may decide that by way of derogation from Article 32.2 monetary income shall be measured according to an alternative method for a period of not more than five years.

32.4. The amount of each national central bank's monetary income shall be reduced by an amount equivalent to any interest paid by that central bank on its deposit liabilities to credit institutions in accordance with Article 19.

The Governing Council may decide that national central banks shall be indemnified against costs incurred in connection with the issue of bank notes or in exceptional circumstances for specific losses arising from monetary policy operations undertaken for the ESCB.

Imdemnification shall be in a form deemed appropriate in the judgment of the Governing Council; these amounts may be offset against the national central bank's monetary income.

32.5. The sum of the national central banks' monetary income shall be allocated to the national central banks in proportion to their paid-up shares in the capital of the ECB, subject to any decision taken by the Governing Council pursuant to Article 33.2.

32.6. The clearing and settlement of the balances arising from the allocation of monetary income shall be carried out by the ECB in accordance with guidelines established by the Governing Council.

32.7. The Governing Council shall take all other measures necessary for the application of this Article.

ARTICLE 33
Allocation of net profits and losses of the ECB

33.1. The net profit of the ECB shall be transferred in the following order:

(a) an amount to be determined by the Governing Council, which may not exceed 20% of the net profit, shall be transferred to the general reserve fund subject to a limit equal to 100% of the capital;

(b) the remaining net profit shall be distributed to the shareholders of the ECB in proportion to their paid-up shares.

33.2. In the event of a loss incurred by the ECB, the shortfall may be offset against the general reserve fund of the ECB and, if necessary, following a decision by the Governing Council, against the monetary income of the relevant financial year in proportion and up to the amounts allocated to the national central banks in accordance with Article 32.5.

CHAPTER VII
GENERAL PROVISIONS

ARTICLE 34
Legal acts

34.1. In accordance with Article 108a of this Treaty, the ECB shall:

— make regulations to the extent necessary to implement the tasks defined in Article 3.1, first indent, Articles 19.1, 22 or 25.2 and in cases which shall be laid down in the acts of the Council referred to in Article 42;

— take decisions necessary for carrying out the tasks entrusted to the ESCB under this Treaty and this Statute;

— make recommendations and deliver opinions.

34.2. A regulation shall have general application. It shall be binding in its entirety and directly applicable in all Member States.

Recommendations and opinions shall have no binding force.

A decision shall be binding in its entirety upon those to whom it is addressed.

Articles 190 and 192 of this Treaty shall apply to regulations and decisions adopted by the ECB.

The ECB may decide to publish its decisions, recommendations and opinions.

34.3. Within the limits and under the conditions adopted by the Council under the procedure laid down in Article 42, the ECB shall be entitled to impose fines or periodic penalty payments on undertakings for failure to comply with obligations under its regulations and decisions.

ARTICLE 35
Judicial control and related matters
35.1. The acts or omissions of the ECB shall be open to review or interpretation by the Court of Justice in the cases and under the conditions laid down in this Treaty.
The ECB may institute proceedings in the cases and under the conditions laid down in this Treaty.
35.2. Disputes between the ECB, on the one hand, and its creditors, debtors or any other person, on the other, shall be decided by the competent national courts, save where jurisdiction has been conferred upon the Court of Justice.
35.3. The ECB shall be subject to the liability regime provided for in Article 215 of this Treaty.
The national central banks shall be liable according to their respective national laws.
35.4. The Court of Justice shall have jurisdiction to give judgment pursuant to any arbitration clause contained in a contract concluded by or on behalf of the ECB, whether that contract be governed by public or private law.
35.5. A decision of the ECB to bring an action before the Court of Justice shall be taken by the Governing Council.
35.6. The Court of Justice shall have jurisdiction in disputes concerning the fulfilment by a national central bank of obligations under this Statute.
If the ECB considers that a national central bank has failed to fulfil an obligation under this Statute, it shall deliver a reasoned opinion on the matter after giving the national central bank concerned the opportunity to submit its observations.
If the national central bank concerned does not comply with the opinion within the period laid down by the ECB, the latter may bring the matter before the Court of Justice.

ARTICLE 36
Staff
36.1. The Governing Council, on a proposal from the Executive Board, shall lay down the conditions of employment of the staff of the ECB.
36.2. The Court of Justice shall have jurisdiction in any dispute between the ECB and its servants within the limits and under the conditions laid down in the conditions of employment.

ARTICLE 37
Seat
Before the end of 1992, the decision as to where the seat of the ECB will be established shall be taken by common accord of the governments of the Member States at the level of Heads of State or of Government.

ARTICLE 38
Professional secrecy
38.1. Members of the governing bodies and the staff of the ECB and the national central banks shall be required, even after their duties have ceased, not to disclose information of the kind covered by the obligation of professional secrecy.
38.2. Persons having access to data covered by Community legislation imposing an obligation of secrecy shall be subject to such legislation.

ARTICLE 39
Signatories
The ECB shall be legally committed to third parties by the President or by two members of the Executive Board or by the signatures of two members of the staff of the ECB who have been duly authorized by the President to sign on behalf of the ECB.

ARTICLE 40
Privileges and immunities
The ECB shall enjoy in the territories of the Member States such privileges and immunities as are necessary for the performance of its tasks, under the conditions laid down in the Protocol on the Privileges and Immunities of the European Communities annexed to the Treaty establishing a Single Council and a Single Commission of the European Communities.

CHAPTER VIII
AMENDMENT OF THE STATUTE
AND COMPLEMENTARY LEGISLATION

ARTICLE 41
Simplified amendment procedure
41.1. In accordance with Article 106(5) of this Treaty, Articles 5.1, 5.2, 5.3, 17, 18, 19.1, 22, 23, 24, 26, 32.2, 32.3, 32.4, 32.6, 33.1(a) and 36 of this Statute may be amended by the Council, acting either by a qualified majority on a recommendation from the ECB and after consulting the Commission, or unanimously on a proposal from the Commission and after consulting the ECB. In either case the assent of the European Parliament shall be required.
41.2. A recommendation made by the ECB under this Article shall require a unanimous decision by the Governing Council.

ARTICLE 42
Complementary legislation
In accordance with Article 106(6) of this Treaty, immediately after the decision on the date for the beginning of the third stage, the Council, acting by a qualified majority either on a proposal from the Commission and after consulting the European Parliament and the ECB, or on a recommendation from the ECB and after consulting the European Parliament and the Commission, shall adopt the provisions referred to in Articles 4, 5.4, 19.2, 20, 28.1, 29.2, 30.4 and 34.3 of this Statute.

CHAPTER IX
TRANSITIONAL AND
OTHER PROVISIONS FOR THE ESCB

ARTICLE 43
General provisions
43.1. A derogation as referred to in Article 109k(1) of this Treaty shall entail that the following Articles of this Statute shall not confer any rights or impose any obligations on the Member State concerned: 3, 6, 9.2, 12.1, 14.3, 16, 18, 19, 20, 22, 23, 26.2, 27, 30, 31, 32, 33, 34, 50 and 52.

43.2. The central banks of Member States with a derogation as specified in Article 109k(1) of this Treaty shall retain their powers in the field of monetary policy according to national law.

43.3. In accordance with Article 109k(4) of this Treaty, 'Member States' shall be read as 'Member States without a derogation' in the following Articles of this Statute: 3, 11.2, 19, 34.2 and 50.

43.4. 'National central banks' shall be read as 'central banks of Member States without a derogation' in the following Articles of the Statute: 9.2, 10.1, 10.3, 12.1, 16, 17, 18, 22, 23, 27, 30, 31, 32, 33.2 and 52.

43.5. 'Shareholders' shall be read as 'central banks of Member States without a derogation' in Articles 10.3 and 33.1.

43.6. 'Subscribed capital of the ECB' shall be read as 'capital of the ECB subscribed by the central banks of Member States without a derogation' in Articles 10.3 and 30.2.

ARTICLE 44
Transitional tasks of the ECB
The ECB shall take over those tasks of the EMI which, because of the derogations of one or more Member States, still have to be performed in the third stage.

The ECB shall give advice in the preparations for the abrogation of the derogations specified in Article 109l of this Treaty.

ARTICLE 45
The General Council of the ECB
45.1. Without prejudice to Article 106(3) of this Treaty, the General Council shall be constituted as a third decision-making body of the ECB.

45.2. The General Council shall comprise the President and Vice-President of the ECB and the Governors of the national central bank. The other members of the Executive Board may participate, without having the right to vote, in meetings of the General Council.

45.3. The responsibilities of the General Council are listed in full in Article 47 of this Statute.

ARTICLE 46
Rules of procedure of the General Council
46.1. The President or, in his absence, the Vice-President of the ECB shall chair the General Council of the ECB.

46.2. The President of the Council and a member of the Commission may participate, without having the right to vote, in meetings of the General Council.

46.3. The President shall prepare the meetings of the General Council.

46.4. By way of derogation from Article 12.3, the General Council shall adopt its Rules of Procedure.

46.5. The Secretariat of the General Council shall be provided by the ECB.

ARTICLE 47
Responsibilities of the General Council
47.1. The General Council shall:
— perform the tasks referred to in Article 44;
— contribute to the advisory functions referred to in Articles 4 and 25.1.

47.2. The General Council shall contribute to:

— the collection of statistical information as referred to in Article 5;
— the reporting activities of the ECB as referred to in Article 15;
— the establishment of the necessary rules for the application of Article 26 as referred to in Article 26.4;
— the taking of all other measures necessary for the application of Article 29 as referred to in Article 29.4;
— the laying down of the conditions of employment of the staff of the ECB as referred to in Article 36.

47.3. The General Council shall contribute to the necessary preparations for irrevocably fixing the exchange rates of the currencies of Member States with a derogation against the currencies, or the single currency, of the Member States without a derogation, as referred to in Article 109l(5) of this Treaty.

47.4. The General Council shall be informed by the President of the ECB of decisions of the Governing Council.

ARTICLE 48
Transitional provisions for the capital of the ECB

In accordance with Article 29.1 each national central bank shall be assigned a weighting in the key for subscription of the ECB's capital. By way of derogation from Article 28.3, central banks of Member States with a derogation shall not pay up their subscribed capital unless the General Council, acting by a majority representing at least two thirds of the subscribed capital of the ECB and at least half of the shareholders, decides that a minimal percentage has to be paid up as a contribution to the operational costs of the ECB.

ARTICLE 49
Deferred payment of capital, reserves and provisions of the ECB

49.1. The central bank of a Member State whose derogation has been abrogated shall pay up its subscribed share of the capital of the ECB to the same extent as the central banks of other Member States without a derogation, and shall transfer to the ECB foreign reserve assets in accordance with Article 30.1. The sum to be transferred shall be determined by multiplying the ECU value at current exchange rates of the foreign reserve assets which have already been transferred to the ECB in accordance with Article 30.1, by the ratio between the number of shares subscribed by the national central bank concerned and the number of shares already paid up by the other national central banks.

49.2. In addition to the payment to be made in accordance with Article 49.1, the central bank concerned shall contribute to the reserves of the ECB, to those provisions equivalent to reserves, and to the amount still to be appropriated to the reserves and provisions corresponding to the balance of the profit and loss account as at 31 December of the year prior to the abrogation of the derogation. The sum to be contributed shall be determined by multiplying the amount of the reserves, as defined above and as stated in the approval balance sheet of the ECB, by the ratio between the number of shares subscribed by the central bank concerned and the number of shares already paid up by the other central banks.

ARTICLE 50
Initial appointment of the members of the Executive Board

When the Executive Board of the ECB is being established, the President, the Vice-President and the other members of the Executive Board shall be appointed by common accord of the governments of the Member States at the level of Heads of State or of Government, on a recommendation from the Council and after consulting the European Parliament and the Council of the EMI. The President of the Executive Board shall be appointed for 8 years. By way of derogation from Article 11.2, the Vice-President shall be appointed for 4 years and the other members of the Executive Board for terms of office of between 5 and 8 years. No term of office shall be renewable. The number of members of the Executive Board may be smaller than provided for in Article 11.1, but in no circumstance shall it be less than four.

ARTICLE 51
Derogation from Article 32
51.1. If, after the start of the third stage, the Governing Council decides that the application of Article 32 results in significant changes in national central banks' relative income positions, the amount of income to be allocated pursuant to Article 32 shall be reduced by a uniform percentage which shall not exceed 60% in the first financial year after the start of the third stage and which shall decrease by at least 12 percentage points in each subsequent financial year.
51.2. Article 51.1 shall be applicable for not more than five financial years after the start of the third stage.

ARTICLE 52
Exchange of bank notes in Community currencies
Following the irrevocable fixing of exchange rates, the Governing Council shall take the necessary measures to ensure that bank notes denominated in currencies with irrevocably fixed exchange rates are exchanged by the national central banks at their respective par values.

ARTICLE 53
Applicability of the transitional provisions
If and as long as there are Member States with a derogation Articles 43 to 48 shall be applicable.

PROTOCOL
ON THE STATUTE OF THE EUROPEAN MONETARY INSTITUTE

THE HIGH CONTRACTING PARTIES,

DESIRING to lay down the Statute of the European Monetary Institute,

HAVE AGREED upon the following provisions, which shall be annexed to the Treaty establishing the European Community:

ARTICLE 1
Constitution and name
1.1. The European Monetary Institute (EMI) shall be established in accordance with Article 109f of this Treaty, it shall perform its functions and carry out its activities in accordance with the provisions of this Treaty and of this Statute.
1.2. The members of the EMI shall be the central banks of the Member States

('national central banks'). For the purposes of this Statute, the Institut monétaire luxembourgeois shall be regarded as the central bank of Luxembourg.
1.3. Pursuant to Article 109f of this Treaty; both the Committee of Governors and the European Monetary Cooperation Fund (EMCF) shall be dissolved. All assets and liabilities of the EMCF shall pass automatically to the EMI.

ARTICLE 2
Objectives
The EMI shall contribute to the realization of the conditions necessary for the transition to the third stage of Economic and Monetary Union, in particular by:
— strengthening the coordination of monetary policies with a view to ensuring price stability;
— making the preparations required for the establishment of the European System of Central Banks (ESCB), and for the conduct of a single monetary policy and the creation of a single currency in the third stage;
— overseeing the development of the ECU.

ARTICLE 3
General principles
3.1. The EMI shall carry out the tasks and functions conferred upon it by this Treaty and this Statute without prejudice to the responsibility of the competent authorities for the conduct of the monetary policy within the respective Member States.
3.2. The EMI shall act in accordance with the objectives and principles stated in Article 2 of the Statute of the ESCB.

ARTICLE 4
Primary tasks
4.1. In accordance with Article 109f(2) of this Treaty, the EMI shall:
— strengthen cooperation between the national central banks;
— strengthen the coordination of the monetary policies of the Member States with the aim of ensuring price stability;
— monitor the functioning of the European Monetary System (EMS);
— hold consultations concerning issues falling within the competence of the national central banks and affecting the stability of financial institutions and markets;
— take over the tasks of the EMCF; in particular it shall perform the functions referred to in Articles 6.1, 6.2 and 6.3;
— facilitate the use of the ECU and oversee its development, including the smooth functioning of the ECU clearing system.
The EMI shall also:
— hold regular consultations concerning the course of monetary policies and the use of monetary policy instruments;
— normally be consulted by the national monetary authorities before they take decisions on the course of monetary policy in the context of the common framework for ex ante coordination.
4.2. At the latest by 31 December 1996, the EMI shall specify the regulatory, organizational and logistical framework necessary for the ESCB to perform its tasks in the third stage, in accordance with the principle of an open market

economy with free competition. This framework shall be submitted by the Council of the EMI for decision to the ECB at the date of its establishment.

In accordance with Article 109f(3) of this Treaty, the EMI shall in particular:

— prepare the instruments and the procedures necessary for carrying out a single monetary policy in the third stage;

— promote the harmonization, where necessary, of the rules and practices governing the collection, compilation and distribution of statistics in the areas within its field of competence;

— prepare the rules for operations to be undertaken by the national central banks in the framework of the ESCB;

— promote the efficiency of cross-border payments;

— supervise the technical preparation of ECU bank notes.

ARTICLE 5
Advisory functions

5.1. In accordance with Article 109f(4) of this Treaty, the Council of the EMI may formulate opinions or recommendations on the overall orientation of monetary policy and exchange rate policy as well as on related measures introduced in each Member State. The EMI may submit opinions or recommendations to governments and to the Council on policies which might affect the internal or external monetary situation in the Community and, in particular, the functioning of the EMS.

5.2. The Council of the EMI may also make recommendations to the monetary authorities of the Member States concerning the conduct of their monetary policy.

5.3. In accordance with Article 109f(6) of this Treaty, the EMI shall be consulted by the Council regarding any proposed Community act within its field of competence.

Within the limits and under the conditions set out by the Council acting by a qualified majority on a proposal from the Commission and after consulting the European Parliament and the EMI, the EMI shall be consulted by the authorities of the Member States on any draft legislative provision within its field of competence, in particular with regard to Article 4.2.

5.4. In accordance with Article 109f(5) of this Treaty, the EMI may publish its opinion and its recommendations.

ARTICLE 6
Operational and technical functions

6.1. The EMI shall:

— provide for the multilateralization of positions resulting from interventions by the national central banks in Community currencies and the multilateralization of intra-Community settlements;

— administer the very short-term financing mechanism provided for by the Agreement of 13 March 1979 between the central banks of the Member States of the European Economic Community laying down the operating procedures for the European Monetary System (hereinafter referred to as 'EMS Agreement') and the short-term monetary support mechanism provided for in the Agreement between the central banks of the Member States of the European Economic Community of 9 February 1970, as amended;

— perform the functions referred to in Article 11 of Council Regulation (EEC)

No 1969/88 of 24 June 1988 establishing a single facility providing medium-term financial assistance for Member States' balances of payments.

6.2. The EMI may receive monetary reserves from the national central banks and issue ECUs against such assets for the purpose of implementing the EMS Agreement. These ECUs may be used by the EMI and the national central banks as a means of settlement and for transactions between them and the EMI. The EMI shall take the necessary administrative measures for the implementation of this paragraph.

6.3. The EMI may grant to the monetary authorities of third countries and to international monetary institutions the status of 'Other Holders' of ECUs and fix the terms and conditions under which such ECUs may be acquired, held or used by Other Holders.

6.4. The EMI shall be entitled to hold and manage foreign exchange reserves as an agent for and at the request of national central banks. Profits and losses regarding these reserves shall be for the account of the national central bank depositing the reserves.

The EMI shall perform this function on the basis of bilateral contracts in accordance with rules laid down in a decision of the EMI.

These rules shall ensure that transactions with these reserves shall not interfere with the monetary policy and exchange rate policy of the competent monetary authority of any Member State and shall be consistent with the objectives of the EMI and the proper functioning of the Exchange Rate Mechanism of the EMS.

ARTICLE 7
Other tasks

7.1. Once a year the EMI shall address a report to the Council on the state of the preparations for the third stage. These reports shall include an assessment of the progress towards convergence in the Community, and cover in particular the adaptation of monetary policy instruments and the preparation of the procedures necessary for carrying out a single monetary policy in the third stage, as well as the statutory requirements to be fulfilled for national central banks to become an integral part of the ESCB.

7.2. In accordance with the Council decisions referred to in Article 109f(7) of this Treaty, the EMI may perform other tasks for the preparation of the third stage.

ARTICLE 8
Independence

The members of the Council of the EMI who are the representatives of their institutions shall, with respect to their activities, act according to their own responsibilities. In exercising the powers and performing the tasks and duties conferred upon them by this Treaty and this Statute, the Council of the EMI may not seek or take any instructions from Community institutions or bodies or governments of Member States.

The Community institutions and bodies as well as the governments of the Member States undertake to respect this principle and not to seek to influence the Council of the EMI in the performance of its tasks.

ARTICLE 9
Administration
9.1. In accordance with Article 109f(1) of this Treaty, the EMI shall be directed and managed by the Council of the EMI.

9.2. The Council of the EMI shall consist of a President and the Governors of the national central banks, one of whom shall be Vice-President. If a Governor is prevented from attending a meeting, he may nominate another representative of his institution.

9.3. The President shall be appointed by common accord of the governments of the Member States at the level of Heads of State or of Government, on a recommendation from, as the case may be, the Committee of Governors or the Council of the EMI, and after consulting the European Parliament and the Council.

The President shall be selected from among persons of recognized standing and professional experience in monetary or banking matters. Only nationals of Member States may be President of the EMI. The Council of the EMI shall appoint the Vice-President. The President and Vice-President shall be appointed for a period of three years.

9.4. The President shall perform his duties on a full-time basis. He shall not engage in any occupation, whether gainful or not, unless exemption is exceptionally granted by the Council of the EMI.

9.5. The President shall:
— prepare and chair the meetings of the Council of the EMI;
— without prejudice to Article 22, present the views of the EMI externally;
— be responsible for the day-to-day management of the EMI.

In the absence of the President, his duties shall be performed by the Vice-President.

9.6. The terms and conditions of employment of the President, in particular his salary, pension and other social security benefits, shall be the subject of a contract with the EMI and shall be fixed by the Council of the EMI on a proposal from a Committee comprising three members appointed by the Committee of Governors or the Council of the EMI, as the case may be, and three members appointed by the Council. The President shall not have the right to vote on matters referred to in this paragraph.

9.7. If the President no longer fulfils the conditions required for the performance of his duties or if he has been guilty of serious misconduct, the Court of Justice may, on application by the Council of the EMI, compulsorily retire him.

9.8. The Rules of Procedure of the EMI shall be adopted by the Council of the EMI.

ARTICLE 10
Meetings of the Council of the EMI and voting procedures
10.1. The Council of the EMI shall meet at least ten times a year. The proceedings of Council meetings shall be confidential. The Council of the EMI may, acting unanimously, decide to make the outcome of its deliberations public.

10.2. Each member of the Council of the EMI or his nominees shall have one vote.

10.3. Save as otherwise provided for in this Statute, the Council of the EMI shall act by a simple majority of its members.

10.4. Decisions to be taken in the context of Articles 4.2, 5.4, 6.2 and 6.3 shall require unanimity of the members of the Council of the EMI.

The adoption of opinions and recommendations under Articles 5.1 and 5.2, the adoption of decisions under Articles 6.4, 16 and 23.6 and the adoption of guidelines under Article 15.3 shall require a qualified majority of two thirds of the members of the Council of the EMI.

ARTICLE 11
Interinstitutional cooperation and reporting requirements
11.1. The President of the Council and a member of the Commission may participate, without having the right to vote, in meetings of the Council of the EMI.

11.2. The President of the EMI shall be invited to participate in Council meetings when the Council is discussing matters relating to the objectives and tasks of the EMI.

11.3. At a date to be established in the Rules of Procedure, the EMI shall prepare an annual report on its activities and on monetary and financial conditions in the Community. The annual report, together with the annual accounts of the EMI, shall be addressed to the European Parliament, the Council and the Commission and also to the European Council.

The President of the EMI may, at the request of the European Parliament or on his own initiative, be heard by the competent Committees of the European Parliament.

11.4. Reports published by the EMI shall be made available to interested parties free of charge.

ARTICLE 12
Currency denomination
The operations of the EMI shall be expressed in ECU.

ARTICLE 13
Seat
Before the end of 1992, the decision as to where the seat of the EMI will be established shall be taken by common accord of the governments of the Member States at the level of Heads of State or of Government.

ARTICLE 14
Legal capacity
The EMI, which in accordance with Article 109f(1) of this Treaty shall have legal personality, shall enjoy in each of the Member States the most extensive legal capacity accorded to legal persons under their law; it may, in particular, acquire or dispose of movable of immovable property and may be a party to legal proceedings.

ARTICLE 15
Legal acts
15.1. In the performance of its tasks, and under the conditions laid down in this Statute, the EMI shall:
— deliver opinions;
— make recommendations;

— adopt guidelines, and take decisions, which shall be addressed to the national central banks.

15.2. Opinions and recommendations of the EMI shall have no binding force.

15.3. The Council of the EMI may adopt guidelines laying down the methods for the implementation of the conditions necessary for the ESCB to perform its functions in the third stage. EMI guidelines shall have no binding force; they shall be submitted for decision to the ECB.

15.4. Without prejudice to Article 3.1, a decision of the EMI shall be binding in its entirety upon those to whom it is addressed. Articles 190 and 191 of this Treaty shall apply to these decisions.

ARTICLE 16
Financial resources

16.1. The EMI shall be endowed with its own resources. The size of the resources of the EMI shall be determined by the Council of the EMI with a view to ensuring the income deemed necessary to cover the administrative expenditure incurred in the performance of the tasks and functions of the EMI.

16.2. The resources of the EMI determined in accordance with Article 16.1, shall be provided out of contributions by the national central banks in accordance with the key referred to in Article 29.1 of the Statute of the ESCB and be paid up at the establishment of the EMI. For this purpose, the statistical data to be used for the determination of the key shall be provided by the Commission, in accordance with the rules adopted by the Council, acting by a qualified majority on a proposal from the Commission and after consulting the European Parliament, the Committee of Governors and the Committee referred to in Article 109c of this Treaty.

16.3. The Council of the EMI shall determine the form in which contributions shall be paid up.

ARTICLE 17
Annual accounts and auditing

17.1. The financial year of the EMI shall begin on the first day of January and end of the last day of December.

17.2. The Council of the EMI shall adopt an annual budget before the beginning of each financial year.

17.3. The annual accounts shall be drawn up in accordance with the principles established by the Council of the EMI. The annual accounts shall be approved by the Council of the EMI and shall thereafter be published.

17.4. The annual accounts shall be audited by independent external auditors approved by the Council of the EMI. The auditors shall have full power to examine all books and accounts of the EMI and to obtain full information about its transactions.

The provisions of Article 188b of this Treaty shall only apply to an examination of the operational efficiency of the management of the EMI.

17.5. Any surplus of the EMI shall be transferred in the following order:

(a) an amount to be determined by the Council of the EMI shall be transferred to the general reserve fund of the EMI;

(b) any remaining surplus shall be distributed to the national central banks in accordance with the key referred to in Article 16.2.

17.6. In the event of a loss incurred by the EMI, the shortfall shall be offset against the general reserve fund of the EMI. Any remaining shortfall shall be made good by contributions from the national central banks, in accordance with the key as referred to in Article 16.2.

ARTICLE 18
Staff
18.1. The Council of the EMI shall lay down the conditions of employment of the staff of the EMI.
18.2. The Court of Justice shall have jurisdiction in any dispute between the EMI and its servants within the limits and under the conditions laid down in the conditions of employment.

ARTICLE 19
Judicial control and related matters
19.1. The acts or omissions of the EMI shall be open to review or interpretation by the Court of Justice in the cases and under the conditions laid down in this Treaty. The EMI may institute proceedings in the cases and under the conditions laid down in this Treaty.
19.2. Disputes between the EMI, on the one hand, and its creditors, debtors or any other person, on the other, shall fall within the jurisdiction of the competent national courts, save where jurisdiction has been conferred upon the Court of Justice.
19.3. The EMI shall be subject to the liability regime provided for in Article 215 of this Treaty.
19.4. The Court of Justice shall have jurisdiction to give judgment pursuant to any arbitration clause contained in a contract concluded by or on behalf of the EMI, whether that contract be governed by public or private law.
19.5. A decision of the EMI to bring an action before the Court of Justice shall be taken by the Council of the EMI.

ARTICLE 20
Professional secrecy
20.1. Members of the Council of the EMI and the staff of the EMI shall be required, even after their duties have ceased, not do disclose information of the kind covered by the obligation of professional secrecy.
20.2. Persons having access to data covered by Community legislation imposing an obligation of secrecy shall be subject to such legislation.

ARTICLE 21
Privileges and immunities
The EMI shall enjoy in the territories of the Member States such privileges and immunities as are necessary for the performance of its tasks, under the conditions laid down in the Protocol on the Privileges and Immunities of the European Communities annexed to the Treaty establishing a Single Council and a Single Commission of the European Communities.

ARTICLE 22
Signatories
The EMI shall be legally committed to third parties by the President or the Vice-President or by the signatures of two members of the staff of the EMI who have been duly authorized by the President to sign on behalf of the EMI.

ARTICLE 23
Liquidation of the EMI
23.1. In accordance with Article 109l of this Treaty, the EMI shall go into liqui-
dation on the establishment of the ECB.
All assets and liabilities of the EMI shall then pass automatically to the ECB.
The latter shall liquidate the EMI according to the provisions of this Article.
The liquidation shall be completed by the beginning of the third stage.

23.2. The mechanism for the creation of ECUs against gold and US dollars as
provided for by Article 17 of the EMS Agreement shall be unwound by the first
day of the third stage in accordance with Article 20 of the said Agreement.
23.3. All claims and liabilities arising from the very short-term financing mechanism
and the short-term monetary support mechanism, under the Agreements referred
to in Article 6.1, shall be settled by the first day of the third stage.
23.4. All remaining assets of the EMI shall be disposed of and all remaining
liabilities of the EMI shall be settled.
23.5. The proceeds of the liquidation described in Article 23.4 shall be distributed
to the national central banks in accordance with the key referred to in Article
16.2, 23.6.
The Council of the EMI may take the measures necessary for the application of
Articles 23.4 and 23.5.
23.7. Upon the establishment of the ECB, the President of the EMI shall relinquish
his office.

PROTOCOL
ON THE EXCESSIVE DEFICIT PROCEDURE

THE HIGH CONTRACTING PARTIES,

DESIRING to lay down the details of the excessive deficit procedure referred to
in Article 104c of the Treaty establishing the European Community,

HAVE AGREED upon the following provisions, which shall be annexed to the
Treaty establishing the European Community:

ARTICLE 1
The reference values referred to in Article 104c(2) of this Treaty are:
— 3% for the ratio of the planned or actual government deficit to gross domestic
product at market prices;
— 60% for the ratio of government debt to gross domestic product at market
prices.

ARTICLE 2
In Article 104c of this Treaty and in this Protocol:
— government means general government, that is central government, regional
or local government and social security funds, to the exclusion of commercial
operations, as defined in the European System of Integrated Economic Accounts;
— deficit means net borrowing as defined in the European System of Integrated
Economic Accounts;
— investment means gross fixed capital formation as defined in the European
System of Integrated Economic Accounts;

— debt means total gross debt at nominal value outstanding at the end of the year and consolidated between and within the sectors of general government as defined in the first indent.

ARTICLE 3
In order to ensure the effectiveness of the excessive deficit procedure, the governments of the Member States shall be responsible under this procedure for the deficits of general government as defined in the first indent of Article 2. The Member States shall ensure that national procedures in the budgetary area enable them to meet their obligations in this area deriving from this Treaty. The Member States shall report their planned and actual deficits and the levels of their debt promptly and regularly to the Commission.

ARTICLE 4
The statistical data to be used for the application of this Protocol shall be provided by the Commission.

PROTOCOL
ON THE CONVERGENCE CRITERIA REFERRED TO IN ARTICLE 109j OF THE TREATY ESTABLISHING THE EUROPEAN COMMUNITY

THE HIGH CONTRACTING PARTIES,

DESIRING to lay down the details of the convergence criteria which shall guide the Community in the decision making on the passage to the third stage of economic and monetary union, referred to in Article 109j(1) of this Treaty,

HAVE AGREED upon the following provisions, which shall be annexed to the Treaty establishing the European Community:

ARTICLE 1
The criterion on price stability referred to in the first indent of Article 109j(1) of this Treaty shall mean that a Member State has a price performance that is sustainable and an average rate of inflation, observed over a period of one year before the examination, that does not exceed by more than 1½ percentage points that of, at most, the three best performing Member States in terms of price stability. Inflation shall be measured by means of the consumer price index (CPI) on a comparable basis, taking in account differences in national definitions.

ARTICLE 2
The criterion on the government budgetary position referred to in the second indent of Article 109j(1) of this Treaty shall mean that at the time of the examination the Member State is not the subject of a Council decision under Article 104c(6) of this Treaty that an excessive deficit exists.

ARTICLE 3
The criterion on participation in the Exchange Rate Mechanism of the European Monetary System referred to in the third indent of Article 109j(1) of this Treaty shall mean that a Member State has respected the normal fluctuation margins

provided for by the Exchange Rate Mechanism of the European Monetary System without severe tensions for at least the last two years before the examination. In particular, the Member State shall not have devalued its currency's bilateral central rate against any other Member State's currency on its own initiative for the same period.

ARTICLE 4

The criterion on the convergence of interest rates referred to in the fourth indent of Article 109j(1) of this Treaty shall mean that, observed over a period of one year before the examination, a Member State has had an average nominal long-term interest rate that does not exceed by more than 2 percentage points that of, at most, the three best performing Member States in terms of price stability. Interest rates shall be measured on the basis of long term government bonds or comparable securities, taking into account differences in national definitions.

ARTICLE 5

The statistical data to be used for the application of this Protocol shall be provided by the Commission.

ARTICLE 6

The Council shall, acting unanimously on a proposal from the Commission and after consulting the European Parliament, the EMI or the ECB as the case may be, and the Committee referred to in Article 109c, adopt appropriate provisions to lay down the details of the convergence criteria referred to in Article 109j of this Treaty, which shall then replace this Protocol.

PROTOCOL
AMENDING THE PROTOCOL ON THE PRIVILEGES AND IMMUNITIES OF THE EUROPEAN COMMUNITIES

THE HIGH CONTRACTING PARTIES,

CONSIDERING that, in accordance with Article 40 of the Statute of the European System of Central Banks and of the European Central Bank and Article 21 of the Statute of the European Monetary Institute, the European Central Bank and the European Monetary Institute shall enjoy in the territories of the Member States such privileges and immunities as are necessary for the performance of their tasks,

HAVE AGREED upon the following provisions, which shall be annexed to the Treaty establishing the European Community:

SOLE ARTICLE

The Protocol on the Privileges and Immunities of the European Communities, annexed to the Treaty establishing a Single Council and a Single Commission of the European Communities, shall be supplemented by the following provisions:

'ARTICLE 23

This Protocol shall also apply to the European Central Bank, to the members of its organs and to its staff, without prejudice to the provisions of the Protocol on the Statute of the European System of Central Banks and the European Central Bank.

The European Central Bank shall, in addition, be exempt from any form of taxation or imposition of a like nature on the occasion of any increase in its capital and from the various formalities which may be connected therewith in the State where the bank has its seat.

The activities of the Bank and of its organs carried on in accordance with the Statute of the European System of Central Banks and of the European Central Bank shall not be subject to any turnover tax.

The above provisions shall also apply to the European Monetary Institute. Its dissolution or liquidation shall not give rise to any imposition.'

PROTOCOL ON DENMARK

THE HIGH CONTRACTING PARTIES,

DESIRING to settle certain particular problems relating to Denmark.

HAVE AGREED UPON the following provisions, which shall be annexed to the Treaty establishing the European Community:

The provisions of Article 14 of the Protocol on the Statute of the European System of Central Banks and of the European Central Bank shall not affect the right of the National Bank of Denmark to carry out its existing tasks concerning those parts of the Kingdom of Denmark which are not part of the Community.

PROTOCOL ON PORTUGAL

THE HIGH CONTRACTING PARTIES,

DESIRING to settle certain particular problems relating to Portugal,

HAVE AGREED upon the following provisions, which shall be annexed to the Treaty establishing the European Community:

1. Portugal is hereby authorized to maintain the facility afforded to the Autonomous Regions of Azores and Madeira to benefit from an interest-free facility with the Banco de Portugal under the terms established by existing Portuguese law.
2. Portugal commits itself to pursue its best endeavours in order to put an end to the abovementioned facility as soon as possible.

PROTOCOL
ON THE TRANSITION TO THE THIRD STAGE
OF ECONOMIC AND MONETARY UNION

THE HIGH CONTRACTING PARTIES,

Declare the irreversible character of the Community's movement to the third stage of Economic and Monetary Union by signing the new Treaty provisions on Economic and Monetary Union.

Therefore all Member States shall, whether they fulfil the necessary conditions for the adoption of a single currency or not, respect the will for the Community to enter swiftly into the third stage, and therefore no Member State shall prevent the entering into the third stage.

If by the end of 1997 the date of the beginning of the third stage has not been set, the Member States concerned, the Community institutions and other bodies involved shall expedite all preparatory work during 1998, in order to enable the Community to enter the third stage irrevocably on 1 January 1999 and to enable the ECB and the ESCB to start their full functioning from this date on.

This Protocol shall be annexed to the Treaty establishing the European Community.

PROTOCOL
ON CERTAIN PROVISIONS RELATING
TO THE UNITED KINGDOM OF GREAT BRITAIN AND NORTHERN
IRELAND

THE HIGH CONTRACTING PARTIES,

RECOGNIZING that the United Kingdom shall not be obliged or committed to move to the third stage of Economic and Monetary Union without a separate decision to do so by its government and Parliament,

NOTING the practice of the government of the United Kingdom to fund its borrowing requirement by the sale of debt to the private sector,

HAVE AGREED the following provisions, which shall be annexed to the Treaty establishing the European Community:

1. The United Kingdom shall notify the Council whether it intends to move to the third stage before the Council makes its assessment under Article 109j(2) of this Treaty.

Unless the United Kingdom notifies the Council that it intends to move to the third stage, it shall be under no obligation to do so.

If no date is set for the beginning of the third stage under Article 109j(3) of this Treaty, the United Kingdom may notify its intention to move to the third stage before 1 January 1998.

2. Paragraphs 3 to 9 shall have effect if the United Kingdom notifies the Council that it does not intend to move to the third stage.

3. The United Kingdom shall not be included among the majority of Member States which fulfil the necessary conditions referred to in the second indent of Article 109j(2) and the first indent of Article 109j(3) of this Treaty.

4. The United Kingdom shall retain its powers in the field of monetary policy according to national law.

5. Articles 3a(2), 104c(1), (9) and (11), 105(1) to (5), 105a, 107, 108, 108a, 109, 109a(1) and (2)(b) and 109(4) and (5) of this Treaty shall not apply to the United Kingdom. In these provisions references to the Community or the Member States shall not include the United Kingdom and references to national central banks shall not include the Bank of England.

6. Articles 109e(4) and 109h and i of this Treaty shall continue to apply to the United Kingdom. Articles 109c(4) and 109m shall apply to the United Kingdom as if it had a derogation.

7. The voting rights of the United Kingdom shall be suspended in respect of acts of the Council referred to in the Articles listed in paragraph 5. For this purpose the weighted votes of the United Kingdom shall be excluded from any calculation of a qualified majority under Article 109k(5) of this Treaty.

The United Kingdom shall also have no right to participate in the appointment of the President, the Vice-President and the other members of the Executive Board of the ECB under Articles 109a(2)(b) and 109l(1) of this Treaty.

8. Articles 3, 4, 6, 7, 9.2, 10.1, 10.3, 11.2, 12.1, 14, 16, 18 to 20, 22, 23, 26, 27, 30 to 34, 50 and 52 of the Protocol on the Statute of the European System of Central Banks and of the European Central Bank ('the Statute') shall not apply to the United Kingdom.

In those Articles, references to the Community or the Member States shall not include the United Kingdom and references to national central banks or shareholders shall not include the Bank of England.

References in Articles 10.3 and 30.2 of the Statute to 'subscribed capital of the ECB' shall not include capital subscribed by the Bank of England.

9. Article 109l(3) of this Treaty and Articles 44 to 48 of the Statute shall have effect, whether or not there is any Member State with a derogation, subject to the following amendments:

(a) References in Article 44 to the tasks of the ECB and the EMI shall include those tasks that still need to be performed in the third stage owing to any decision of the United Kingdom not to move to that stage.

(b) In addition to the tasks referred to in Article 47 the ECB shall also give advice in relation to and contribute to the preparation of any decision of the Council with regard to the United Kingdom taken in accordance with paragraphs 10(a) and 10(c).

(c) The Bank of England shall pay up its subscription to the capital of the ECB as a contribution to its operational costs on the same basis as national central banks of Member States with a derogation.

10. If the United Kingdom does not move to the third stage, it may change its notification at any time after the beginning of that stage.

In that event:

(a) The United Kingdom shall have the right to move to the third stage provided only that it satisfies the necessary conditions. The Council, acting at the request of the United Kingdom and under the conditions and in accordance with the procedure laid down in Article 109k(2) of this Treaty, shall decide whether it fulfils the necessary conditions.

(b) The Bank of England shall pay up its subscribed capital, transfer to the ECB foreign reserve assets and contribute to its reserves on the same basis as the national central bank of a Member State whose derogation has been abrogated.

(c) The Council, acting under the conditions and in accordance with the procedure laid down in Article 109l(5) of this Treaty, shall take all other necessary decisions to enable the United Kingdom to move to the third stage.

If the United Kingdom moves to the third stage pursuant to the provisions of this protocol, paragraphs 3 to 9 shall cease to have effect.

11. Notwithstanding Articles 104 and 109e(3) of this Treaty and Article 21.1 of the Statute, the government of the United Kingdom may maintain its Ways and Means facility with the Bank of England if and so long as the United Kingdom does not move to the third stage.

PROTOCOL
ON CERTAIN PROVISIONS RELATING TO DENMARK

THE HIGH CONTRACTING PARTIES,

DESIRING to settle, in accordance with the general objectives of the Treaty establishing the European Community, certain particular problems existing at the present time,

TAKING INTO ACCOUNT that the Danish Constitution contains provisions which may imply a referendum in Denmark prior to Danish participation in the third stage of Economic and Monetary Union,

HAVE AGREED on the following provisions, which shall be annexed to the Treaty establishing the European Community:

1. The Danish Government shall notify the Council of its position concerning participation in the third stage before the Council makes its assessment under Article 109j(2) of this Treaty.

2. In the event of a notification that Denmark will not participate in the third stage, Denmark shall have an exemption. The effect of the exemption shall be that all Articles and provisions of this Treaty and the Statute of the ESCB referring to a derogation shall be applicable to Denmark.

3. In such case, Denmark shall not be included among the majority of Member States which fulfil the necessary conditions referred to in the second indent of Article 109j(2) and the first indent of Article 109j(3) of this Treaty.

4. As for the abrogation of the exemption, the procedure referred to in Article 109k(2) shall only be initiated at the request of Denmark.

5. In the event of abrogation of the exemption status, the provisions of this Protocol shall no longer be applicable.

PROTOCOL ON FRANCE

THE HIGH CONTRACTING PARTIES,

DESIRING to take into account a particular point relating to France,

HAVE AGREED upon the following provisions, which shall be annexed to the Treaty establishing the European Community:

France will keep the privilege of monetary emission in its overseas territories under the terms established by its national laws, and will be solely entitled to determine the parity of the CFP franc.

PROTOCOL ON SOCIAL POLICY

THE HIGH CONTRACTING PARTIES,

NOTING that eleven Member States, that is to say the Kingdom of Belgium, the Kingdom of Denmark, the Federal Republic of Germany, the Hellenic Republic, the Kingdom of Spain, the French Republic, Ireland, the Italian Republic, the Grand Duchy of Luxembourg, the Kingdom of the Netherlands, the Portuguese Republic, wish to continue along the path laid down in the 1989 Social Charter, that they have adopted among themselves an Agreement to this end: that this Agreement is annexed to this Protocol; that this Protocol and the said Agreement are without prejudice to the provisions of this Treaty, particularly those which relate to social policy which constitute an integral part of the 'acquis communautaire':

1. Agree to authorize those eleven Member States to have recourse to the institutions, procedures and mechanisms of the Treaty for the purposes of taking among themselves and applying as far as they are concerned the acts and decisions required for giving effect to the abovementioned Agreement.
2. The United Kingdom of Great Britain and Northern Ireland shall not take part in the deliberations and the adoption by the Council of Commission proposals made on the basis of this Protocol and the abovementioned Agreement.
By way of derogation from Article 148(2) of the Treaty, acts of the Council which are made pursuant to this Protocol and which must be adopted by a qualified majority shall be deemed to be so adopted if they have received at least forty-four votes in favour.
The unanimity of the members of the Council, with the exception of the United Kingdom and Northern Ireland, shall be necessary for acts of the Council which must be adopted unanimously and for those amending the Commission proposal.
Acts adopted by the Council and any financial consequences other than administrative costs entailed for the institutions shall not be applicable to the United Kingdom of Great Britain and Northern Ireland.
3. This Protocol shall be annexed to the Treaty establishing the European Community.

AGREEMENT ON SOCIAL POLICY CONCLUDED BETWEEN THE MEMBER STATES OF THE EUROPEAN COMMUNITY WITH THE EXCEPTION OF THE UNITED KINGDOM OF GREAT BRITAIN AND NORTHERN IRELAND

The undersigned eleven HIGH CONTRACTING PARTIES, that is to say the Kingdom of Belgium, the Kingdom of Denmark, the Federal Republic of

Germany, the Hellenic Republic, the Kingdom of Spain, the French Republic, Ireland, the Italian Republic, the Grand Duchy of Luxembourg, the Kingdom of the Netherlands and the Portuguese Republic (hereinafter referred to as 'the Member States'),

WISHING to implement the 1989 Social Charter on the basis of the 'acquis communautaire',

CONSIDERING the Protocol on social policy,

HAVE AGREED as follows:

ARTICLE 1
The Community and the Member States shall have as their objectives the promotion of employment, improved living and working conditions, proper social protection, dialogue between management and labour, the development of human resources with a view to lasting high employment and the combatting of exclusion. To this end the Community and the Member States shall implement measures which take account of the diverse forms of national practices, in particular in the field of contractual relations, and the need to maintain the competitiveness of the Community economy.

ARTICLE 2
1. With a view to achieving the objectives of Article 1, the Community shall support and complement the activities of the Member States in the following fields:
— improvement in particular of the working environment to protect workers' health and safety;
— working conditions;
— the information and consultation of workers;
— equality between men and women with regard to labour market opportunities and treatment at work;
— the integration of persons excluded from the labour market, without prejudice to Article 127 of the Treaty establishing the European Community (hereinafter referred to as 'the Treaty').
2. To this end, the Council may adopt, by means of directives, minimum requirements for gradual implementation, having regard to the conditions and technical rules obtaining in each of the Member States.
Such directives shall avoid imposing administrative, financial and legal constraints in a way which would hold back the creation and development of small and medium-sized undertakings.
The Council shall act in accordance with the procedure referred to in Article 189c of the Treaty after consulting the Economic and Social Committee.
3. However, the Council shall act unanimously on a proposal from the Commission, after consulting the European Parliament and the Economic and Social Committee, in the following areas:
— social security and social protection of workers;
— protection of workers where their employment contract is terminated;
— representation and collective defence of the interests of workers and employers, including co-determination, subject to paragraph 6;

— conditions of employment for third-country nationals legally residing in Community territory;
— financial contributions for promotion of employment and job-creation, without prejudice to the provisions relating to the Social Fund.
4. A Member State may entrust management and labour, at their joint request, with the implementation of directives adopted pursuant to paragraphs 2 and 3.
In this case, it shall ensure that, no later than the date on which a directive must be transposed in accordance with Article 189, management and labour have introduced the necessary measures by agreement, the Member State concerned being required to take any necessary measure enabling it at any time to be in a position to guarantee the results imposed by that directive.
5. The provisions adopted pursuant to this Article shall not prevent any Member State from maintaining or introducing more stringent preventive measures compatible with the Treaty.
6. The provisions of this Article shall not apply to pay, the right of association, the right to strike or the right to impose lock-outs.

ARTICLE 3
1. The Commission shall have the task of promoting the consultation of management and labour at Community level and shall take any relevant measure to facilitate their dialogue by ensuring balanced support for the parties.
2. To this end, before submitting proposals in the social policy field, the Commission shall consult management and labour on the possible direction of Community action.
3. If, after such consultation, the Commission considers Community action advisable, it shall consult management and labour on the content of the envisaged proposal. Management and labour shall forward to the Commission an opinion or, where appropriate, a recommendation.
4. On the occasion of such consultation, management and labour may inform the Commission of their wish to initiate the process provided for in Article 4. The duration of the procedure shall not exceed nine months, unless the management and labour concerned and the Commission decide jointly to extend it.

ARTICLE 4
1. Should management and labour so desire, the dialogue between them at Community level may lead to contractual relations, including agreements.
2. Agreements concluded at Community level shall be implemented either in accordance with the procedures and practices specific to management and labour and the Member States or, in matters covered by Article 2, at the joint request of the signatory parties, by a Council decision on a proposal from the Commission. The Council shall act by qualified majority, except where the agreement in question contains one or more provisions relating to one of the areas referred to in Article 2(3), in which case it shall act unanimously.

ARTICLE 5
With a view to achieving the objectives of Article 1 and without prejudice to the other provisions of the Treaty, the Commission shall encourage cooperation between the Member States and facilitate the coordination of their action in all social policy fields under this Agreement.

ARTICLE 6

1. Each Member State shall ensure that the principle of equal pay for male and female workers for equal work is applied.

2. For the purpose of this Article, 'pay' means the ordinary basic or minimum wage or salary and any other consideration, whether in cash or in kind, which the worker receives directly or indirectly, in respect of his employment, from his employer.

Equal pay without discrimination based on sex means:

(a) that pay for the same work at piece rates shall be calculated on the basis of the same unit of measurement;

(b) that pay for work at time rates shall be the same for the same job.

3. This Article shall not prevent any Member State from maintaining or adopting measures providing for specific advantages in order to make it easier for women to pursue a vocational activity or to prevent or compensate for disadvantages in their professional careers.

ARTICLE 7

The Commission shall draw up a report each year on progress in achieving the objectives of Article 1, including the demographic situation in the Community. It shall forward the report to the European Parliament, the Council and the Economic and Social Committee.

The European Parliament may invite the Commission to draw up reports on particular problems concerning the social situation.

DECLARATIONS

1. Declaration on Article 2(2)

The eleven High Contracting Parties note that in the discussions on Article 2(2) of the Agreement it was agreed that the Community does not intend, in laying down minimum requirements for the protection of the safety and health of employees, to discriminate in a manner unjustified by the circumstances against employees in small and medium-sized undertakings.

2. Declaration on Article 4(2)

The eleven High Contracting Parties declare that the first of the arrangements for application of the agreements between management and labour Community-wide — referred to in Article 4(2) — will consist in developing, by collective bargaining according to the rules of each Member State, the content of the agreements, and that consequently this arrangement implies no obligation on the Member States to apply the agreements directly or to work out rules for their transposition, nor any obligation to amend national legislation in force to facilitate their implementation.

PROTOCOL
ON ECONOMIC AND SOCIAL COHESION

THE HIGH CONTRACTING PARTIES,

RECALLING that the Union has set itself the objective of promoting economic and social progress, inter alia, through the strengthening of economic and social cohesion;

RECALLING that Article 2 of this Treaty includes the task of promoting economic and social cohesion and solidarity between Member States and that the strengthening of economic and social cohesion figures among the activities of the Community listed in Article 3;

RECALLING that the provision of Part Three, Title XIV, on economic and social cohesion as a whole provide the legal basis for consolidating and further developing the Community's action in the field of economic and social cohesion, including the creation of a new fund;

RECALLING that the provisions of Part Three, Title XII on trans-European networks and Title XVI on environment envisage a Cohesion Fund to be set up before 31 December 1993;

STATING their belief that progress towards Economic and Monetary Union will contribute to the economic growth of all Member States;

NOTING that the Community's Structural Funds are being doubled in real terms between 1987 and 1993, implying large transfers, especially as a proportion of GDP of the less prosperous Member States;

NOTING that the EIB is lending large and increasing amounts for the benefit of the poorer regions;

NOTING the desire for greater flexibility in the arrangements for allocations from the Structural Funds;

NOTING the desire for modulation of the levels of Community participation in programmes and projects in certain countries;

NOTING the proposal to take greater account of the relative prosperity of Member States in the system of own resources,

REAFFIRM that the promotion of economic and social cohesion is vital to the full development and enduring success of the Community, and underline the importance of the inclusion of economic and social cohesion in Articles 2 and 3 of this Treaty;

REAFFIRM their conviction that the Structural Funds should continue to play a considerable part in the achievement of Community objectives in the field of cohesion;

REAFFIRM their conviction that the European Investment Bank should continue to devote the majority of its resources to the promotion of economic and social cohesion, and declare their willingness to review the capital needs of the European Investment Bank as soon as this is necessary for that purpose;

REAFFIRM the need for a thorough evaluation of the operation and effectiveness of the Structural Funds in 1992, and the need to review, on that occasion, the appropriate size of these Funds in the light of the tasks of the Community in the area of economic and social cohesion;

AGREE that the Cohesion Fund to be set up before 31 December 1993 will provide Community financial contributions to projects in the fields of environment and trans-European networks in Member States with a per capita GNP of less than 90% of the Community average which have a programme leading to the fulfilment of the conditions of economic convergence as set out in Article 104c;

DECLARE their intention of allowing a greater margin of flexibility in allocating financing from the Structural Funds to specific needs not covered under the present Structural Funds regulations;

DECLARE their willingness to modulate the levels of Community participation in the context of programmes and projects of the Structural Funds, with a view to avoiding excessive increases in budgetary expenditure in the less prosperous Member States;

RECOGNIZE the need to monitor regularly the progress made towards achieving economic and social cohesion and state their willingness to study all necessary measures in this respect;

DECLARE their intention of taking greater account of the contributive capacity of individual Member States in the system of own resources, and of examining means of correcting, for the less prosperous Member States, regressive elements existing in the present own resources system;

AGREE to annex this Protocol to this Treaty.

PROTOCOL
ON THE ECONOMIC AND SOCIAL COMMITTEE
AND THE COMMITTEE OF THE REGIONS

THE HIGH CONTRACTING PARTIES,

HAVE AGREED upon the following provision, which shall be annexed to this Treaty establishing the European Community:
The Economic and Social Committee and the Committee of the Regions shall have a common organizational structure.

PROTOCOL
ANNEXED TO THE TREATY ON EUROPEAN UNION
AND TO THE TREATIES ESTABLISHING THE EUROPEAN COMMUNITIES

THE HIGH CONTRACTING PARTIES,

HAVE AGREED upon the following provision, which shall be annexed to the Treaty on European Union and to the Treaties establishing the European Communities;
Nothing in the Treaty on European Union, or in the Treaties establishing the European Communities, or in the Treaties or Acts modifying or supplementing those Treaties, shall affect the application in Ireland of Article 40.3.3. of the Constitution of Ireland.

FINAL ACT OF THE CONFERENCE

1. The Conferences of the Representatives of the Governments of the Member States convened in Rome on 15 December 1990 to adopt by common accord the amendments to be made to the Treaty establishing the European Economic Community with a view to the achievement of political union and with a view to the final stages of economic and monetary union, and those convened in Brussels on 3 February 1992 with a view to amending the Treaties establishing respectively the European Coal and Steel Community and the European Atomic Energy Community as a result of the amendments envisaged for the Treaty establishing the European Economic Community have adopted the following texts:

I. the Treaty on European Union
II. Protocols
1. Protocol on the acquisition of property in Denmark
2. Protocol concerning Article 119 of the Treaty establishing the European Community
3. Protocol on the Statute of the European system of central banks and of the European Central Bank
4. Protocol on the Statute of the European Monetary Institute
5. Protocol on the excessive deficit procedure
6. Protocol on the convergence criteria referred to in Article 109j of the Treaty establishing the European Community
7. Protocol amending the Protocol on the privileges and immunities of the European Communities
8. Protocol on Denmark
9. Protocol on Portugal
10. Protocol on the transition to the third stage of economic and monetary union
11. Protocol on certain provisions relating to the United Kingdom of Great Britain and Northern Ireland
12. Protocol on certain provisions relating to Denmark
13. Protocol on France
14. Protocol on social policy, to which is annexed an agreement concluded between the Member States of the European Community with the exception

of the United Kingdom of Great Britain and Northern Ireland, to which two declarations are attached

15. Protocol on economic and social cohesion
16. Protocol on the Economic and Social Committee and the Committee of the Regions
17. Protocol annexed to the Treaty on European Union and to the Treaties establishing the European Communities
   The conferences agreed that the Protocols referred to in 1 to 16 above will be annexed to the Treaty establishing the European Community and that the Protocol referred to in 17 above will be annexed to the Treaty on Political Union and to the Treaties establishing the European Communities.

2. At the time of signature of these texts, the Conferences adopted the declaration listed below and annexed to this Final Act:

III. Declarations

1. Declaration on civil protection, energy and tourism
2. Declaration on nationality of a Member State
3. Declaration on Part Three, Titles III and VI, of the Treaty establishing the European Community
4. Declaration on Part Three, Title VI, of the Treaty establishing the European Community
5. Declaration on monetary cooperation with non-Community countries
6. Declaration on monetary relations with the Republic of San Marino, the Vatican City and the Principality of Monaco
7. Declaration on Article 73d of the Treaty establishing the European Community
8. Declaration on Article 109 of the Treaty establishing the European Economic Community
9. Declaration on Part Three, Title XVI, of the Treaty establishing the European Community
10. Declaration on Articles 109, 130r and 130y of the Treaty establishing the European Community
11. Declaration on the Directive of 24 November 1988 (Emissions)
12. Declaration on the European Development Fund
13. Declaration on the role of national Parliaments in the European Union
14. Declaration on the Conference of the Parliaments
15. Declaration on the number of members of the Commission and of the European Parliament
16. Declaration on the hierarchy of Community Acts
17. Declaration on the right of access to information
18. Declaration on estimated costs under Commission proposals
19. Declaration on the implementation of Community law
20. Declaration on assessment of the environmental impact of Community measures
21. Declaration on the Court of Auditors
22. Declaration on the Economic and Social Committee
23. Declaration on cooperation with charitable associations
24. Declaration on the protection of animals
25. Declaration on the representation of the interests of the overseas countries and territories referred to in Article 227(3) and (5)(a) and (b) of the Treaty establishing the European Community

26. Declaration on the outermost regions of the Community
27. Declaration on voting in the field of the common foreign and security policy
28. Declaration on practical arrangements in the field of the common foreign and security policy
29. Declaration on the use of languages in the field of the common foreign and security policy
30. Declaration on Western European Union
31. Declaration on asylum
32. Declaration on police cooperation
33. Declaration on disputes between the ECB and the EMI and their servants

Done at Maastricht this seventh day of February in the year one thousand nine hundred and ninety-two.

DECLARATION
ON CIVIL PROTECTION, ENERGY AND TOURISM

The Conference declares that the question of introducing into the Treaty establishing the European Community Titles relating to the spheres referred to in Article 3(t) of that Treaty will be examined, in accordance with the procedure laid down in Article N(2) of the Treaty on European Union, on the basis of a report which the Commission will submit to the Council by 1996 at the latest.

The Commission declares that Community action in those spheres will be pursued on the basis of the present provisions of the Treaties establishing the European Communities.

DECLARATION
ON NATIONALITY OF A MEMBER STATE

The Conference declares that, wherever in the Treaty establishing the European Community reference is made to nationals of the Member States, the question whether an individual possesses the nationality of a Member State shall be settled solely by reference to the national law of the Member State concerned. Member States may declare, for information, who are to be considered their nationals for Community purposes by way of a declaration lodged with the Presidency and many amend any such declaration when necessary.

DECLARATION ON PART THREE,
TITLES III AND VI, OF THE TREATY
ESTABLISHING THE EUROPEAN COMMUNITY

The Conference affirms that, for the purposes of applying the provisions set out in Part Three, Title III, Chapter 4 on capital and payments, and Title VI on economic and monetary policy, of this Treaty, the usual practice, according to which the Council meets in the composition of Economic and Finance Ministers, shall be continued, without prejudice to Article 109j(2) to (4) and Article 109k(2).

DECLARATION ON PART THREE, TITLE VI, OF THE TREATY ESTABLISHING THE EUROPEAN COMMUNITY

The Conference affirms that the President of the European Council shall invite the Economic and Finance Ministers to participate in European Council meetings when the European Council is discussing matters relating to Economic and Monetary Union.

DECLARATION ON MONETARY COOPERATION WITH NON-COMMUNITY COUNTRIES

The Conference affirms that the Community shall aim to contribute to stable international monetary relations. To this end the Community shall be prepared to cooperate with other European countries and with those non-European countries with which the Community has close economic ties.

DECLARATION ON MONETARY RELATIONS WITH THE REPUBLIC OF SAN MARINO, THE VATICAN CITY AND THE PRINCIPALITY OF MONACO

The Conference agrees that the existing monetary relations between Italy and San Marino and the Vatican City and between France and Monaco remain unaffected by the Treaty establishing the European Community until the introduction of the ECU as the single currency of the Community.

The Community undertakes to facilitate such renegotiations of existing arrangements as might become necessary as a result of the introduction of the ECU as a single currency.

DECLARATION ON ARTICLE 73d OF THE TREATY ESTABLISHING THE EUROPEAN COMMUNITY

The Conference affirms that the right of Member States to apply the relevant provisions of their tax law as referred to in Article 73d(1)(a) of this Treaty will apply only with respect to the relevant provisions which exist at the end of 1993.

DECLARATION ON ARTICLE 109 OF THE TREATY ESTABLISHING THE EUROPEAN COMMUNITY

The Conference emphasizes that the use of the term 'formal agreements' in Article 109(1) is not intended to create a new category of international agreement within the meaning of Community law.

DECLARATION ON PART THREE, TITLE XVI,
OF THE TREATY ESTABLISHING THE EUROPEAN COMMUNITY

The Conference considers that, in view of the increasing importance of nature conservation at national, Community and international level, the Community should, in exercising its powers under the provisions of Part Three, Title XVI, take account of the specific requirements of this area.

DECLARATION ON ARTICLES 109, 130r AND 130y
OF THE TREATY ESTABLISHING THE EUROPEAN COMMUNITY

The Conference considers that the provisions of Article 109(5), Article 130r(4), second subparagraph, and Article 130y do not affect the principles resulting from the judgment handed down by the Court of Justice in the AETR case.

DECLARATION
OF THE DIRECTIVE OF 24 NOVEMBER 1988 (Emissions)

The Conference declares that changes in Community legislation cannot undermine the derogations granted to Spain and Portugal until 31 December 1999 under the Council Directive of 24 November 1988 on the limitation of emissions of certain pollutants into the air from large combustion plants.

DECLARATION
ON THE EUROPEAN DEVELOPMENT FUND

The Conference agrees that the European Development Fund will continue to be financed by national contributions in accordance with the current provisions.

DECLARATION
ON THE ROLE OF NATIONAL PARLIAMENTS IN THE EUROPEAN UNION

The Conference considers that it is important to encourage greater involvement of national Parliaments in the activities of the European union.

To this end, the exchange of information between national Parliaments and the European Parliament should be stepped up. In this context, the governments of the Member States will ensure, inter alia, that national Parliaments receive Commission proposals for legislation in good time for information or possible examination.

Similarly, the Conference considers that it is important for contacts between the national Parliaments and the European Parliament to be stepped up, in particular through the granting of appropriate reciprocal facilities and regular meetings between members of Parliament interested in the same issues.

DECLARATION
ON THE CONFERENCE OF THE PARLIAMENTS

The Conference invites the European Parliament and the national Parliaments to meet as necessary as a Conference of the Parliaments (or 'Assises').

The Conference of the Parliaments will be consulted on the main features of the European Union, without prejudice to the powers of the European Parliament and the rights of the national Parliaments. The President of the European Council and the President of the Commission will report to each session of the Conference of the Parliaments on the state of the Union.

DECLARATION ON THE NUMBER OF MEMBERS
OF THE COMMISSION AND OF THE EUROPEAN PARLIAMENT

The Conference agrees that the Member States will examine the questions relating to the number of members of the Commission and the number of members of the European Parliament no later than at the end of 1992, with a view to reaching an agreement which will permit the establishment of the necessary legal basis for fixing the number of members of the European Parliament in good time for the 1994 elections. The decisions will be taken in the light, inter alia, of the need to establish the overall size of the European Parliament in an enlarged Community.

DECLARATION
ON THE HIERARCHY OF COMMUNITY ACTS

The Conference agrees that the Intergovernmental Conference to be convened in 1996 will examine to what extent it might be possible to review the classification of Community acts with a view to establishing an appropriate hierarchy between the different categories of act.

DECLARATION
ON THE RIGHT OF ACCESS TO INFORMATION

The Conference considers that transparency of the decision-making process strengthens the democratic nature of the institutions and the public's confidence in the administration. The Conference accordingly recommends that the Commission submit to the Council no later than 1993 a report on measures designed to improve public access to the information available to the institutions.

DECLARATION
ON ESTIMATED COSTS UNDER COMMISSION PROPOSALS

The Conference notes that the Community undertakes by basing itself where appropriate on any consultations it considers necessary and by strengthening its system for evaluating Community legislation, to take account in its legislative proposals of costs and benefits to the Member States' public authorities and all the parties concerned.

DECLARATION
ON THE IMPLEMENTATION OF COMMUNITY LAW

1. The Conference stresses that it is central to the coherence and unity of the process of European construction that each Member State should fully and accurately transpose into national law the Community Directives addressed to it within the deadlines laid down therein. Moreover, the Conference, while recognizing that it must be for each Member State to determine how the provisions of Community law can best be enforced in the light of its own particular institutions, legal system and other circumstances, but in any event in compliance with Article 189 of the Treaty establishing the European Community, considers it essential for the proper functioning of the Community that the measures taken by the different Member States should result in Community law being applied with the same effectiveness and rigour as in the application of their national law.

2. The Conference calls on the Commission to ensure, in exercising its powers under Article 155 of this Treaty, that Member States fulfil their obligations. It asks the Commission to publish periodically a full report for the Member States and the European Parliament.

DECLARATION ON ASSESSMENT
OF THE ENVIRONMENTAL IMPACT OF COMMUNITY MEASURES

The Conference notes that the Commission undertakes in its proposals, and that the Member States undertake in implementing those proposals, to take full account of their environmental impact and of the principle of sustainable growth.

DECLARATION ON THE COURT OF AUDITORS

The Conference emphasizes the special importance it attaches to the task assigned to the Court of Auditors by Articles 188a, 188b and 206 of the Treaty establishing the European Community.
It requests the other Community institutions to consider, together with the Court of Auditors, all appropriate ways of enhancing the effectiveness of its work.

DECLARATION ON THE ECONOMIC AND SOCIAL COMMITTEE

The Conference agrees that the Economic and Social Committee will enjoy the same independence with regard to its budget and staff management as the Court of Auditors has enjoyed hitherto.

DECLARATION ON COOPERATION WITH CHARITABLE ASSOCIATIONS

The Conference stresses the importance, in pursuing the objectives of Article 117 of the Treaty establishing the European Community, of cooperation between the latter and charitable associations and foundations as institutions responsible for social welfare establishments and services.

DECLARATION ON THE PROTECTION OF ANIMALS

The Conference calls upon the European Parliament, the Council and the Commission, as well as the Member States, when drafting and implementing Community legislation on the common agricultural policy, transport, the internal market and research, to pay full regard to the welfare requirements of animals.

DECLARATION
on the representation of the interests of the overseas countries and territories referred to in Article 227(3) and (5)(a) and (b) of the Treaty establishing the European Community

The Conference, noting that in exceptional circumstances divergences may arise between the interests of the Union and those of the overseas countries and territories referred to in Article 227(3) and (5)(a) and (b), agrees that the Council will seek to reach a solution which accords with the position of the Union. However, in the event that this proves impossible, the Conference agrees that the Member State concerned may act separately in the interests of the said overseas countries and territories, without this affecting the Community's interests. The Member State concerned will give notice to the Council and the Commission where such a divergence of interests is likely to occur and, when separate action proves unavoidable, make it clear that it is acting in the interests of an overseas territory mentioned above. This declaration also applies to Macao and East Timor.

DECLARATION
ON THE OUTERMOST REGIONS OF THE COMMUNITY

The Conference acknowledges that the outermost regions of the Community (the French overseas departments, Azores and Madeira and Canary Islands) suffer from major structural backwardness compounded by several phenomena (remoteness, island status, small size, difficult topography and climate, economic dependence on a few products), the permanence and combination of which severely restrain their economic and social development.
It considers that, while the provisions of the Treaty establishing the European Community and secondary legislation apply automatically to the outermost regions, it is nonetheless possible to adopt specific measures to assist them inasmuch and as long as there is an objective need to take such measures with a view to the economic and social development of those regions. Such measures should have as their aim both the completion of the internal market and the recognition

of the regional reality to enable the outermost regions to achieve the average economic and social level of the Community.

DECLARATION ON VOTING IN THE FIELD
OF THE COMMON FOREIGN AND SECURITY POLICY

The Conference agrees that, with regard to Council decisions requiring unanimity. Member States will, to the extent possible, avoid preventing a unanimous decision where a qualified majority exists in favour of that decision.

DECLARATION ON PRACTICAL ARRANGEMENTS IN THE FIELD
OF THE COMMON FOREIGN AND SECURITY POLICY

The Conference agrees that the division of work between the Political Committee and the Permanent Representatives Committee will be examined at a later stage, as will the practical arrangements for merging the Political Cooperation Secretariat with the General Secretariat of the Council and for cooperation between the latter and the Commission.

DECLARATION ON THE USE OF LANGUAGES IN THE FIELD
OF THE COMMON FOREIGN AND SECURITY POLICY

The Conference agrees that the use of languages shall be in accordance with the rules of the European Communities.

For COREU communications, the current practice of European Political Cooperation will serve as a guide for the time being.

All common foreign and security policy texts which are submitted to or adopted at meetings of the European Council and of the Council as well as all texts which are to be published are immediately and simultaneously translated into all the official Community languages.

DECLARATION ON WESTERN EUROPEAN UNION
The Conference notes the following declarations:
I. DECLARATION

**of Belgium, Germany, Spain, France, Italy, Luxembourg,
the Netherlands, Portugal and the United Kingdom of Great Britain and Northern
Ireland, which are members of the Western European Union and also members
of the European Union on**

THE ROLE OF THE WESTERN EUROPEAN UNION AND ITS RELATIONS
WITH THE EUROPEAN UNION AND WITH THE ATLANTIC ALLIANCE

Introduction

1. WEU Member States agree on the need to develop a genuine European security and defence identity and a greater European responsibility on defence matters. This identity will be pursued through a gradual process involving successive phases. WEU will form an integral part of the process of the development of the European Union and will enhance its contribution to solidarity within the Atlantic Alliance.

WEU Member States agree to strengthen the role of WEU, in the longer term perspective of a common defence policy within the European Union which might in time lead to a common defence, compatible with that of the Atlantic Alliance.

2. WEU will be developed as the defence component of the European Union and as the means to strengthen the European pillar of the Atlantic Alliance. To this end, it will formulate common European defence policy and carry forward its concrete implementation through the further development of its own operational role.

WEU Member States take note of Article J.4 relating to the common foreign and security policy of the Treaty on European Union which reads as follows:
'1. The common foreign and security policy shall include all questions related to the security of the Union, including the eventual framing of a common defence policy, which might in time lead to a common defence.
2. The Union requests the Western European Union (WEU), which is an integral part of the development of the Union, to elaborate and implement decisions and actions of the Union which have defence implications. The Council shall, in agreement with the institutions of the WEU, adopt the necessary practical arrangements.
3. Issues having defence implications dealt with under this Article shall not prejudice the procedures set out in Article J.3.
4. The policy of the Union in accordance with this Article shall not prejudice the specific character of the security and defence policy of certain Member States and shall respect the obligations of certain Member States under the North Atlantic Treaty and be compatible with the common security and defence policy established within that framework.
5. The provisions of this Article shall not prevent the development of closer cooperation between two or more Member States on a bilateral level, in the framework of the WEU and the Atlantic Alliance, provided such cooperation does not run counter to or impede that provided for in this Title.
6. With a view to furthering the objective of this Treaty, and having in view the date of 1998 in the context of Article XII of the Brussels Treaty, the provisions of this Article may be revised as provided for in Article N(2) on the basis of a report to be presented in 1996 by the Council to the European Council, which shall include an evaluation of the progress made and the experience gained until then.'

A. WEU's relations with European Union

3. The objective is to build up WEU in stages as the defence component of the European Union. To this end, WEU is prepared, at the request of the European

Union, to elaborate and implement decisions and actions of the Union which have defence implications.

To this end, WEU will take the following measures to develop a close working relationship with the Union:
— as appropriate, synchronization of the dates and venues of meeting and harmonization of working methods;
— establishment of close cooperation between the Council and Secretariat-General of WEU on the one hand, and the Council of the Union and General Secretariat of the Council on the other;
— consideration of the harmonization of the sequence and duration of the respective Presidencies;
— arranging for appropriate modalities so as to ensure that the Commission of the European Communities is regularly informed and, as appropriate, consulted on WEU activities in accordance with the role of the Commission in the common foreign and security policy as defined in the Treaty on European Union;
— encouragement of closer cooperation between the Parliamentary Assembly of WEU and the European Parliament.

The WEU Council shall, in agreement with the competent bodies of the European Union, adopt the necessary practical arrangements.

B. WEU's relations with the Atlantic Alliance

4. The objective is to develop WEU as a means to strengthen the European pillar of the Atlantic Alliance. Accordingly WEU is prepared to develop further the close working links between WEU and the Alliance and to strengthen the role, responsibilities and contributions of WEU Member States in the Alliance. This will be undertaken on the basis of the necessary transparency and complementarity between the emerging European security and defence identity and the Alliance. WEU will act in conformity with the positions adopted in the Atlantic Alliance.
— WEU Member States will intensify their coordination on Alliance issues which represent an important common interest with the aim of introducing joint positions agreed in WEU into the process of consultation in the Alliance which will remain the essential forum for consultation among its members and the venue for agreement on policies bearing on the security and defence commitments of Allies under the North Atlantic Treaty.
— Where necessary, dates and venues of meetings will be synchronized and working methods harmonized.
— Close cooperation will be established between the Secretariats-General of WEU and NATO.

C. Operational role of WEU

5. WEU's operational role will be strengthened by examining and defining appropriate missions, structures and means, covering in particular:
— WEU planning cell;
— closer military cooperation complementary to the Alliance in particular in the fields of logistics, transport, training and strategic surveillance;

— meetings of WEU Chiefs of Defence Staff;
— military units answerable to WEU.

Other proposals will be examined further, including:
— enhanced cooperation in the field of armaments with the aim of creating a European armaments agency;
— development of the WEU Institute into a European Security and Defence Academy. Arrangements aimed at giving WEU a stronger operational role will be fully compatible with the military dispositions necessary to ensure the collective defence of all Allies.

D. Other measures

6. As a consequence of the measures set out above, and in order to facilitate the strengthening of WEU's role, the seat of the WEU Council and Secretariat will be transferred to Brussels.
7. Representation on the WEU Council must be such that the Council is able to exercise its functions continuously in accordance with Article VIII of the modified Brussels Treaty. Member States may draw on a double-hatting formula, to be worked out, consisting of their representatives to the Alliance and to the European Union.
8. WEU notes that, in accordance with the provisions of Article J.4(6) concerning the common foreign and security policy of the Treaty on European Union, the Union will decide to review the provisions of this Article with a view to furthering the objective to be set by it in accordance with the procedure defined. The WEU will re-examine the present provisions in 1996. This re-examination will take account of the progress and experience acquired and will extend to relations between WEU and the Atlantic Alliance.

II. DECLARATION
of Belgium, Germany, Spain, France, Italy, Luxembourg, the Netherlands,
Portugal and the United Kingdom of Great Britain and Northern Ireland
which are members of the Western European Union

'The Member States of WEU welcome the development of the European security and defence identity. They are determined, taking into account the role of WEU as the defence component of the European Union and as the means to strengthen the European pillar of the Atlantic Alliance, to put the relationship between WEU and the other European States on a new basis for the sake of stability and security in Europe. In this spirit, they propose the following:

States which are members of the European Union are invited to accede to WEU on conditions to be agreed in accordance with Article XI of the modified Brussels Treaty, or to become observers if they so wish. Simultaneously, other European Member States of NATO are invited to become associate members of WEU in a way which will give them the possibility of participating fully in the activities of WEU.

The Member States of WEU assume that treaties and agreements corresponding with the above proposals will be concluded before 31 December 1992.'

DECLARATION ON ASYLUM

1. The Conference agrees that, in the context of the proceedings provided for in Articles K.1 and K.3 of the provisions on cooperation in the fields of justice and home affairs, the Council will consider as a matter of priority questions concerning Member States' asylum policies with the aim of adopting, by the beginning of 1993, common action to harmonize aspects of them, in the light of the work programme and timetable contained in the report on asylum drawn up at the request of the European Council meeting in Luxembourg on 28 and 29 June 1991.

2. In this connection, the Council will also consider, by the end of 1993 on the basis of a report, the possibility of applying Article K.9 to such matters.

DECLARATION ON POLICE COOPERATION

The Conference confirms the agreement of the Member States on the objectives underlying the German delegation's proposals at the European Council meeting in Luxembourg on 28 and 29 June 1991.

For the present, the Member States agree to examine as a matter of priority the drafts submitted to them, on the basis of the work programme and timetable agreed upon in the report drawn up at the request of the Luxembourg European Council, and they are willing to envisage the adoption of practical measures in areas such as those suggested by the German delegation, relating to the following functions in the exchange of information and experience:
— support for national criminal investigation and security authorities, in particular in the coordination of investigations and search operations;
— creation of data bases;
— central analysis and assessment of information in order to take stock of the situation and identify investigative approaches;
— collection and analysis of national prevention programmes for forwarding to Member States and for drawing up Europe-wide prevention strategies;
— measures relating to further training, research, forensic matters and criminal records departments.
Member States agree to consider on the basis of a report, during 1994 at the latest, whether the scope of such cooperation should be extended.

DECLARATION ON DISPUTES BETWEEN
THE ECB AND THE EMI AND THEIR SERVANTS

The Conference considers it proper that the Court of First Instance should hear this class of action in accordance with Article 168a of the Treaty establishing the European Community. The Conference therefore invites the institutions to adapt the relevant rules accordingly.

TREATY ON EUROPEAN UNION

The full text of the 'Treaty on European Union' as decided at the Council of Europe in Maastricht, was published in its definitive version, under No1759/1760 of EUROPE/Documents. Since, the Conference of Representatives of Member States has reviewed it one last time in its different linguistic versions, bringing final corrections. These essentially concern form.

So that our subscribers can have precise texts, we are publishing below the corrections made by the Conference.

Page 6
— Article 73g (1), line 1:
For 'case', read 'cases'.

Page 7
— Article 100c
The first sentence of paragraph 3 shall read:
'3. From 1 January 1996, the Council shall adopt the decisions referred to in paragraph 1 by a qualified majority.'
— In paragraphs 4, 6 and 7, 'matters' shall be replaced by *'areas'*.
— Article 103
In the second subparagraph of paragraph 2, 'this report' shall read *'the* report'.
— Article 104 (1)
A comma shall be inserted after 'law'.
— The beginning of paragraph 2 shall read:
'2. *Paragraph 1* shall not apply to publicly-owned credit institutions which, in the context of the supply of reserves by central banks, shall . . .'
— Article 104a (1)
A comma shall be inserted after 'law'.

Page 8
— Article 104 (c) 11
The first indent shall begin: '— to require the Member State concerned to publish . . .'.
The third indent shall begin:
'— to require the Member State concerned to make . . .'.
— Article 104 (c) 12
Delete 'as' in line 1;
For 'previously has', read *'has previously'*.
— Article 104 (c) 13
A comma shall be inserted after 'Article 148 (2)' and the word 'and' deleted.
— Article 105 (4)
For 'within'
Read: *'in'*.

Page 9
— Article 106 (6)
In line 3, the comma shall be deleted.
— Article 108a (1)
In line 2 of the first indent, 'or' shall read *'and'*.

— Article 109 (2)
In line 4, the comma shall be deleted.
— Article 109 (5)
In line 2, read 'economic and *m*onetary *u*nion'.

Page 10
— Article 109 (f) (3)
In the third indent, for 'in', read '*within*'.

Page 11
— Article 109 (f) (4)
In line 2, a comma shall be inserted after 'Council'.

Page 12
— Article 109 (k) (1)
In line 3, 'as' shall be deleted.
— Article 109 (k) (5)
In line 1, for 'The voting rights of the Member States', read 'The voting rights *of Member States*'.
— Article 109 (1) (2)
In line 2, for 'functions', read '*tasks*'.

Page 13
— Article 126 (3)
In line 3, for 'sphere', read '*field*'.
— Article 126 (4)
The beginning of the second indent shall read: '— acting by *a* qualified majority . . .'.

Page 20
— Article 189b (2)
In line 2 of the second subparagraph, for 'Opinion', read '*o*pinion'.
Idem for page 21, Article 189c (a), second line.

Page 21
— Article 189b (2) (c), in line 4,
for 'paragraph 3', read 'paragraph *4*'.

Page 22
— Article 198
The third sentence of the first subparagraph shall begin: 'It may issue an opinion on its own initiative in cases . . .'.
Idem in Article 198c and in Article 170.
— Article 198a
In line 2, for 'Committee of the Regions', read '*the* Committee of the Regions'.
— Article 199
Second subparagraph, line 1, for 'The administrative . . .', read '*Administrative* . . .'.
In line 3, for 'spheres', read '*fields*'.

Page 23
— Article 209 (b), in line 3,
for 'to the Communities' own resources', read 'to the Community's own resources'.
— Article 228 (3)
In the first subparagraph, for 'Opinion', read 'opinion' (twice).
— Article 228 (4)
In line 2, for 'empower', read 'authorize', and in line 6, for 'empowerment', read 'authorization'.

Page 25
— Article 32
The word 'judges' shall be replaced by 'Judges' each time it occurs and 'chambers' shall be replaced by 'Chambers' in line 3. Idem for Article 137.

Page 26
— Article 45c(3)
In the second subparagraph 'department' shall read 'departments' and 'as' 'at' in line 3.

Page 27
— Article 78h
In line 2 of (b), 'for' shall be deleted.

Page 28
— Article 123
In line 1, read 'acting by a qualified majority'.
In line 3, insert 'of' between 'and' and 'the'.

Page 30
— Article 173
The first subparagraph shall be replaced by the following: 'Without prejudice to other revenue, the budget shall be financed wholly from own resources'.

Page 31
— Article 180b(1) and (2). In line 3, for 'budgets', read 'budget'.
— Article 180b(2)
In line 5, for 'maintenance', read 'operation'.
— Article 183
In (b), delete 'for'.
— Article 183 (a)
For 'implementing the budgets' read 'implementing the budget'.
In the last line of the second subparagraph, for 'services', read 'departments'.
— Article 183 (b)
For 'the Communities' own resources' read 'the Community's own resources'.

Page 33
— Article J.11 (1). In line 1 For 'Articles 137, 138 to 142, 146,' read 'Articles 137 138, 139 to 142, 146,'
— In the first indent of paragraph 2, for 'operating', read 'operational'.
Idem for Article K.8

— Article K.8 (1). In line 1,
For 'Articles 137, 138 to 142, 146,' read 'Articles 137, *138, 139 to 142*, 146'.

Page 37
— Article 21.1.
In line 5, a comma shall be inserted after 'public law'.

Page 38
— Article 27.2.
For 'Article 188b', read 'Article 188c'.
— Article 29.1.
For: '0,05% points', read '*0.05 percentage* points'.

Page 40
— Article 42.
In line 5, the comma after 'ECB' shall be deleted, and in line 7, '29,2' shall read '29.2'.
— Article 44
In the second subparagraph, the reference shall be to 'Article 109*k*'.

Page 42
— Article 5.4. The words '*decide to*' shall be inserted between 'may' and 'publish'.

Page 43
— Article 12. 'ECU' shall read 'ECU*s*'.

Page 44
— In the Protocol on the convergence criteria, the beginning of the preamble shall read:
'DESIRING to lay down the details of the convergence criteria which shall guide the Community *in taking decisions* on the passage . . .'.
— Article 1. In line 8, '(CPI)' shall be deleted.

Page 46
In the Protocol on the transition to the third stage of EMU, in the last line of the third subparagraph, 'on' shall be deleted.

Page 47
— Protocol on certain provisions relating to Denmark.
In point 5, for 'no longer be applicable', read '*cease to apply*'.
— Protocol on social policy.
After 'Netherlands' in line 5 of the recital, the word '*and*' shall be added; in line 10, for 'which relate', read '*relating*'.

Page 48
— Article 2(5).
In line 3, 'preventive' shall read '*protective*'.
In line 3 of the second Declaration, 'Community-wide' shall read '*at Community level*'.

Page 49
— Protocol on economic and social cohesion.
The beginning of the second subparagraph shall read:
'RECALLING that Article 2 of *the* Treaty *establishing the European Community* includes . . .'.
— In line 14, 'EIB' shall read *'European Investment Bank'*.
— The final words on this page shall read:
'AGREE to annex this Protocol *to the Treaty establishing the European Community'*.

Page 51
— For 'FINAL ACT OF THE CONFERENCE', read 'FINAL ACT'.
— In the last subparagraph of point 17, 'Political Union' shall read *'European Union'*.

Page 52
— Declaration on article 73 d. The following sentence shall be added to this Declaration:
'However, this Declaration shall apply only to capital movements between Member States and to payments effected between Member States'.

Page 54
— Declaration on the Court of Auditors.
For 'Articles 188a, 188b and 206', read 'Articles 188a, 188b, *188c* and 206'.
— Declaration on the outermost regions of the Community. In line 4 of the second subparagraph, for 'the recognition', read *'a* recognition'.

Page 55
— Declaration on practical Arrangements in the field of the common foreign and security policy or 'Permanent Representatives Committee', read *'Committee of Permanent Representatives'*.
— Declaration on western european union.
— For 'I. DECLARATION of', read 'I. DECLARATION *by'*.
Idem in the second declaration, on page 56.
— In paragraph 2, 'the means' shall read *'a* means'.

Page 56
— In point 3, for 'shall not prejudice', read *'shall not be subject to'*.

Appendix 2

DECLARATIONS ADOPTED AT THE UNITED STATES/EC SUMMITOF 9 NOVEMBER IN THE HAGUE

On 9 November 1991, the half yearly summit was held in The Hague bringing together the President of the United States, the President-in-Office of the European Council and the President of the European Commission. On this occasion, George Bush, Ruud Lubbers and Jacques Delors adopted three declarations that we are publishing in full: on the Uruguay Round, the changes in Central and Eastern Europe, and the establishment within the UN of a register on the transfer of conventional arms (also see other news in EUROPE Bulletin No 5607 dated 12–13 November 1991).

DECLARATION OF THE GATT AND THE URUGUAY ROUND

The United States and the European Community are more than ever committed to an ambitious, global and balanced result of the Uruguay Round. Through the strengthening of the multilateral trading system, they aim at creating the conditions for more economic growth for all nations and more particularly for the developing countries as well as for the Central and Eastern European countries thereby enabling them to progress towards market economies and full participation in the world economy. In order to give new momentum to the negotiations they have decided to endeavour to overcome divergencies which still separate them.

We welcome the recent intensification of the negotiations under the leadership of GATT Director General Dunkel, and we are willing to show flexibility to bring this round to a successful conclusion by the end of this year. Accordingly, we have instructed our negotiators to lead by example and work with our other trading partners to fashion an ambitious package on the basis of the following platform:

On *Agriculture* we have made some progress on a package of measures being discussed. The remaining gap will not be easy to close, but we are both committed to do so. Thus the United States and the EC have made progress in narrowing their differences and instruct their negotiators to continue in Geneva.

The US and the EC share the objective of *strengthening the existing rules of the GATT* and of adapting them to today's economic realities. We are close to agreement on how this should be accomplished in all areas. On *subsidies* we have agreed to seek a solution that improves discipline on trade distorting subsidies, while meeting each other's major concerns.

We also both agreed that it is vital to achieve an effective and more binding system of resolving our *trade disputes*, one that reduces the dangers of retaliatory actions by effectively channeling our differences into a multilateral, rule-based system.

We strongly feel that liberalization to *tariff and non-tariff barriers* by all GATT partners would be a major incentive to restore business confidence and stimulate global economic growth. We noted real progress in the bilateral US/EC market access negotiations. We have decided to move boldly to meet one another's key objectives in this area. Specifically, we have instructed our negotiators to develop an agreement substantially reducing peak tariffs, eliminating tariffs in key sectors, and harmonizing them at very low levels in others.

We call on all nations to match the ambitions of the US and EC in market access. Too many countries maintain high tariff structures, and these barriers to world trade can no longer be justified. A trading system in which all participants have binding commitments to maintain low tariff structures will benefit both developing and developed economies alike.

Finally, we reaffirmed the necessity of significant results in the new areas of intellectual property, investment, and service.

On *intellectual property*, we are in virtual agreement on the elements of a substantial agreement that would contain a high level of protection for copyrights, patents, integrated circuits, trade secrets geographical indications and trademarks.

On *services*, which represents a vital and growing share of the world economy, we agreed on a common objective: a strong framework of rules regarding such matters as effective national treatment and MFN, combined with a substantial package of market access commitments from all participants. We agreed that coverage of a services framework should be universal, including financial services, and should form an integral part of the multilateral trading system. We have agreed in principle to seek maximum liberalization and to minimize derogations. We also discussed certain key services sectors where problems still exist, in the negotiations, and agreed to resolve quickly our differences in these sectors so as to finalize the negotiations.

We instruct our negotiators to move quickly in Geneva to bridge any remaining differences and to work with our trading partners to conclude the ambitious package we all seek. We also agreed that we stand ready to intervene again as and when necessary.

EC-US STATEMENT ON PEACEFUL AND DEMOCRATIC TRANSFORMATION IN THE EAST

We, the European Community and its member States and the United States support the citizens of the new democracies of Central and Eastern Europe and the Soviet Union and its Republics in their struggle to rebuild their societies and their economies on a democratic basis after decades of dictatorship and decay. We reaffirm our willingness to assist them as they confront the challenges they must overcome on the path to democracy and free-market economies.

One of the greatest of those challenges is dealing with ethnic diversity and the rights of persons belonging to national minorities. Ethnic diversity had enriched immensely the member States of the European Community and the United States.

In Central and Eastern Europe and the Soviet Union and its Republics, however, communism suppressed the legitimate concerns of those who sought to express and exercise their human rights and fundamental freedoms. Many States of the region now face the re-emergence of inter-ethnic tensions, which can lead to ethnic intolerance and aggressive nationalism and other dangers. The problem is currently most acute, and most dangerous, in Yugoslavia where the full benefits of democratic reform have not yet been realized. It also exists elsewhere and threatens to undermine progress toward democracy and prosperity in all the countries of the region.

The potential for inter-ethnic tensions and aggressive nationalism to destabilize the emerging democracies of the region can best be addressed through adherence to the principles and commitments enunciated through the CSCE process, including as reaffirmed at the recent Geneva meeting of experts on national minorities. Failure to observe these can, as we have seen in Yugoslavia, lead only to tragedy and human suffering.

We specifically want to underline that political freedom is not the cause of such problems but is the necessary pre-condition for achieving durable solutions in the spirit of compromise and mutual tolerance.

We call on the government and citizens of the region to join them in openly and publicly confirming their support for CSCE norms, including, specifically:

* The resolution of disputes consistent with democratic values, principles and practices.

* Reliance on dialogue and negotiation rather than the use of force to settle political differences. The use of force in such matters is absolutely unacceptable and will result in the international isolation of those who resort to it.

* Respect for all existing borders, both internal and external, and agreement to change them only through peaceful means and by the agreement of the parties concerned.

* Rebuilding their societies based on democracy and the rule of Law, including in particular democratic practices such as free and fair elections, due process of law, free media and fostering tolerance and cross-cultural understanding. Democracy is based not only on the principle of majority rule, but also on the protection of the fundamental human rights of those in the minority.

* Safeguarding of human rights, with full respect for the individual, including fair and equal treatment of members of national minorities.

* Respect for international law and obligations, as well as the values, principles and commitments enunciated through the CSCE process, especially those contained in the Helsinki Final Act, the Charter of Paris, and the Copenhagen, Geneva and Moscow Documents.

We note that the full observance and implementation of all CSCE principles and commitments and the respect for the diversity of minorities in a spirit of tolerance are essential to the development of close, cooperative and mutually beneficial relations in the new Europe.

As the CSCE proclaimed categorically and irrevocably in Moscow, respect for fundamental human rights in any CSCE State is a legitimate concern of the CSCE community. Indeed, they are among the primary obligations of responsible government. The citizens and governments of Central and Eastern Europe and the Soviet Union and its Republics should understand that the respect for these principles will be fundamental to the development of our relations.

EC-US STATEMENT ON UN CONVENTIONAL ARMS TRANSFER REGISTER

We agree to work closely together to establish an arms transfer registry under U. N. auspices as proposed in the EC-Japan initiative. Greater transparency in the transfer of arms can help to build international confidence and stability and reduce regional tensions. We urge worldwide support for the current resolution and for other efforts that seek to enhance the transparency of conventional arms transfers.

Appendix 3

DECLARATION ON EC-US RELATIONS

The United States of America on one side and, on the other, the European Community and its member States,
— mindful of their common heritage and of their close historical, political, economic and cultural ties,
— guided by their faith in the values of human dignity, intellectual freedom and civil liberties, and in the democratic institutions which have evolved on both sides of the Atlantic over the centuries,
— recognizing that the transatlantic solidarity has been essential for the preservation of peace and freedom and for the development of free and prosperous economies as well as for the recent developments which have restored unity in Europe,
— determined to help consolidate the new Europe, undivided and democratic,
— resolved to strengthen security, economic cooperation and human rights in Europe in the framework of the CSCE, and in other fora,
— noting the firm commitment of the United States and the EC Member States concerned to the North Atlantic Alliance and to its principles and purposes,
— acting on the basis of a pattern of cooperation proven over many decades, and convinced that by strengthening and expanding this partnership on an equal footing they will greatly contribute to continued stability, as well as to political and economic progress in Europe and in the world,
— aware of their shared responsibility, not only to further common interests but also to face transnational challenges affecting the well-being of all mankind,
— bearing in mind the accelerating process by which the European Community is acquiring its own identity in economic and monetary matters, in foreign policy and in the domain of security,
— determined further to strengthen transatlantic solidarity, through the variety of their international relations,
   have decided to endow their relationship with long-term perspectives.

Common goals
The United States of America and the European Community and its member States solemnly reaffirm their determination further to strengthen their partnership in order to:
— support democracy, the rule of law and respect for human rights and individual liberty, and promote prosperity and social progress world-wide;
— safeguard peace and promote international security, by cooperating with other nations against aggression and coercion, by contributing to the settlement of conflicts in the world and by reinforcing the role of the United Nations and other international organisations;
— pursue policies aimed at achieving a sound world economy marked by sustained economic growth with low inflation, a high level of employment, equitable social conditions, in a framework of international stability;
— promote market principles, reject protectionism and expand, strengthen and further open the multilateral trading system;
— carry out their resolve to help developing countries by all appropriate means in their efforts towards political and economic reforms;
— provide adequate support, in cooperation with other states and organisations, to the nations of Eastern and Central Europe undertaking economic and political reforms and encourage their participation in the multilateral institutions of international trade and finance.

Principles of US-EC partnership
To achieve their common goals, the European Community and its member States and the United States of America will inform and consult each other on important matters of common interest, both political and economic, with a view to bringing their positions as close as possible, without prejudice to their respective independence. In appropriate international bodies, in particular, they will seek close cooperation.

The EC-US partnership will, moreover, greatly benefit from the mutual knowledge and understanding acquired through regular consultations as described in this Declaration.

Economic cooperation
Both sides recognize the importance of strengthening the multilateral trading system. They will support further steps towards liberalization, transparency, and the implementation of GATT and OECD principles concerning both trade in goods and services and investment.

They will further develop their dialogue, which is already underway, on other matters such as technical and non-tariff barriers to industrial and agricultural trade, services, competition policy, transportation policy, standards, telecommunications, high technology and other relevant areas.

Education, scientific and cultural cooperation
The partnership between the European Community and its member States on the one hand, and the United States on the other, will be based on continuous efforts to strengthen mutual cooperation in various other fields which directly affect the present and future well-being of their citizens, such as exchanges and joint projects in science and technology, including, inter alia, research in medicine, environment

protection, pollution prevention, energy, space, high-energy physics, and the safety of nuclear and other installations, as well as in education and culture, including academic and youth exchanges.

Trans-national challenges
The United States of America and the European Community and its member States will fulfil their responsibility to address trans-national challenges, in the interest of their own peoples and of the rest of the world. In particular, they will join their efforts in the following fields:
— combatting and preventing terrorism;
— putting an end to the illegal production, trafficking and consumption of narcotics and related criminal activities, such as the laundering of money;
— cooperating in the fight against international crime;
— protecting the environment, both internationally and domestically, by integrating environmental and economic goals;
— preventing the proliferation of nuclear armaments, chemical and biolgical weapons, and missile technology.

Institutional framework for consultation
Both sides agree that a framework is required for regular and intensive consultation. They will make full use of and further strengthen existing procedures, including those established by the President of the European Council and the President of the United States on 27 February 1990, namely:
— bi-annual consultations to be arranged in the United States and in Europe between, on the one side, the President of the European Council and the President of the Commission, and on the other side, the President of the United States;
— bi-annual consultations between the European Community Foreign Ministers, with the Commission, and the US Secretary of State, alternately on either side of the Atlantic;
— ad hoc consultations between the Presidency Foreign Minister or the Troika and the US Secretary of State;
— bi-annual consultations between the Commission and the US Government at Cabinet level;
— briefings, as currently exist, by the Presidency to US Representatives on European Political Cooperation (EPC) meetings at the Ministerial level.
Both sides are resolved to develop and deepen these procedures for consultation so as to reflect the evolution of the European Community and of its relationship with the United States.
They welcome the actions taken by the European Parliament and the Congress of the United States in order to improve their dialogue and thereby bring closer together the peoples on both sides of the Atlantic.

Appendix 4

TRANSPARENCY AND OPENNESS CHARACTERISE THE EUROPE 1992 PROGRAMME, ACCORDING TO SENIOR STATE DEPARTMENT OFFICIAL

On 20 February, Mr. *Eugene McAllister*, Assistant Secretary of State for Economic and Business Affairs, testified in front of three subcommittees of the House of Representatives Foreign Affairs Committee (Europe and the Middle East, International Economic Policy and Trade). He spoke about moves towards implementing the programme for 1992 after a first audience in May 1989. His remarks and conclusions on the main questions up for discussion are particularly encouraging and give the Community a very different impression than that which has been fashionable for some time of a 'fortress'. This is why we are reproducing the entire text of this testimony.

TESTIMONY BY ASSISTANT SECRETARY OF STATE MCALLISTER

I am Eugene J. McAllister, Assistant Secretary of State for Economic and Business Affairs. I am pleased to review for you changes in the European Community's 1992 policies since my last appearance before you in May of 1989. I will also discuss the impact of events in Eastern Europe upon EC 1992, our efforts to upgrade our relationship with the EC, and the administration's strategy for dealing with the EC's Single Market program.

Let me say from the outset that we welcome the Congresss' role in advising on EC 1992. The hearings that this Committee sponsored last year were especially valuable in providing us with the views of Congress and private industry, and in understanding the need to do everything possible to ensure that the Single Market program does not disadvantage U.S. interests.

There are three main points that I would like to make in my presentation:

1. We are generally pleased with the direction of EC 1992. Of the 279 directives in the Single Market program, only 18 remain to be drafted, and over half have been passed. For the most part, the program has opened the EC market to greater

competition. On a number of occasions, notably banking, produce standards, and trucking, the Commission has responded to objections or requests raised by the U.S. government. I do not mean to suggest the EC's track record is perfect. The broadcasting directive certainly comes to mind. But the Single Market program has on the whole marked a big step in the direction of greater openness.

2. We have seen no evidence of a 'pasue' or a slowdown in the Community's progress toward 1992, despite the tumultuous events in Eastern Europe. In recent months, the EC has approved major legislation on banking, mergers, and road haulage and moved toward liberalization of insurance and investment services. The Commission intends to draft all remaining internal market legislation by the end of this year.

It is worthwhile to point out that we can make progress in assuring a Single Market that is open through a successful Uruguay Round of the GATT. As we enter the final nine months of the new Round, the Administration will intensify our efforts on behalf of negotiating objectives that affect both the GATT and the evolving EC market.

3. One of the most encouraging developments of the past year has been the strengthening of our relationship with the EC. We share a common purpose in promoting and assisting the transition to democratic market-based societies in Eastern Europe. This common purpose has had a beneficial side effect on more mundane, yet important, issues. Secretary Baker stated in his Berlin speech on December 12, 'As Europe moves toward its goal of a common internal market, and as its insitutions for political and security cooperation evolve, the link between the United States and European Community will become more important. We want our transatlantic cooperation to keep pace with European integration and institutional reform.' For that purpose, the Secretary proposed discussions on 'a strengthened set of institutional and consultative links' in economics, foreign policy, the environment, science and other areas that would 'proceed in parallel with Europe's efforts to achieve by 1992 a common internal market so that plans for U.S.-EC interaction would evolve with changes in the Community.'

Let me elaborate on these themes.

EC 1992 to date points to not only a more intregrated Europe, but a more open Europe. In many instances, the Community has responded to our concerns when we have had the opportunity to present our views, as on banking or product standards. Most of the developments on the Single Market since I testified last May have provided greater transparency and openness, and promoted greater competition:
— The EC has passed directives on road haulage that will permit U.S. trucking companies to compete in the Community on a non-discriminatory basis. Addressing U.S. objections, the EC dropped a proposed condition that road haulage firms be controlled and majority-owned by EC nationals before they could operate in a member state.
— We were concerned that the EC would use a merger control directive to pursue its industrial policy. However, the regulation passed in late December will use established antitrust criteria, similar to those used by U.S. antitrust authorities,

to evaluate mergers and acquisitions. Among these criteria are market structure, market position and financial power of firms, barriers to entry, actual or potential competition from both within and outside the EC, and the interests of consumers.
— U.S. industry is meeting with EC standards-setting organizations, and talks are underway to coordinate testing and certification regimes. If the EC has an open process, all — including U.S. firms — will benefit.
— The Community agreed to a dialogue on the controversial issue of the proposed introduction of socioeconomic criteria — in this instance, the impact of higher productivity upon the Common Agricultural Policy — into food health and safety decisions. The battle is far from over on this issue, but we have won allies in the Commission to the idea that product approval should depend upon the traditional criteria of health, safety, and efficacy — that is to say, accepted scientifically based considerations.
— In December, the EC finally removed mirror-image reciprocity provisions from the Second Banking Directive. U.S. bank subsidiaries will enjoy approximate national treatment in the Community, so long as EC banks in the U.S. receive national treatment and the same competitive opportunities as domestic credit institutions.
— In a related area, if not strictly part of the EC 1992 program, the Commission has moved to reduce member states' subsidies to several smokestack industries. Since 1989, the EC has required Commission approval before a subsidy of more than 14 million dollars can be granted to an auto, textile, or shipbuilding firm. In one case, the Community required an Italian steel company to slash capacity and cut employment by 20,000 (28 percent of workforce) as a condition for receiving 5.5 billion dollars in continued state aid.

We see 1992 as moving in the right direction, in part because the U.S. government has aggressively protected and pursued our interests. We intend to continue addressing the remaining areas of concern about the Single Market.

While the situation has improved, we believe that the relative lack of transparency in the EC legislative and regulatory process may disadvantage American business competing in the European market. Without explicit provision for acceptance for U.S. testing, and in some cases certification, U.S. firms could face major barriers to exporting to the Community. Certain rules of origin, in combination with anti-dumping statutes, have led some U.S. companies to believe they must invest in the EC in order to do business there. And of course, we were very disappointed over the EC's decision on the broadcasting directive, when the EC voted to require majority European programming in the transmission of entertainment television. We do not, however, consider this matter closed.

Even though over half of the EC 1992 program is complete, and the Commission has drafted over 90 percent of the 279 directives in the Single Market program, some of the most difficult, and for the U.S. important, issues remain unresolved. Let me give a few exmaples:
— We are pressing the EC to open up its vast (10 percent of EC GNP) and relatively closed public procurement sectors that are not covered by the GATT procurement code to non-EC bidders. While the Commission's proposed directives would significantly liberalize what are now virtually national markets for transport,

water, telecom, and energy, they would nonetheless discriminate against the U.S. by excluding bids that contain less than 50 percent EC content and offering a 3 percent price preference to EC suppliers. Negotiations on the GATT procurement code afford an opportunity to resolve favorably this problem.

— Harmonization of telecommunications equipment standards should benefit competitive U.S. producers, but the EC's procurement directive would still favor EC producers of big-ticket switching equipment. Against the Commission's wishes, EC member states are also holding out to reserve monopoly powers over telecom services to the PTTs — that is, to the benefit of government monopolies in the Community. This clearly could result in discrimination against U.S. providers of telecom services.

— The EC may replace national auto import quotas with a transitional VRA with Japan. We have made it clear that Japanese nameplate cars made in the U.S. should not be covered by quotas or VRAs. Secretary Baker raised this issue in December at the U.S.-EC Ministerial in Brussels, and we will continue to pursue it at the highest levels.

— Working with the European Community is the most promising means to expand civil aviation opportunities in the U.S.-European market. The Commission has been forcing the pace of liberalization within the Community, and we are strongly encouraging them to extend that policy to aviation relations with us. At the same time, we have made it very clear to the Europeans that all of the bilateral aviation rights that we now enjoy with individual countries in Europe must continue to be respected.

— Following the approval of the Second Banking Directive, we are seeking similar treatment for U.S. firms engaged in insurance and investment services in the EC. We understand that the Commission intends to remove the mirror-image reciprocity provisions, which are part of the insurance and investment directives. We are working to ensure that the Commission fulfils its pledge to open financial markets.

— A draft EC proposal on biotechnological inventions seeks to harmonize patent laws of EC member states applying to microorganisms, plants, and animals produced through human intervention in biological processes. However, the proposal offers only limited patent protection for biotechnologically produced plants and animals. The U.S believes this approach could threaten research and commercialization of new products in a field in which U.S. firms are the leaders. We have urged the Commission to tighten its proposal and are continuing to work toward that end.

— On computer software, we are engaged in detailed consultations with U.S. industry on an EC proposal to harmonize EC copyright protection for software. A large segment of U.S. industry opposes reverse engineering of software codes, but a vocal minority supports amendments to the proposed directive that would ensure compatibility of different systems. The Administration is in the process of formulating a position that we will communicate to the EC shortly. The EC Commission has agreed to work with industry, including U.S. firms in Europe, towards a compromise.

The Bush Administration is working very hard to ensure that these issues are resolved in ways that further U.S. business and commercial interests. As I have suggested, the record so far is encouraging.

The EC 1992 program is not proceeding against a static backdrop in Europe. The collapse of the Iron Curtain has expanded the meaning of 'European integration' to include the possibility of closer relationships between Eastern Europe and the European Community.

At first, many observers feared that preoccupation with developments in the East would slow the momentum of the internal market program. Instead, the prospect of German reunification in particular has led some member states to intensify efforts to finish the EC 1992 program on time. French President Mitterrand called together EC heads of state before the EC's Strasbourg Summit in December expressly to signal that developments in Eastern Europe should not deflect the Community's attention from completion of the Single Market.

The bottleneck in 1992 has not been in the policy formulation and adoption process, but in the member states, where implementing legislation is lagging. Only a handful of directives have been passed by all 12 of the member states. Commission officials who recently visited Washington told us, however, that this delay largely reflects parliamentary deadlock in the individual countries, and was a problem long before the dramatic events in Eastern Europe started to unfold. Both the EC Commission and the Irish in their role as the current EC President are pushing member states to pick up the pace of implementation.

As important as EC 1992 and the developments in Eastern Europe are, it is imperative that neither the U.S. nor the EC lose sight of the importance of the Uruguay Round, which is scheduled to end in December of this year. The strengthened and expanded multilateral trading framework that we seek in the Round would put in place international rules and disciplines that would go far to reinforce the EC 1992 exercise as a liberalizing process in many areas of vital concern to the U.S. Current multilateral rules are inadequate or non-existent, for example, for agricultural and services trade, protection of intellectual property rights, and rules of origin, among others. These issues are the very core of what we feel a successful Uruguay Round package should include. Agreement on how to approach these issues would help resolve many current and potential trade disputes with the EC.

The rapidly evolving political situation on the Continent has underscored the need to design a new ch on December 12. 'The example of Western cooperation through the European Community has already had a dramatic effect on Eastern attitudes toward economic liberty.' As the EC moves toward its goal of a common internal market and assumes increasing responsibility in certain foreign policy areas, our transatlantic relationship must evolve as well. For this purpose, Secretary Baker proposed at Berlin that the United States and the European Comunity should strive to achieve 'a significantly strengthened set of institutional and consultative links.'

We are now considering how U.S. interests can best be advanced in our evolving relationship with the European Community. Some of the obvious steps, such as increasing the level and number of contacts, have already occurred. For example, the status of the chief EC representative in Washington has been raised to Ambassadorial rank. Significantly, we are planning to hold the next U.S.-EC

Ministerial for the first time in Washington on April 23. Increasingly, today's agenda requires greater cooperation between the U.S. and the EC:
— We share common interests and objectives on the rapidly developing events in Eastern Europe. Both the EC and the U.S. are determined to assure the smoothest possible transition to pluralistic democracies with free markets, and at the same time ensure stability and peace.
— We need to enhance cooperation on environmental issues — issues that are global in nature, but call for greater dialogue across the Atlantic. There are also possibilities for greater cooperation in scientific and technical areas.
— There are other foreign policy issues — for instance, Third World development — in which the exchange of views could enhance coordination of our efforts.

The high-level contacts between the U.S. and the EC are just part of our far-reaching dialogue with the EC. We are aware that there were concerns in Congress a year ago about whether the U.S. government was adequately equipped to deal effectively with EC 1992. Since then, we have taken into account your many useful observations — to develop a pro-active strategy, put more people on the job in Washington and Europe to deal with EC 92, and use the Uruguay Round to solve those EC–92 problems that are appropriately handled in the GATT. I believe that the Executive Branch is extremely well organized on the Single Market.

I believe you are already familiar with how the U.S. government (USG) is set up to deal with EC 1992. Our mission to the EC in Brussels, USEC, has 29 professional staff, soon to be augmented by Commerce representatives. We receive extensive reporting from our dozen Embassies in the EC countries, and they have made a concerted effort to support Washington in conveying USG views on key issues like broadcasting and reciprocity. Finally, there is the interagency task force, consisting of a dozen working groups at the staff level, as well as an Assistant Secretary-level Trade Policy Review Group on EC 1992. Together, these efforts have ensured that the U.S. government knows what is going on in the 1992 process and can most effectively represent U.S. interests to the EC Commission and member states.

We also have a very close and extremely productive relationship with U.S. business. Thanks to the contribution of the private sector, we were able to persuade the Community to make critical changes in the Second Banking Directive — changes that should redound to the benefit of U.S. firms in the insurance and investment directives as well. U.S. business is also playing a key role in EC standards-setting.

Last week, we met with the Advisory Committee on Trade Policy Negotiations (ACTPN) to receive its recommendations on standards, public procurement, local content, reciprocity, and other issues. We have or will implement most of their ideas and hope to maintain a close relationship with this and the many other business groups we have consulted on EC 1992. For instance, we are meeting shortly with representatives of the auto industry to hear their views on the proposed EC auto VRA on Japanese nameplate autos.

We have also sought out the views of third countries. I have personally led interagency delegations to Ottawa, Bern, and Geneva to consult with officials of Canada and the EFTA countries on EC 1992.

In conclusion, we believe the EC 1992 program will benefit U.S. business. We remain vigilant that certain policies of the Community do not disadvantage U.S. interests. European integration is in the U.S. interest: indeed, the remarkable events in Eastern Europe today, and the Community's positive contribution to them, are a tribute to the correctness of U.S. policies toward Europe since the Marshall Plan. In this instance, it may be safe to say that politics follow economics: the example of an integrated and prosperous West has stimulated the fundamental changes now taking place among its eastern neighbors.

Appendix 5

'A NEW EUROPE, A NEW ATLANTICISM: ARCHITECTURE FOR A NEW ERA'

On Tuesday 12 December, American Secretary of State James Baker gave a speech to the West Berlin 'press club' on Europe in light of the upheavals underway in Eastern Europe.

During this speech, the head American diplomat called for a reinforcement of links between the United States and the European Community, possibly through a treaty.

Because of the importance of this speech, we are publishing it in its entirety below.

It is truly an honor for an American to speak at this time in this city. For me and for millions of my fellow citizens, Berlin, Freedom's City, is the crucible of half a century of history.
— Here we have seen clearly what elswhere hid in the shadows.
— Here the ambiguous disclosed its true nature
— And here, together, we made the choices and we took the stands that shaped today's world.

In 1945, pictures of a bombed-out Berlin brought home to us the terrible cost of war.

In 1948, the Soviet Union stalked out of the Four Power Control Commission and blockaded Berlin — a clear declaration of cold war.

In 1953, Berliners staged the first popular revolt against Soviet tyranny in Eastern Europe.

In 1961, the Berlin Wall closed the last escape hatch from the prison camp of nations which Eastern Europe had become.

In 1971, the Quadripartite Agreement on Berlin epitomized the terrible dilemma of detente — the proposition that cooperation between East and West assumed the continued division of this continent.

And then in 1989, the most important event — certainly the most dramatic event — of the postwar era occurred, right here in Freedom City.

On November 9, the Wall became a gateway. Berliners celebrated history's largest and happiest family reunion. And all of us who watched these scenes felt, once again: We are all Berliners.

Once more images from Berlin flashed around the world, images that heralded a new reality. This new reality has its roots in those older Berlin scenes — the scenes of West Berlin's dramatic postwar reconstruction; the scenes of allied aircraft supplying a blockaded city; the scenes if you will of American and Soviet tanks facing off at Checkpoint Charlie.

By standing together in Berlin as elsewhere, Western nations created the essential preconditions for overcoming the division of this city, the division of this nation, and indeed the division of this continent.

As these recent events have unfolded, the Soviet Union has demonstrated a remarkable degree of realism. And President Gorbachev deserves credit for being the first Soviet leader to have the courage and to have the foresight to permit the lifting of repression in Eastern Europe.

But the real impulse for change comes from an altogether different source: it comes from the peoples of Poland, of Hungary, of Czechoslovakia, of Bulgaria, and yes of East Germany.

They have in effect freed themselves.

From the Baltic to the Adriatic, an irresistible movement has gathered force — it is a movement of, by, and for the people. In their peaceful urgent mutlitude, the peoples of Eastern Europe have held up a mirror to the West and they have reflected the enduring power of our own best values. In the words of Thomas Jefferson who was the first American secretary of State. 'Nothing is more certainly written in the book of fate than that these people are to be free.'

The changes amount to nothing less than a peaceful revolution.

And now, as President Bush stated last week, 'the task before us is to consoldiate the fruits of this peaceful revolution and to provide the architecture for continued peaceful change.'

The first step is for free men and women to create free governments. The path may appear difficult, at times even confusing, but we must travel it and we must travel it with understanding. For true stability requires governments with legitimacy, governments in other words that are based on the consent of the governed.

The peoples of Eastern Europe are trying to build such governments. Our view, as President Bush told President Gorbachev, is that the political and economic reforms in the East can enhance both long-term stability in Europe and the prospects for perestroika. A legitimate and stable European order will help, it will help not threaten, legitimate Soviet interests. And, of course, an illegitimate order will provide no order at all.

Free men and free governments are the building blocks of a Europe whole and free. But hopes for a Europe whole and free are tinged with concern by some that a Europe undivided may not necessarily be a Europe peaceful and prosperous. Many of the guideposts that brought us securely through four sometimes tense and threatening decades are now coming down. Some of the divisive issues that once brought conflict to Europe are reemerging.

As Europe changes, the instruments for Western cooperation have got to adapt. Working together, it is up to us to design and gradually to put into place what I refer to as a new architecture for this new era.

This new architecture must have a place for old foundations and structures that remain very valuable like NATO — while recognizing that they can also serve new collective purposes. The new architecture must continue the construction of institutions — like the European Community — that can help draw together the West while also serving as an open door to the East. And the new architecture must build up frameworks — like the CSCE process — that can overcome the division of Europe and that at the same time can bridge the Atlantic Ocean.

This new structure must also accomplish two special purposes. First, as a part of overcoming the division of Europe there must be an opportunity to overcome through peace and freedom the division of Berlin and of Germany. The United States and NATO have stood for unification for 40 years, and we will not waiver from that goal.

Second, the architecture should reflect that America's security — politically, militarily, and economically remains linked to Europe's security. The United States and Canada share Europe's neighborhood.

As President Bush stated in May, 'The United States is and the United States will remain a European power.' And as he added last week, 'The United States will maintain significant military forces in Europe as long as our Allies desire our presence as part of a common security effort.' This is our commitment to a common future, a recognition of a need for an active U.S. role in Europe, a need acknowledged even by President Gorbachev.

The change for us all then is to work together, to work together toward the New Europe and the New Atlanticism.

New Missions for NATO
In May of this year, President Bush suggested to his NATO colleagues that it was time to begin considering some new missions for NATO.

For over 40 years, the North Atlantic Treaty Organization has secured peace in Europe through both deterrence and dialogue with the East. Today, NATO is working in Vienna to build a new security structure for Europe, one in which the military component is reduced and the political is enhanced. This, of course, is NATO's first mission.

A convenential forces agreement is the keystone of this new security structure. In May, NATO adopted President Bush's suggestion to seek such an agreement and to seek it on an accelerated timetable. President Gorbachev has responded to this opportunity in a positive way. And we have moved significantly closer to concluding an agreement limiting conventional armaments from the Atlantic to the Urals. In Malta, President Bush proposed a summit meeting to sign such an agreement sometime during the year 1990.

Today, I further propose that the ministers of the 23 NATO and Warsaw Pact nations take advantage of our February meeting in Ottawa, where we will launch the Open Skies negotiations, to review the status and to give a further push to the conventional forces talks going on in Vienna.

As we construct a new security architecture that maintains the common defense, the non-military component of European security will grow. Arms control agreements, confidence-building measures and other political consultative arrangements are going to become more important. It is in such a world that the role of NATO is going to evolve. NATO will become the forum where Western nations cooperate: where Western nations cooperate to negotiate, to implement, to verify and to extend agreements between East and West.

In this context, the implementation and verification monitoring of a conventional forces agreement will present a major challenge for enduring security. NATO is going to have to make an important contribution to that.

I, therefore, also invite allied governments to consider establishing a NATO Arms Control Verification Staff. Verification will, of course, remain a national responsibility. But such a new staff would be able to assist member governments in monitoring compliance with arms control and confidence building measures in Europe. A NATO organization of this sort could be valuable; valuable in assisting all allies and in coordinating the implementation of inspections. It could provide a clearinghouse for information contributed by national governments, perhaps, joining with collective European efforts through the Western European Union.

As the East-West confrontation recedes, and as the prospects for East-West cooperation advance, other challenges for European and Atlantic security are going to arise. These point to NATO's second mission. Regional conflicts — along with the proliferation of missiles and nuclear, chemical and biological weapons present us with ever-growing dangers. Intensified NATO consultations on these issues can play an important role in forming common Western approaches to these various threats.

Third, NATO should also begin considering further initiatives the West might take, through the CSCE process in particular, to build economic and political ties with the East, to promote respect for human rights, to help build democratic instutitions, and to fashion, consistent with Western security interests, a more open environment for East-West trade and investment.

And finally, NATO may have its greatest and most lasting effect on the pattern of change by demonstrating to the nations of the East a fundamentally different approach to security. NATO's four decades offer a vision of cooperation, not coercion; of open borders, not iron curtains. The reconciliation of ancient enemies, which has taken place under the umbrella of NATO's collective security, offers the nations of Eastern Europe an appealing model of international relations.

Whatever security relationships the governments of Eastern Europe choose, NATO will continue to provide Western governments the optimal instrument to coordinate their efforts at defense and arms control, and to build a durable European order of peace. The interests of Eastern Europe, and indeed the interests of the Soviet Union, will be served by the maintenance of a vigorous North Atlantic Treaty Organization.

The Role of the European Community
The future development of the European Community will also play a central role in shaping the new Europe.

The example of Western cooperation through the European Community has already had a dramatic effect on Eastern attitudes toward economic liberty. The success of this great European experiment, perhaps more than any other factor, has caused Eastern Europeans to recognize that people as well as nations cooperate more productively when they are free to choose. The ballot box and the free market are of course the fundamental instruments of choice. Naturally, the United States seeks a European Community which is open to cooperation with others. But the European experiment has succeeded not just because it has appealed to the enlightened self-interest of European producers and consumers. This experiment has succeeded because the vision of its founders encompassed and yet transcended the material. This experiment has succeeded because it also held out the higher goal of political as well as economic barriers overcome, that is of a Europe united.

This was the goal of Monnet and Schumann. This was the goal supported by the United States of Marshall and Acheson. This was the goal contained in the Treaty of Rome and more recently in the Single European Act. The United States supports this goal today with the same energy that it did 40 years ago.

We think that Americans will profit from access to a single European market, just as Europeans have long profited from their access to a single American market. However, it is vital to us all — vital to us all that both these markets remain open — and indeed that both become even more open.

As Europe moves toward its goal of a common internal market, and as its institutions for political and security cooperation evolve, the link between the United States and the European Community will become even more important. We want our transatlantic cooperation to keep pace with European integration and with institutional reform.

To this end, we propose that the United States and the European Community work together to achieve, whether its in treaty or some other form, a significantly strengthened set of institutional and consultative links. Working from shared ideals and common values, we face a set of mutual challenges — in economics, in foreign policy, the environment, science, and a host of other fields. So it makes sense for us to fashion our responses together as a matter of common course.

We suggest that our discussions about this idea proceed in parallel with Europe's efforts to achieve by 1992 a common internal market so that plans for U.S.-EC interaction would evolve along with changes in the community.

The United States also encourages the European Comunity to continue to expand cooperation with the nations of the East. The promotion of a political and economic reform in the East is a natural vocation for the European Community. That is why we were exceptionally pleased with the agreement at the Paris Economic Summit that the European Commission should assume a special role in the Group of 24 effort to promote reform in Poland and Hungary.

The United States has worked closely with the European Community in mobilizing economic and financial support for Poland and Hungary. Indeed, the United States has authorized almost 1,000 million dollars of assistance to these two nations. This week, we look at the Group of 24 meeting to move as close as possible toward achieving the additional 1,000 million dollar stabilization fund that Poland requested to support its major move toward currency convertibility and macreoeconomic reform.

That should be just the start of our common labor. Poland and Hungary have 40 years of economic stagnation to overcome, and this is going to take time and it's going to take the steady support of all of us. As Czechoslovakia, Bulgaria and the German Democratic Republic undertake political and economic reforms comparable to those already underway in Poland and Hungary, we believe the activities of the Group of 24, centered around the EC, should be expanded to support peaceful change in these countries as well.

As the nations of Europe achieve more open political and economic systems, they may seek new relationships with the European Community, with the Council of Europe and with other institutions serving both Europe and the broader international community. In fact, such ties could be fundamental to our strategy of rebuilding the economies of Eastern Europe through private capital and private initiative: Private investors in Eastern Europe are going to want to know that they can sell their products in Western markets.

I am confident that creative new arrangements can be devised to encourage and sustain the process of political and economic reform in the countries of Eastern Europe, while at the same time preserving the integrity and the vitality of existing institutions. We need to offer the nations of the East hope, opportunities that can be seized as they take steps toward democracy and economic liberty. Perhaps the recent work on an agreement between the EC and the six nations of the European Free Trade Association will set a pattern for improved ties with others.

We see no conflict between the process of European integration and an expansion of cooperation between the European Community and its neighbors to the

East and West. Indeed, we believe that the attraction of the European Community for the countries of the East depends most on its continued vitality. And the vitality of the Economic Community depends in turn on its continued commitment to the goal of a united Europe envisaged by its founders — free, democratic and closely linked to its North American partners.

The Helsinki Process — The New Role of CSCE
The one institution that brings all the nations of the East and West together in Europe, the Conference on Security and Cooperation in Europe, is in fact an ongoing process launched over 14 years ago in Helsinki. There have been different perceptions as to the functions of this CSCE process. Some saw the Helsinki Final Act of 1975 as a ratification of the status the equivalent if you will of a peace treaty concluding World War II, and thus the legitimization of Europe's permanent division. Others, however, saw this process as a device by which these divisions could be overcome.

The dynamic concept of the CSCE process has prevailed. In 1975, the governments of Eastern Europe may not have taken seriously their commitments to respect a wide range of fundamental human rights. But their populations did. The standards of conduct set by the Helsinki Final Act are increasingly being met through international pressure and domestic ferment. Last month, here in Berlin, of course we witnessed one of the proudest achievements of the CSCE process as the GDR fulfilled its commitment to allow its people to travel freely.

Now it's time for the CSCE process to advance further. I think we can look toward filling each of its three baskets with new substance.

First, we can give the security basket further content through the 35-nation negotiations on confidence-building measures which are currently underway in Vienna. The agreements under consideration there should help prevent force, or the threat of force, from being used again in an effort to intimidate any European nation. Apart from reducing further the risk of war, new confidence-building measures can create greater openness. They can insititutionalize a predictable pattern of military interaction, a pattern that is difficult to reverse and that builds a new basis for trust.

Second, the relatively underdeveloped economic basket can assume new responsibilities. President Bush suggested to President Gorbachev at Malta that we could breath new life into this CSCE forum by focusing it on the conceptual and practical questions involved in the transition from stalled, planned economies to free, competitive markets. When our nations meet in Bonn in May of next year to discuss economic cooperation, I suggest we concentrate on this issue.

Third, the CSCE process has made its most distinctive mark in the field of human rights. One fundamental right, however, has not yet been fully institutionalized. This is the right for people to choose, through regular, free, open, multiparty elections, those who will govern them.

This, of course, is an ultimate human right, the right that secures all others.

Without free elections, no rights can be long guaranteed. With free elections, no rights can be long be denied.

On May 31, in Mainz, President Bush announced a major new Helsinki intiative to help end the division of Europe. He called for free elections and political pluralism in all the countries of Europe. Now, this is beginning to come to pass.

In June, the United States and the United Kingdom co-sponsored a free elections initiative at the CSCE human rights meeting in Paris. This proposal called on all 35 CSCE participating states to allow periodic, genuine and contested elections based on universal and equal suffrage, by secret ballot, with international observers. Individuals would be allowed to establish and maintain their own political parties in order to ensure fully democratic procedures.

Free elections should now become the highest priority in the CSCE process. In 1945, Josef Stalin promised free elections and self-determination for the peoples of Eastern Europe. The fact that those elections were not free, and the fact that those peoples were not allowed to determine their destiny, was a fundamental cause of the Cold War.

Now this Stalinst legacy is being removed: being removed by people determined to reclaim their birthright to freedom. They should not be denied and they will not be denied.

As all or nearly all the CSCE states move toward fully functioning representative governments, I suggest we consider another step: We could involve parliamentarians more directly in CSCE processes, not only as observers as at present, but perhaps through their own meetings. To sustain the movement toward democracy, we need to reinforce the institutions of democracy.

Germany and Berlin in a New Europe
A new Europe, a Europe that is whole and free, must include of course arrangements that satisfy the aspirations of the German people and meet the legitimate concerns of Germany's neighbors. Before the Bundestag on November 28, Chancellor Kohl laid out an approach designed to achieve German aspirations in peace and freedom. At last week's NATO Summit, President Bush reaffirmed America's long-standing support for the goal of German reunification. He enunciated four principles — four principles that guide our policy, and I am pleased to note these ideas were incorporated into the statements issued last week by the leaders of the European Community nations at Strasbourg.

— One, self-determination must be pursued without prejudice to its outcome. We should not at this time endorse nor should we exclude any particular vision of unity.

— Two, unification should occur in the context of Germany's continued commitment to NATO and an increasingly integrated European Community, and with due regard of course for the legal role and responsibilities of the allied powers.

— Three, in the interests of genral European stability, moves toward unification must be peaceful, they must be gradual, and part of a step-by-step process.

— Four, and finally, on the question of borders, we should reiterate our support for the principles of the Helsinki Final Act.

President Bush concluded that 'an end to the unnatural division of Europe, and of Germany, must proceed in accordance with and be based upon the values that are becoming universal ideals, as all the countries of Europe become part of a commonwealth of free nations.'

As an American, ladies and gentlemen, I am very proud of the role my nation has played and will continue to play standing with you. Yet this very positive course will not be easy, nor can it be rushed. It must be peaceful. It must be democratic. And, of course, it must respect the legitimate concerns of all the participants in the New Europe.

As Berlin has stood at the center of a divided Europe, so may it stand at the center of a Europe which is whole and free – no longer the embattled bastion of freedom, but instead a beacon of hope — a beacon of hope to people around the world for a better life.

A New Europe, A New Atlanticism
And so my friends, we see changes today underway in the East which are a great source of great hope. But a new era brings different concerns for all of us. Some of these are as old as Europe itself. Others are themselves the new products of changes.

Were the West to abandon the patterns of cooperation that we have built up over four decades, these concerns could grow into problems. But the institutions that we have created — NATO, the European Community, and the CSCE process — are alive. Rooted in democratic values, they fit well with the people power that is shaping history's new course.

More important, these institutions are also flexible and they are capable of adapting to rapidly changing circumstances. As we adapt, as we update and expand our cooperation with each other and with the nations of the East, we will create a new Europe — a new Europe on the basis of a new Atlanticism.

NATO will remain North America's primary link with Europe. As arms control and political arrangements increasingly supplement the vital military component of European security, NATO will take on new roles.

The European Community is already an economic pillar of the transatlantic relationship. It will also take on, perhaps in concert with other European institutions, increasingly important political roles. Indeed, it has already done so, as evidenced by the community's coordination of a Western effort to support reform in Eastern Europe. And as it continues to do so, the link between the United States and the European Community should grow more strong, the issues we discuss more diversified, and our common endeavors more important.

At the same time, the substantive overlap between NATO and European institutions will grow. This overlap must lead to synergy, not to friction. Better communication among European and transatlantic institutions will thus become more urgent.

The CSCE process could become the most important forum of East-West cooperation. Its mandate will grow as this cooperation takes root.

And as these changes proceed, as they overcome the division of Europe, so too will the divisions of Germany and Berlin be overcome in peace and freedom.

Ladies and gentlemen, this fall a powerful cry went up from the huge demonstrations in Leipzig, Dresden and Berlin. 'We are the people,' the crowds chanted at the party that ruled in their name. On the other side of the globe, Lech Walesa was addressing the U.S. Congress, thanking America for supporting Polish liberty. He began with words written two hundred years ago, the words that open the U.S. Constitution: 'We the people.'

Between 1789 and 1989, between the expressions 'We the people' and 'We are the people,' runs one of history's deepest currents. What the American founding fathers knew, the people of East Germany and Eastern Europe now also know — that freedom is a blessing, but not a gift. That the work of freedom is never done, and it is never done alone. Between the America of 'We the people' and the Europe of 'We are the people.' There can be no division. On this basis a new Atlanticism will flourish, and a new Europe will be born.

Appendix 6

Section 1301 of the Omnibus Trade and Competitiveness Act of 1988

LAWS OF 100th CONG. — 2nd SESS.

Subtitle C — Response to Unfair International Trade Practices

PART 1 — ENFORCEMENT OF UNITED STATES RIGHTS UNDER TRADE AGREEMENTS AND RESPONSE TO CERTAIN FOREIGN TRADE PRACTICES

19USC 2411. SEC. 1301. REVISIION OF CHAPTER I OF TITLE III OF THE TRADE ACT OF 1974

(a) IN GENERAL — Chapter 1 of title III of the Trade Act of 1974 (19 U.S.C. 2411 et seq.) is amended to read as follows:

'CHAPTER 1 — ENFORCEMENT OF UNITED STATES RIGHTS UNDER TRADE AGREEMENTS AND RESPONSE TO CERTAIN FOREIGN TRADE PRACTICES

'SEC. 301. ACTIONS BY UNITED STATES TRADE REPRESENTATIVE.

'(a) MANDATORY ACTION. —
'(1) If the United States Trade Representative determines under section 304(a)(1) that —
'(A) the rights of the United States under any trade agreement are being denied; or
'(B) an act, policy, or practice of a foreign country —
'(i) violates, or is inconsistent with, the provisions of, or otherwise denies benefits to the United States under, any trade agreement, or
'(ii) is unjustifiable and burdens or restricts United States commerce;
the Trade Representative shall take action authorized in subsection (c), subject to the specific direction, if any, of the President regarding any such action, and shall take all other appropriate and feasible action within the power of the President that

the President may direct the Trade Representative to take under this subsection, to enforce such rights or to obtain the elimination of such act, policy, or practice.

'(2) The Trade Representative is not required to take action under paragraph (1) in any case in which —

'(A) the Contracting Parties to the General Agreement on Tariffs and Trade have determined, a panel of experts has reported to the Contracting Parties, or a ruling issued under the formal dispute settlement proceeding provided under any other trade agreement finds, that —

'(i) the rights of the United States under a trade agreement are not being denied, or

'(ii) the act, policy, or practice —

'(I) is not a violation of, or inconsistent with, the rights of the United States, or

'(II) does not deny, nullify, or impair benefits to the United States under any trade agreement; or

'(B) the Trade Representative finds that —

'(i) the foreign country is taking satisfactory measures to grant the rights of the United States under a trade agreement

'(ii) the foreign country has —

'(I) agreed to eliminate or phase out the act, policy, or practice, or

'(II) agreed to an imminent solution to the burden or restriction on United States commerce that is satisfactory to the Trade Representative,

'(iii) it is impossible for the foreign country to achieve the results described in clause (i) or (ii), as appropriate, but the foreign country agrees to provide to the United States compensatory trade benefits that are satisfactory to the Trade Representative,

'(iv) in extraordinary cases, where the taking of action under this subsection would have an adverse impact on the United States economy substantially out of proportion to the benefits of such action, taking into account the impact of not taking such action on the credibility of the provisions of this chapter, or

'(v) the taking of action under this subsection would cause serious harm to the national security of the United States.

'(3) Any action taken under paragraph (1) to eliminate an act, policy, or practice shall be devised so as to affect goods or services of the foreign country in an amount that is equivalent in value to the burden or restriction being imposed by that country on United States commerce.

'(b) DISCRETIONARY ACTION. — If the Trade Representative determines under section 304(a)(1) that —

'(1) an act, policy, or practice of a foreign country is unreasonable or discriminatory and burdens or restricts United States commerce, and

'(2) action by the United States is appropriate, the Trade Representative shall take all appropriate and feasible action authorized under subsection (c), subject to the specific direction, if any, of the President regarding any such action, and all other appropriate and feasible action within the power of the President that the President may direct the Trade Representative to take under this subsection, to obtain the elimination of that act, policy, or practice.

'(c) SCOPE OF AUTHORITY. —

'(1) For purposes of carrying out the provisions of subsection (a) or (b), the Trade Representative is authorized to —

'(A) suspend, withdraw, or prevent the application of, benefits of trade agreement concessions to carry out a trade agreement with the foreign country referred to in such subsection;

'(B) impose duties or other import restrictions on the goods of, and, notwithstanding any other provision of law, fees or restrictions on the services of, such foreign country for such time as the Trade Representative determines appropriate; or

'(C) enter into binding agreements with such foreign country that commit such foreign country to —

'(i) eliminate, or phase out, the act, policy, or practice that is the subject of the action to be taken under subsection (a) or (b),

'(ii) eliminate any burden or restriction on United States commerce resulting from such act, policy, or practice, or

'(iii) provide the United States with compensatory trade benefits that —

'(I) are satisfactory to the Trade Representative, and

'(II) meet the requirements of paragraph (4).

'(2)(A) Notwithstanding any other provision of law governing any service sector access authorization, and in addition to the authority conferred in paragraph (1), the Trade Representative may, for purposes of carrying out the provisions of subsection (a) or (b) —

'(i) restrict, in the manner and to the extent the Trade Representative determines appropriate, the terms and conditions of any such authorization, or

'(ii) deny the issuance of any such authorization.

'(B) Actions described in subparagraph (A) may only be taken under this section with respect to service sector access authorizations granted or applications therefor pending, on or after the date on which —

'(i) a petition is filed under Section 302(a), or

'(ii) a determination to initiate an investigation is made by the Trade Representative under section 302(b).

'(C) Before the Trade Representative takes any action under this section involving the imposition of fees or other restrictions on the services of a foreign country, the Trade Representative shall, if the services involved are subject to regulation by any agency of the Federal Government or of any State, consult, as appropriate, with the head of the agency concerned.

'(3) The actions the Trade Representative is authorized to take under subsection (a) or (b) may be taken against any goods or economic sector —
Discrimination, prohibition

'(A) on a nondiscriminatory basis or solely against the foreign country described in such subsection, and

'(B) without regard to whether or not such goods or economic sector were involved in the act, policy, or practice that is the subject of such action.

'(4) Any trade agreement described in paragraph (1)(C)(iii) shall provide compensatory trade benefits that benefit the economic sector which includes the domestic industry that would benefit from the elimination of the act, policy, or practice that is the subject of the action to be taken under subsection (a) or (b), or benefit the economic sector as closely related as possible to such economic sector, unless —

'(A) the provision of such trade benefits is not feasible, or

'(B) trade benefits that benefit any other economic sector would be more satisfactory than such trade benefits.

'(5) In taking actions under subsection (a) or (b), the Trade Representative shall —

'(A) give preference to the imposition of duties over the imposition of other import restrictions, and

'(B) if an import restriction other than a duty is imposed, consider substituting, on an incremental basis, an equivalent duty for such other import restriction.

'(6) Any action taken by the Trade Representative under this section with respect to export targeting shall, to the extent possible, reflect the full benefit level of the export targeting to the beneficiary over the period during which the action taken has an effect.

(d) DEFINITIONS AND SPECIAL RULES — For purposes of this chapter —

'(1) The term 'commerce' includes, but is not limited to —

'(A) services (including transfers of information) associated with international trade, whether or not such services are related to specific goods, and

'(B) foreign direct investment by United States persons with implications for trade in goods or services.

'(2) An act, policy, or practice of a foreign country that burdens or restricts United States commerce may include the provision, directly or indirectly, by that foreign country of subsidies for the construction of vessels used in the commercal transportation by water of goods between foreign countries and the United States.

Maritime affairs.

'(3)(A) An act, policy, or practice is unreasonable if the act, policy, or practice, while not necessarily in violation of, or inconsistent with, the international legal rights of the United States, is otherwise unfair and inequitable.

'(B) Acts, policies, and practices that are unreasonable include, but are not limited to, any act, policy, or practice, or any combination of acts, policies, or practices, which —

'(i) denies fair and equitable —

'(I) opportunities for the establishment of an enterprise,

'(II) provision of adequate and effective protection of intellectual property rights, or

Copyrights. Patents and trademarks.

'(III) market opportunities, including the toleration by a foreign government of systematic anticompetitive activities by private firms or among private firms in the foreign country that have the effect of restricting, on a basis that is inconsistent with commercial considerations, access of United States goods to purchasing by such firms,

'(ii) constitutes export targeting, or

'(iii) consitutes a persistent pattern of conduct that —

'(I) denies workers the right of association,

'(II) denies workers the right to organize and bargain collectively,

'(III) permits any form of forced or compulsory labor,

'(IV) fails to provide a minimum age for the employment of children, or

Children and youth

Wages. Safety.

'(V) fails to provide standards for minimum wages, hours of work, and occupational safety and health of workers.

'(C)(i) Acts, policies, and practices of a foreign country described in subparagraph

(B)(iii) shall not be treated as being unreasonable if the Trade Representative determines that —

'(I) the foreign country has taken, or is taking, actions that demonstrate a significant and tangible overall advancement in providing throughout the foreign country (including any designated zone within the foreign country) the rights and other standards described in the subclauses of subparagraph (B)(iii), or

'(II) such acts, policies, and practices are not inconsistent with the level of economic development of the foreign country.

Federal Register, publication.

'(ii) The Trade Representative shall publish in the Federal Register any determination made under clause (i), together with a description of the facts on which such determination is based.

'(D) For purposes of determining whether any act, policy, or practice is unreasonable, reciprocal opportunities in the United States for foreign nationals and firms shall be taken into account, to the extent appropriate.

'(E) The term 'export targeting' means any government plan or scheme consisting of a combination of coordinated actions (whether carried out severally or jointly) that are bestowed on a specific enterprise, industry, or group thereof, the effect of which is to assist the enterprise, industry, or group to become more competitive in the export of a class or kind of merchandise.

'(4)(A) An act, policy, or practice is unjustifiable if the act, policy, or practice is in violation of, or inconsistent with, the international legal rights of the United States.

Copyrights. Patents and trademarks.

'(B) Acts, policies, and practices that are unjustifiable include, but are not limited to, any act, policy, or practice described in subparagraph (A) which denies national or most-favored-nation treatment or the right of establishment or protection of intellectual property rights.

'(5) Acts, policies, and practices that are discriminatory include, when appropriate, any act, policy, and practice which denies national or most-favored-nation treatment to United States goods, services, or investment.

'(6) The term 'service sector access authorization' means any license, permit, order, or other authorization, issued under the authority of Federal law, that permits a foreign supplier of services access to the United States market in a service sector concerned.

'(7) The term 'foreign country' includes any foreign instrumentality. Any possession or territory of a foreign country that is administered separately for customs purposes shall be treated as a separate foreign country.

'(8) The term 'Trade Representative' means the United States Trade Representative.

'(9) The term 'interested persons', only for purposes of sections 302(a)(4)(B), 304(b)(1)(A), 306(c)(2), and 307(a)(2), includes, but is not limited to, domestic firms and workers, representatives of consumer interests, United States product exporters, and any industrial user of any goods or services that may be affected by actions taken under subsection (a) or (b).

19 usc 2412

'SEC. 302. INITIATION OF INVESTIGATIONS.

'(a) PETITIONS. —

'(1) Any interested person may file a petition with the Trade Representative requesting that action be taken under section 301 and setting forth the allegations in support of the request.

'(2) The Trade Representative shall review the allegations in any petition filed under paragraph (1) and, not later than 45 days after the date on which the Trade Representative received the petition, shall determine whether to initiate an investigation.

Index